JEFFERSON

CHAMPION OF THE FREE MIND

BY

Phillips Russell

ILLUSTRATED WITH PHOTOGRAPHS

DODD, MEAD & COMPANY

NEW YORK · 1956

LIBRARY OF CONGRESS CATALOG CARD NUMBER: 56-10535

PRINTED IN THE UNITED STATES OF AMERICA
BY VAIL-BALLOU PRESS, INC., BINGHAMTON, N. Y.

CONTENTS

v

ILLUSTRATIONS

JEFFERSON

CHAMPION OF THE FREE MIND

CHAPTER 1

STUDENT DAYS

PETER JEFFERSON WAS doubtless just the sort of father his son Thomas would have chosen, had the choice been his.

In the first place, Peter was a master farmer, and Thomas Jefferson was extravagant in his preference for farmers above men of all other classes and occupations. Peter Jefferson was one of those pioneers who early in the eighteenth century had deserted the Tidewater country of Virginia because its soil was becoming exhausted and its land prices were high, and moved up the river James into the hilly Piedmont country. Here he patented and speculated in land until he owned several thousand acres over which he placed a steward and five overseers. He bought books until he had a small but respectable library,[1] and made a friend of a former William and Mary professor, Joshua Fry, with whom he was employed to continue the dividing line between Virginia and North Carolina, following the surveys left incomplete by the celebrated William Byrd.

Jefferson professed to be careless about matters of lineage. "The tradition in my father's family," he wrote, "was that their ancestor came to this country from Wales, and from near the mountain of Snowden, the highest in Great Britain. . . . The first particular information I have of any ancestor was my grandfather. . . . He had three sons, Thomas who died young, Field who settled on the waters of Roanoke and left numerous descendants, and Peter my father, who settled on the lands I still own called Shadwell and

---

[1] Among these books were Rapin's *History of England*, Solomon's *State Tryals*, Ogilvie's *Description of America*, Treht's *Astronomy*, *History of Queen Anne's Ministers*, Anson's *Voyage around the World*, and bound volumes of the *Spectator*, *Tatler and Guardian*.

1

adjoining my present residence. He was born on Feb. 29, 1707–08, and intermarried 1739, with Jane Randolph, of the age of 19. They [the Randolphs] trace their pedigree far back in England and Scotland, to which let every one ascribe the faith and merit he chooses."

This indulgent reference to the pedigree-lovers has to some commentators appeared to be contemptuous, as befitting a democrat; first of all he was a republican: that is, one who believes republics are superior to monarchies or other forms of one-man or one-class rule.

Jefferson's pride in his father was ever evident, though Peter's book education "had been quite neglected." It is an adage that behind great men stand great mothers; but we know almost nothing of Jane, the daughter of genial Isham Randolph of Dungeness, except that at twenty-three she gave birth to her eldest son, Thomas. In all of Jefferson's vast writings he barely mentions his mother. But she must have given her son something of the Randolph genius, for William Randolph of Warwickshire, England, who emigrated to Turkey Island, twenty miles below Richmond, in 1660, was the father of a great line of eminent and intellectual men, some of whom traced their lineage back to Pocahontas.[2]

Thomas was born on April 2, 1743, on his father's farm at Shadwell on the Rivanna River. Jefferson's lifelong interest in schools and schooling probably went back to the time when at the age of five he went to his first school at Tuckahoe on the river James, a few miles above Richmond. His father was then living on and operating the Tuckahoe farm, having been requested to do so by his close friend, Colonel William Randolph, the owner. When Thomas was nine, his father returned to his own farm at Shadwell. He placed the boy under the Reverend William ("Parson") Douglas, a Scotch dominie, at sixteen pounds a year. One of the other pupils in

---

[2] Included were not only Jefferson but Chief Justice John Marshall; General Robert E. Lee; William Stith, the historian; John Randolph of Roanoke; Thomas Nelson Page; and any number of burgesses, Congress members, speakers, governors of Virginia, diplomats, authors and orators. It is a curious fact that two of Jefferson's bitterest critics were related to him on the Randolph side—John Randolph of Roanoke and Justice Marshall.

the school was Thomas Meriwether, who lived on a neighboring farm. He remembered the parson saying to him one day:

"Tommy, why can't you be clever like Tommy Jefferson?" [3]

Peter Jefferson died when fifty years old. His son Thomas was only fourteen and was then a pupil of the Reverend James Maury, whose school and family became famous. Maury, of a liberal Huguenot ancestry, had an unusually good library, also an interest in natural history, which may have influenced young Jefferson not a little. Under his classical instruction Thomas remained two years, and then, soon after the new year, 1760, he wrote a plaintive letter to his guardian, John Harvie of Belmont, in which we catch a glimpse of the burdensome visitors, or "company," that plagued him all his life and at the end almost ate him out of the house. In this note is also seen a hint of that sageness which distinguished Jefferson his life long and which was apparently already well developed when he was only seventeen:

"Shadwell, January 14th, 1760
"I was at Col. Peter Randolph's about a Fortnight ago, and my schooling falling into Discourse, he said he thought: [it] would be to my Advantage to go to the College, and was desirous I should go, as indeed I am myself for several Reasons. In the first place, as long as I stay at the mountain, the loss of one-fourth of my time is inevitable, by Company's coming here and detaining me from school. And likewise my absence will, in a great measure, put a stop to so much Company, and by that Means lessen the expenses of the estate in Housekeeping. And on the other Hand by going to the College, I shall get a more universal acquaintance, which may hereafter be serviceable to me; I suppose I can pursue my studies in the Greek and Latin as well there as here, and likewise learn something of the mathematics. I shall be glad of your opinion. And remain, Sir, your most humble servant,

"Thomas Jefferson"

Jefferson was subsequently enrolled in the College of William and Mary at Williamsburg, Virginia.

"Eager after information." In these terms Thomas Jefferson once described his father. But the same description might as well have

[3] *Virginia Magazine of History and Biography*, XLV, 4.

been applied to himself. For all his life, in whatever activity or re-
lationship, Jefferson was avid in pursuit of "science," which was often
his term for learning or knowledge. He was born at a time when the
world was reacting against emotional revelation as the only source
of knowledge and was giving birth to the practical-minded Benjamin
Franklins who pursued truth in objective things and in the workings
of nature.

As his teachers, Jefferson always delighted to name three men belonging to his student days at Williamsburg. They were his admired
trio, his sacred trinity, his grand triumvirate—Dr. William Small,
George Wythe and Peyton Randolph. So deep had been their impression on his mind that when in doubt or dilemma he was accustomed
to ask himself: "What would Dr. Small, Mr. Wythe, Peyton Randolph, do in this situation?"

Of these three models we have vivid portraits sketched by Jefferson himself. Of Peyton Randolph, afterward speaker of the Virginia
house of burgesses and later speaker of Congress, Jefferson wrote:
"He was indeed a most excellent man; and none was ever more beloved and respected by his friends. Somewhat cold and coy towards
strangers, but of the sweetest affability when ripened into acquaintance. Of Attic pleasantry in conversation, always good-humored
and conciliatory."

Of Wythe, Jefferson's law teacher, and afterward signer of the
Declaration of Independence and chancellor of Virginia, he wrote:
"In pleading he never indulged himself with a useless or declama-
tory thought or word—and became as distinguished by correctness
and purity of conduct in his profession, as he was by his industry
and fidelity to those who employed him."

But of these three men Jefferson declared he owed most to Dr.
William Small, the Scottish professor of mathematics at William
and Mary who after returning to Birmingham, England, became a
medical man and the friend of James Watt and Erasmus Darwin.
In his meeting with Small, Jefferson discerned something like destiny. He wrote in his *Autobiography*:

*"It was my great good fortune, and what probably fixed the des-
tinies of life, that Dr. William Small of Scotland was then Professor of Mathematics, a man profound in most of the useful branches*

of science, with a happy talent of communication, correct and gentlemanly manners, and an enlarged and liberal mind."

Dr. Small liked the eager lad from the hill country, talked with him as an equal, and made him his companion outside of class hours. This was just what the absorptive boy, who three years previously had lost an attentive and guiding father, most craved; and it may be imagined that Jefferson listened avidly when the Scotch professor gave him his "first views of the expansion of science, and of the system of things in which we are placed"; all his life Jefferson was a gourmand of knowledge and a glutton for sheer information, loving to know what was the average weight of an American buffalo (1,800 pounds) no less than to discover the annual per capita cost of government in Virginia at the close of the Revolutionary War (21¢ to 40¢).

But Dr. Small did more for young Jefferson than to instruct him in science: he procured the lad's reception by Wythe as a student of law, and Small crowned his attentions by introducing him to the table and conversation of the most elegant man then living in Virginia, Lieutenant Governor Francis Fauquier. There, wrote Jefferson, "I have heard more good sense, more rational and philosophical conversation than in all my life besides."

Fauquier was a gambler, but he was also a man with tastes in literature and music. He gave weekly concerts in which Jefferson, who loved the violin, was invited to take part. With Fauquier, Dr. Small and Wythe, Jefferson, though only a youth, was the fourth member of a genial *partie quarrée*.

"To the habitual conversations on these occasions," said Jefferson in his *Memoirs*, "I owed much instruction."

No doubt this was an understatement. Mature men do not ordinarily trouble themselves to show attention to a youth in his teens, however promising; hence there must have been something singularly winning and capable about Jefferson at this early age to have gained admittance to a circle so brilliant. Young Jefferson was mentally well equipped to take full advantage of the companionship of these learned men. His father, Peter Jefferson, who, in his son's words, had been "of a strong mind, sound judgement, and eager after information," had encouraged Tom, who was his third child, to read the classics and study the world around him.

So many of Jefferson's letters and papers are written in a serious tone that it is hard to imagine him taking part in gaieties and dissipations. Yet after he had at the age of seventeen become a student at William and Mary, he was, by his own statement, often thrown into the society of horse racers, card players and fox hunters.

Williamsburg, the colonial capital of Virginia, was a center of frivolity as well as of politics and learning—Jefferson himself sometimes called it "Devilsburg"; and at first the reckless men who frequented Henry Wedderburn's tavern there fascinated the country boy who had come down from the Piedmont Hills one hundred and fifty miles distant. Having already a taste for good clothes and horses, as well as books, Thomas's bills often were high, and sometimes he felt a twinge of conscience. After his first year at the college, indeed, he was so troubled that he wrote to his guardian suggesting that his expenses should be charged to his inheritance from his father. But his proffer was waved aside.

"If you have sowed your wild oats in this way," said the reply, "the estate can well afford to pay the bill."

During his second year in college Jefferson studied hard; sometimes for fifteen hours a day. He took his only exercise after sundown when he ran a mile out of town, then back. He was absorbed by mathematics, and read copiously in Greek and Latin authors. Of the speculations and metaphysical writings grouped at the time under the head of "moral philosophy," he once remarked that he thought it "lost time to attend lectures on this branch."

"A boy goes to college," wrote Emerson, "and the students educate him."

At Williamsburg Jefferson met not only those idealized elders, Dr. Small, George Wythe and Peyton Randolph, but fellow-students of his own age and station, the sons of Tidewater planters, who became his friends for life. Among them were John Page, afterward governor of Virginia, to whom Jefferson wrote many letters at that time of life when to young men the most important things in the world are girls; Dabney Carr, Jefferson's closest boyhood friend; John Tyler, also a later governor of Virginia; John Walker, son of

Peter Jefferson's favorite physician; Benjamin Harrison; William Fleming; Warner Lewis; and other sons of established families living in the rich river valleys of Virginia.

Jefferson once wrote Page that affairs at William and Mary had fallen "in the greatest confusion" because of charges of misbehavior brought by the president and masters of the college against certain students, among whom were Walker, Burwell and Lewis. Walker was rusticated or temporarily suspended, while Burwell and Lewis had fled as Jefferson put it, "to escape flagellation."

From this we may conclude that Jefferson's companions at William and Mary were much like well-to-do college boys anywhere and any time—preferring amusement to books and mischief to instructions. No wonder he was moved in 1808 to write to a grandson: "When I recollect that at 14 years of age, the whole care and direction of myself was thrown on myself entirely, without a relation or a friend qualified to advise or guide me, and recollect the various sorts of bad company with which I associated from time to time, I am astonished I did not turn off with some of them, and become as worthless to society as they were."

Altogether Jefferson could not have been satisfied with his schooling or other academic experiences. In his riper years he wrote to James Maury, son of his old teacher, suggesting they meet and renew their recollections: *"Reviewing the course of a long and sufficiently successful life, I find in it no portion of it happier moments than those were."* But in the same letter he made it plain he was not thinking of books, or studies, but of *"youthful exploits, our hunts on Peter's Mountain, with a long train of et cetera in addition."* If only we knew what Jefferson meant by that "et cetera," we would know about the things that shaped his boyish mind at this period.

He left William and Mary at the end of his second year, in the spring of 1762. But his education was just beginning.

CHAPTER 2

BACK TO ANCIENT
BRITISH LIBERTIES

ALTHOUGH JEFFERSON WAS only nineteen years old when he departed from college, he was already, in his own words, "bold in pursuit of knowledge, never fearing to follow truth and reason whatever results they led [to], and bearding every authority which stood in their way." In this he was not unique: all spirited and healthy young fellows at some stage are radicals and rebels; yet one of Jefferson's distinctions was that increasing age found him neither cynical nor conservative. During a long life he remained an inquirer and student. He believed that intelligence is given to man not only to have but to use.

On leaving William and Mary, Jefferson hung up his three-cornered hat in the law office of the learned George Wythe, whose firm signature can be read to this day high on the Declaration of Independence. Jefferson loved the companionship of Wythe, then thirty-four years old; but he could have begun the study of law with no gaiety. In his secret heart he probably would have preferred to be an architect, for all his life he loved to design and build; or he might have chosen to be a teacher of science. But at dusty little Williamsburg there was no outlet for either architectural or scientific tastes. Even the college buildings, Jefferson saw as "wide, mis-shapen piles, which, but they have roofs, would be taken for brick kilns." He had no taste for the practice of law, and looked down on lawyers and their jargon; but Jefferson's instinct was to be thorough, and soon he was deep in Coke's digest of English law. He also read diligently in other legal and lay volumes owned by Wythe. Jefferson found Coke dry but appealing; in dealing with the common law and

8

the growth of liberty Coke was almost eloquent. But when Jefferson
came to Blackstone, he detected something sinister.

"Coke Lyttleton," he wrote, *"was the universal elementary book
of law students; and a sounder Whig never wrote, nor of profounder
learning in the orthodox doctrines of the British Constitution, or in
what were called British liberties. Our lawyers were then all Whigs.
But when his black-letter text, and uncouth but cunning learning,
got out of fashion, and the honeyed Mansfieldism of Blackstone became the student's hornbook, from that moment that profession (the
nursery of our Congress) began to slide into Toryism, and nearly all
the young brood of lawyers are now of that line. They suppose themselves indeed to be Whigs, because they no longer know what
Whiggism or Republicanism means."*

In reading English law, Jefferson was amazed to learn that the
Bible was part of the law of the realm. In the words of Sir Matthew
Hale, "Christianity is parcel of the laws of England," and this dictum
had been used by Lord Mansfield in his decisions. "The essential
principles of revealed religion," Mansfield once ruled, "are part of
the common law," and Blackstone in his commentaries had rubri-
cated this precept. In this field precedent had been piled upon
precedent, so that it occurred to no one at that day to question the
saying. But Jefferson questioned it; moreover, he tracked it to its
cradle. And he decided it had been founded on fraud. He called
it a "pious fraud" because the old monks of England in copying
King Alfred's Saxon laws had inserted five chapters from the Book
of Exodus, the 20th to the 24th. "This string of authorities," he
remarked of Blackstone, Mansfield and Hale, "all hang on the same
hook, a perverted expression of Prisot's." Prisot had written in an old
law book that the common law was derived in part from *ancien
scripture.* Jefferson showed these words were merely the French for
"ancient writings." But the translator had made it read "Holy
Scripture," thus justifying a belief in witches, demons, sorceries
and other medieval furniture. Jefferson concluded this was an example of "the alliance between Church and State in England" which
"has ever made their judges accomplices in the frauds of the clergy."

We can imagine the young Jefferson at this time making up his
mind that if ever opportunity offered, he would cut in two the link

between church and state in Virginia. In this excoriating remark there are other germs of his subsequent thought. One was a distrust of official England. The other was a scorn of official clergymen, a feeling which the clergy hotly returned.

But all this study was dry fare for a nineteen-year-old lad of vigorous health and not a little personal charm; and one day his feelings burst from the end of his quill pen in a letter to John Page:

"Well, Page, I do wish the devil had old Coke, for I am sure I never was so tired of an old dull scoundrel in my life."

For this tedium nature had a remedy, and young Jefferson soon found it. Its components were named in his letters of this period— Rebecca Burwell, Sukey Potter, Sally Nicholas, Alice Corbin, Jane Nelson, Betsy Page and other colonial maids. Of these Rebecca, daughter of the president of the Virginia council, was his chief concern. He could not make up his mind about her. He tried to conceal his interest in her by curious cyphers. "Belinda" was a favorite pseudonym for her. This name he converted into Latin syllables—"campana in die," and then again he reversed it and wrote it in Greek letters as "Adnileb." This was a curious trait in Jefferson; an instinct to conceal followed him through life. Not only he never wore his heart upon his sleeve, but tried to lead the approaches to it through a maze. He was not satisfied now to write his love-tremors to Page in ordinary language, but hinted: "We must fall on some scheme of communicating our thoughts to each other, which shall be totally unintelligible to every one but ourselves. I will send you some of these days Shelton's Tachygraphical Alphabet, and directions." [Tachygraphy, "speed writing," was later known as short-hand.]

We know little about Rebecca Burwell except that Jefferson called her "the devil; if not the devil she's one of his imps." Hence we can guess she was vivacious and mischievous. She liked him well enough to give him a "watch-paper"—possibly a self-cut silhouette of herself —made to fit inside his watch-case. When in Williamsburg, she liked to dance at the Apollo Room of the Raleigh Tavern, which housed most of the capital's social as well as political events. She was an orphan, the daughter of Lewis Burwell of Fairfield, a plantation on

Carter's Creek on the north side of the York river; and she was a sister of that younger Lewis Burwell who, as already noted, once fled from William and Mary College to escape disciplinary measures.

Of the other girls of her set young Jefferson was fond enough, but none so teased his heart and imagination as the little Belinda. Once when he was on a visit to Shadwell, where his mother lived with her brood of nine other children, soon after the new year in 1763, he was bored with the quietude of the place ("I am scarcely sensible that I exist," he wrote Page), and could not resist asking his confidant, who seems also to have been his advocate with Rebecca: "How does R. B. do?" Jefferson's indecision was pitiable. He who inscribed himself "bold in pursuit of knowledge, never fearing to follow truth" was anything but bold in his pursuit of Belinda, while in trying to make up his mind to follow her he was a laggard. "Had I better stay here," he implored Page, "and do nothing, or go down and do less? . . . Inclination tells me to go, receive my sentence, and be no longer in suspense; but reason says, if you go, and your attempt proves unsuccessful, you will be ten times more wretched than ever."

At moments he fancied he would, and could, marry Rebecca. He conjured up rosy pictures of a life together. "Dear Will," he wrote Fleming, another college mate, "I have thought of the cleverest plan of life that can be imagined. You exchange lands for Edgehill, or I mine for Fairfield, you marry S——y P——r [Sukey Potter], I marry R—— B——, join and get a pole chair and a pair of keen horses, practise the law in the same courts, and drive about to all the dances in the country together." But such imaginings would then be rejected in favor of devices for curing love as a sort of distemper.

"Have you any inclination for travel, Page?" he wrote. "Because if you have, I shall be glad of your company. For you must know that as soon as the Rebecca (the name I intend to give the vessel above mentioned) is completely finished, I intend to hoist sail and away. I shall visit particularly England, Holland, France, Spain, Italy (where I would buy me a good fiddle) and Egypt, and return through the British provinces to the northward, home. This, to be sure, would take us two or three years, and if we should not both be cured of love in that time, I think the devil would be in it."

It is possible that he hoped Page would drop in the right quarter a hint about his proposed departure for foreign lands, so that he, Jefferson, might judge of the effect on Belinda. Page seems to have recommended that the suitor come down to Williamsburg and present his case in person, for a possible rival was on the horizon. Jefferson's reply was:

"The rival you mention I know not whether to think formidable or not, as there has been so great an opening for him during my absence. I say has been, because I expect there is one no longer. . . . No, no, Page: whatever assurances I may give her in private of my esteem for her, or whatever assurances I may ask in return from her, depend on it—they must be kept in private. . . . If Belinda will not accept of my service, it shall never be offered another. That she may, I pray most sincerely; but that she will, she gave me no reason to hope."

And then, revealing his reading of the Stoic philosophy mingled with a Christian resignation perhaps taught by the masters under whom he had labored, he wrote to Page this bit from a young man's sadness:

"Perfect happiness, I believe, was never intended by the Deity to be the lot of one of his creatures in this world; but that he has very much put in our power the nearness of our approaches to it, is what I have steadfastly believed.

"The most fortunate of us, on our journey through life, frequently meet with calamities and misfortunes which may greatly afflict us; and, to fortify our minds against the attacks of these calamities and misfortunes, should be one of the principal studies and endeavors of our lives. The only method of doing this is to assume a perfect resignation to the Divine will, to consider that whatever does happen, must happen. . . . Such, dear Page, will be the language of the man who considers this situation in life, and such should be the language of every man who would wish to render that situation as easy as the nature of it will admit. Few things will disturb him at all; nothing will disturb him much."

Certainly Jefferson, with his extreme sensibility, needed all his

early Stoic philosophy to enable him to bear up under all the
attacks that fate had prepared for him.

After an absence of almost nine months at Shadwell, Jefferson
returned to Williamsburg in October, 1763. One evening in that
month William Nelson of Yorktown, Rebecca's uncle with whom
she lived, was in town to attend a meeting of the council, and
Rebecca was able to attend a ball given in the Apollo Room of
the Raleigh Tavern, a chamber soon to house important political
as well as social events.

Jefferson had had word she was to be there and had prepared a
series of neat little speeches intended for her intimate ear—speeches
designed to impress her, but not so designed as to commit himself
unduly in case she should lack response.

Everything went well. The occasion was jolly; the lady showed
herself ready to listen. It may be assumed that Jefferson, who although he could be careless about his appearance, could also dress
himself meticulously, looked his redheaded best—young, slim and
self-conscious. But when at length Belinda was dancing in his arms,
when the moment came that had been for months prepared for,
Jefferson found the situation to be wretched beyond his control.
What he was saying lacked point, and despite his laborious effort
to say something effective, dreadful pauses crept in that drew themselves out to dismal lengths. In short, the evening was a failure, and
Thomas confessed to Page:

"In the most melancholy fit that ever any poor soul was, I sit
down to write to you. Last night, as merry as agreable company and
dancing with Belinda in the Apollo could make me, I never could
have thought the succeeding sun would have seen me so wretched
as I now am! I was prepared to say a great deal. . . . But, good
God! When I had an opportunity of writing them, a few broken
sentences, uttered in great disorder, and interrupted with pauses of
uncommon length, were the two visible marks of my strange confusion!"

Several weeks later he wrote again to Page as a result of some
sort of warning letter received from him: "The contents of your
letter has not a little alarmed me, and really upon seriously weigh-

ing them with what has formerly passed between —— and myself, I am somewhat at a loss what to conclude; your *semper saltat, semper videt, semper loquitur, semper solicitat, etc.* appear a little suspicious; but good God! it is impossible. . . . I asked no question which would admit of a categorical answer; but I assured Belinda that such questions would one day be asked—in short were I to have another interview with him, I could say nothing now which I did not say then. . . . He is satisfied that I shall make him an offer, and if he intends to accept of it, he will disregard those made by others. . . ."

In this priggish letter it can be seen that Jefferson not only gave Miss Burwell the disguise of Belinda, but went to the length of referring to her by a masculine pronoun. This might have been done in order to throw any casual reader of his letter off the track; or it might have been in line with Jefferson's habitual love of secrecy. In the spring of that year, 1764, Jefferson in a letter to Fleming had to write a final brief chapter to this formless romance:

"With regard to the scheme which I proposed to you sometime since, I am sorry to tell you it is totally frustrated by Miss R. B's marriage with Jacquelin Ambler, which the people here tell me they daily expect: I say the people here tell me so, for (can you believe it?) I have been so abominably indolent as not to have seen her since last October, wherefore I cannot affirm I knew it from herself, though I am as well satisfied if it is true as if she had told me. Well, the Lord bless her, I say!" Thus were Jefferson's first matrimonial intentions cut short by his own laggardness and indecision.

Jacquelin Ambler was afterward the Virginia provincial treasurer. As for Rebecca Burwell, she became the mother-in-law of Justice John Marshall, one of the most implacable of Jefferson's critics.

For all his admitted indolence as a suitor, Jefferson could not have escaped a heart wound, although not deep, in this affair; for soon afterward he began to fill his literary *Commonplace Book* with quotations critical of, and derogatory to, the female sex. Woman was put down as "the front of all human frailty," and marriage was described as a last human resort.

"When I am old and weary of the world," he wrote, "I may grow desperate, and take a wife to mortify withal."

Just as a cynic may be regarded as a disappointed idealist turned wrong side out, so a derider of women and marriage may be regarded as not far from the altar. How close Jefferson was at this time, we shall soon see. Meantime, as a young man in his late teens and early twenties, he must have had a famous time. He was related to some of the chief families of the pleasure-loving Tidewater country, where a hundred doors were ready to open at his touch; he found ample occasion to play his violin—in a letter of the period he speaks of half a dozen minuets he had just got; he could ride out from Shadwell or Williamsburg and within a couple of hours get off his horse at plantation houses where he could stay indefinitely and be welcome; he was under the admiring eye of several of the province's eminent men, while in a circle of well-born and well-to-do youths he was held in respect and affection. His account book shows he went often to the playhouse, attended races and shootings, and played cards and chess.

He writes of having "passed perhaps a fortnight together at the revelries of the neighborhood and season" during a Christmas holiday at Colonel Nathan Dandridge's house in Hanover county. Here he met a young and ungainly country merchant who had recently failed in business. He was named Patrick Henry, who, though of obvious intelligence, affected uncouth, rustic ways and loved to tell broad jokes that made his friends slap their breeches with delight. He always had a circle of admirers about him, and he talked in a broader dialect than they: he pronounced "learning" *larnin'*, "earth" was *yearth* and "cart" had the intrusive Virginia "y" which made it *cyart*.

Henry remained aloof from the gentry and affected the company of backwoodsmen. Yet when the dancing started, he made himself the center of the fun, whether he was doing the fiddling or leading the figure in a Sir Roger de Coverley. Behind this rustic storekeeper's unhandsome appearance lay some fierce inner energy; he afterward took one of Colonel Dandridge's daughters for wife, winning her away from John Paul Jones, the naval captain. Jefferson watched Henry and was fascinated by him. Yet Patrick Henry was Jefferson's opposite in almost every respect, and they seemed to have nothing in common save a love of fiddling. Jefferson later wrote of Henry one of his swift and searching sketches:

"On his visits to court, he used always to put up with me. On one occasion of the breaking up in November, to meet again in the spring, as he was departing in the morning, he looked among my books and observed 'Mr. J., I will take two volumes of Hume's Essays, and try to read them this winter.' On his return he brought them, saying he had not been able to get half way into them.

"His great delight was to put on his hunting shirt, collect a parcel of overseers and such like people, and spend weeks in the 'piny woods,' camping at night, and cracking jokes round a light-wood fire."

There was another respect in which Patrick Henry fascinated the lad from Shadwell: in speaking he had an enormous gift of acceleration, leaping into the middle of his subject and rivetting attention instantly. *"He spoke as Homer wrote,"* said Jefferson, who on his feet could utter logic but no eloquence, having a voice that had not the strength for long speech. "I have frequently shut my eyes while he spoke," wrote Jefferson of Henry, "and when he was done asked myself what he had said, without being able to recollect a word of it."

All these encounters, social and political, while he danced attendance on the Virginia girls at great houses where punctilio was often mixed with the most hospitable informality, were part of young Jefferson's education. They gave him ease and assurance, so that when as envoy to France he met the cleverest women and most sophisticated men of Paris, they accepted him as an equal and friend.

CHAPTER 3

STILL A STUDENT

WHEN JEFFERSON WAS still a very young man, he began making entries in the first of those private records that reveal his love of detail. No other such master of the particular ever sat in the White House. Jefferson was forever counting, weighing and measuring. He loved to estimate. He was a born figurer. Late in life he confessed that mathematics had been his first intellectual love, and that he had returned to it with the old zest if not the old facility. Mathematics, be it noted, is the mark of the self-contained mind, of the individual dependent on nothing beyond himself.

One of the first of the long line of blank books Jefferson brought to his desk was a *Garden Book*.[1] In this he kept up his entries for fifty-eight years. Even when he was president of the United States he annually noted for eight years the dates of the earliest and latest appearances of the vegetables commonest on the Washington market. Thus he recorded sprouts on February 22, corn "sallad" on March 4, and radishes on March 28, while cauliflower and cresses appeared in December.

When he was just past his majority, Jefferson felt the first attack by that enemy which in subsequent years so frequently beset his household—death. Jane Jefferson, his eldest sister, died when she was only twenty-five years old. He was twenty-two. It was for her that he wrote the tender epitaph:

> *"Ah, Joanna, puellarum optima,*
> *Ah, aevi virentis flore praerepta,*

---

[1] This book has been annotated by Professor Edwin Morris Betts of the Miller School of Biology, University of Virginia.

17

Sit tibi terra laevis;
Longe, longeque valeto!" [2]

In his old age, Jefferson loved to tell his grandchildren about this best of sisters. It was probably she who fostered his early love of music; they often played together, he on the violin, the psalmic melodies, convincing Jefferson that ordinary hymns were "far less suited to the dignity of religious worship."

In this year, 1765, occurred another event of importance in Jefferson's life: his sister Martha married Dabney Carr, of whose modest home Jefferson wrote this affectionate picture to John Page:

"This friend of ours, Page, in a very small house, with a table, half a dozen chairs, and one or two servants, is the happiest man in the universe. Every incident in life he so takes as to render it a source of pleasure. With as much benevolence as the heart of men will hold, but with an utter neglect of the costly apparatus of life, he exhibits to the world a new phenomenon in philosophy—the Senecan sage in the tub of the cynic."

Dabney Carr was a man whom the soul of Jefferson loved. Two miles from Shadwell, Jefferson's home, rose a lone, low mountain which then had no name but which Jefferson afterward called Monticello. To the top of this little wooded mountain the two friends often went for intimate conversation. There they made one of those compacts that imaginative and fond young men are wont to devise for the tighter forging of mutual bonds. It was agreed that on this spot the one who died first should be buried by the other. Dabney Carr lies there today and not far away is Jefferson.

In 1767, when Jefferson was twenty-four years old, he began the practice of law. In this first year he had sixty-eight cases. He made himself into an excellent office lawyer. But for the broils and tempests of court trials he had no talent. He hated undignified strife; and for success as an advocate before the bar he lacked vigor of delivery. Rarely at any time during a long life did he speak in public. After a few minutes his voice was apt to weaken and grow

---

[2] Ah, my Jane, best of maidens,
  Ah, cut off in thy green youth,
    May earth rest lightly upon you;
    A fond, fond farewell!

husky. His was a temperament which at certain times inclined him toward silence and solitude. It was a student's temperament. Concerning this period he afterward wrote:

"When I was a student of the law . . . after getting through Coke Littleton, whose matter cannot be abridged, I was in the habit of abridging and commonplacing what I read meriting it, and of sometimes mixing my own reflections on the subject."

It was some time during these years, perhaps between 1764 and 1772, that something strangely maturing happened to Jefferson. In its way it was a metamorphosis as complete as that which transforms a creeping caterpillar into a winged butterfly. The moon-touched lad, concerned with girls and frolics, disappeared; the love-struck youth, yearning after a Belinda flying across a ballroom floor, left the stage; instead there developed a steady-minded lawyer versed in history and a critic of governments and societies. Where there was a priggish and hesitant young man, we find the grave and careful student of laws and histories; where there was an immature youth dreaming of a typical upper-class Englishman's grand tour of Europe, we find a searcher of the lock-boxes of civilizations.

What caused this change in Jefferson we do not certainly know. About particular phases of his life he was candid enough; over others he clamped the most steely covers. The Rebecca Burwell who rejected him for another man was possibly a factor. And so perhaps was the shock of Jane Jefferson's death. A third contributing cause may have been the complete destruction by fire of his mother's house at Shadwell in 1770. In this disaster, he told John Page, he had lost "every paper I had in the world, and almost every book." If we knew what were the contents of those papers and what was the nature of those books, we should know better the process of development that went on in Jefferson's mind during those critical and fixing years. Lacking them, we can only surmise. And yet we have one plain clue visible in this letter to John Page wherein Jefferson went on to say: "To make the loss more sensible, it fell principally on my books of Common Law, of which I have but one left, at that time lent out." This book was recovered subsequently, and it is a revelation of Jefferson's maturing mind. In fact, it is the very key to Jefferson's firmest conclusions and beliefs. He called it his *Commonplace Book*.

CHAPTER 4

WHENCE JEFFERSON DREW
HIS IDEAS

WHEN THE HOUSE at Shadwell burned, Jefferson moved to Monticello where for the rest of his active years he worked upon the main house, the satellite buildings or the grounds. At first he thought of calling his place on the little mountain the "Hermitage," which fact is in itself significant: for never in life was he free of streams of visitors. He used the name Monticello for the first time in an entry on August 3, 1767, when he was beginning to practice law.

He rapidly replaced his burned books, so that by August 4, 1773, he was able to record that his new library contained 1,244 books, not including "volumes of music, nor my books in Williamsburg." The authors or titles of most of these volumes are known, but we should not know what books, either before or after the fire, most impressed or influenced young Jefferson, were it not for the discovery in recent years of his *Commonplace Book*. It is the reprint of this book that enables us to trace the source of some of Jefferson's characteristic political and social tenets. Also it reveals how truly Jefferson the youth was father of Jefferson the man. This *Commonplace Book* furnishes evidence that Jefferson's opinions crystallized very early in life, and that his views regarding human societies he was able to retain from youth to old age with remarkable consistency.

After Jefferson had become nationally prominent, it was often and acrimoniously charged by his enemies that while resident in France he had become unduly swayed by foul French notions stemming out of the soil of subversion and revolution. But his *Commonplace Book* furnishes abundant proof that in his studies of governments and other political structures he went back not to French but to English sources; that in seeking the origins of American law and custom he traced them back to the very Angles and Saxons who invaded Britain; and that although he gave due attention to Montesquieu and his *Spirit of Laws,* he damned the French writer as often as he praised him, and gave the greater respect to King Alfred as framer and establisher of the common law of England, which in Saxon was called the "folk-right" or people's right.

"We know that the Common law," wrote Jefferson in his notes, "is that system of law which was introduced by the Saxons on their settlement in England, and altered from time to time by proper legislative authority from that to the date of the Magna Charta which terminates the period of the Common law, or *Lex non scripta,* and commences that of the Statute law, or *Lex scripta.*" [1]

It was when unwritten law became written law that the liberties of men began to suffer; Jefferson convinced himself of that by his studies of English political writers. Unwritten law, which grew out of custom on the one hand and the natural rights of peoples on the other, had permitted men to live freely and to be freely active, developing institutions suited to their needs.

This was what he learned from English writers concerning their Saxon ancestors; and this was in accord with his own observations among American Indians, whom Jefferson admired for certain primitively democratic customs and whom he always treated with special consideration. It was when unwritten law was taken in hand by sharp lawyers and biased judges, and by nobles and sycophantic priests, that wisdom and justice began to deteriorate. Jefferson believed that these clever or corrupt gentry converted, or twisted at the behest of kings and conquerors, unwritten law into written law, which in time became fixed, so that it worked oppression upon peoples, goading them at last into rebellion and insurrection. It was in this belief that Jefferson subsequently wrote these passages in *A Summary View of the Rights of British America:*

". . . Our ancestors, before their emigration to America, were the free inhabitants of the British Dominions in Europe, and possessed a right, which nature has given to all men, of departing from the country in which chance, not choice, had placed them, of going in

---

[1] *The Commonplace Book of Thomas Jefferson,* ed. Chinard, Baltimore, 1926.

quest of new habitations, and of there establishing new societies, under such laws and regulations as, to them, shall seem most likely to promote public happiness.

". . . Their Saxon ancestors had, under this universal Law, in like manner, left their native wilds and woods in the north of Europe, had possessed themselves of the Island of Britain, then less charged with inhabitants, and had established there a system of laws which has been so long the glory and protection of that country."

Here are terms and phrases often to be encountered in Jefferson's later writings; and here is proof that in his young manhood he was just a loyal young colonial Briton.

Natural rights . . . The rights of human nature . . . The rights of man.

These are phrases Jefferson loved to dwell upon. Whence came they? In his *Commonplace Book* Jefferson made extensive notes from the writings of Lord Kames ("Kaims," Jefferson spelled it), the Scottish jurist, especially Kames's histories of the criminal law, of property and of privileges; he abstracted chapters from Dalrymple's *Essay Toward a General History of Federal Property in Great Britain,* published in London in 1757; and he studied Pelloutier's histories of the rise of popular sovereignty among early peoples. From each of these writers he learned something substantial; and it can be imagined that he took particular note of Kames's saying, "Man by his nature is fitted for society"; of Dalrymple's prophecy that "our entails will share the fate of almost all the other remains of feudal law"; and of Pelloutier's descriptions of tribes which were able to be free and independent without having either military organizations or captains except when attacked.

And finally he noted Blackstone's observations on English liberties, summarizing the essayist's view that "English liberties are not infringements merely of the King's prerogative, extorted from our princes by taking advantage of their weakness; but a restoration of that antient [sic] constitution, of which our ancestors had been defrauded by the art and finesse of the Norman Lawyers, rather than deprived by the force of the Norman arms."

There is nothing in Jefferson's *Commonplace Book* to indicate

Thomas Jefferson in fashionable Parisian dress. Painted by John Trumbull for Maria Cosway. Previously unpublished, this portrait was found in the convent for girls at Lodi, Italy, established by Mrs. Cosway.

Photo by Ralph Thompson

View of the Rivanna River near Shadwell, Virginia, Jefferson's birthplace. Taken at about the site where he had his mill.

that at this time he was in any rebellious mood against his sovereign, George III; or that he was gathering force for any flaming outburst against monarchs or governments; he was just a young colonial lawyer collecting abstracts and noting precedents. These things he copied and filed in his characteristically thorough and orderly way. The abstracted laws, customs and opinions thus gathered were in no way radical. They merely reflected what the late eighteenth century was thinking of; registered what was the temper and content of the mental climate. But these plodding notes ably prepared young Jefferson for what was to come; so that when the occasion arrived, he was armed for it and spoke with so much of the thunder of Jove that his associates recognized his Olympian power.

One of Jefferson's longest and most careful studies dealt with the history of property. It covered many pages and concluded with remarks on "the thirst of man . . . to perpetuate his memory and his wealth," evidenced in England by the statute of entails and the locking up of land. He could foresee the time when the whole available land would thus be taken out of use.

"How pernicious this event must be need not be explained," he wrote. "Land-property, naturally one of the greatest blessings of life, is thus converted into a curse."

Entailed land, he noted, finally subverts "that liberty and independency, to which all men aspire, with respect to their possessions as well as their persons." Hence it is not surprising to find Jefferson a few years later attacking the system that gave rise to entailed and locked-up land in Virginia. In the *Commonplace Book* were entered many curious passages and cullings from authors both ancient and modern. One abstract of particular interest was taken from James Wilson's *Considerations on the Nature and Extent of the Legislative Authority of the British Parliament* published in Philadelphia in 1774. It concluded: "Will it then ensure and increase the happiness of the American colonies that the parliament of Great Britain should possess a supreme irresistible, uncontrouled [*sic*] authority over them?" A passage from the discussion by Wilson, who was a Pennsylvania signer of the Declaration of Independence, contains these sentences not quoted by Jefferson in his notes:

"All men are, by nature, equal and free: No one has a right to any authority over another without his consent; All lawful government is founded on the consent of those, who are subject to it: Such consent was given with a view to ensure and to increase the happiness of the governed above what they could enjoy in an independent and unconnected state of nature. The consequence is, that the happiness of the society is the first law of every government." The echoes that lie in this quotation are patent.

CHAPTER 5

WHAT JEFFERSON ADMIRED
MOST IN A WOMAN

THERE ARE STILL many things we do not know about Jefferson. One question that arises is: How did such a well-born, well-to-do young colonial Englishman grow up to be a teacher of republicanism and a philosopher of democracy?

Another question to be answered is: What caused this prospering young bachelor, who might have been a leader at dances, races and hunting, to drop all such diversions to experiment with gardening and agriculture, and to start a solitary home for himself atop a mountain on the other side of the Rivanna, two miles from his mother's house at Shadwell?

A third question is: How did he meet and win the young widow who became his wife?

Beyond a few legends, all we know is that at the end of 1771 he applied at Charles City county court for a license to marry Martha Wayles Skelton, twenty-three years old. She had been the widow of Bathurst Skelton, a planter, for three years. Her father was John Wayles, an affable English-born lawyer with a practice at Williamsburg and an estate nearby on the James, called The Forest. He was the owner of large farm properties and many slaves. Of his daughter, Martha, we know little except that a visitor, the Marquis de Chastellux, found her "amiable," that she was sought by several suitors, and that two of them met one evening at her doorstep. When through a window they saw her playing a spinet while the tall Jefferson accompanied her on his violin, something told them they could as suitors spare themselves further pains, whereupon they silently stole away. If Jefferson's heart was ardent, his head on his wedding day was

25

cool enough; for in his account book he set down every item of marriage expense, even the fees handed to the clergymen, fiddlers and servants. The wedding journey was a cold drive in January, 1772, for more than a hundred miles to Monticello, where they arrived over a snow-covered road at a cold and silent one-room brick cottage built there by Jefferson. Luckily they found a bottle of wine, and this and youth and hope warmed them and made them merry.

As for Jefferson's ideas of what a woman and wife should be, we get an inkling from letters he wrote. In truth, he had a plain eighteenth-century, indeed a patriarchal, concept of woman as a companionate vassal of her husband. The right sort of American women, he once reminded the ambitious Mrs. William Bingham of Philadelphia, "are contented to soothe and calm the minds of their husbands returning ruffled from political debate. . . . Compare [the women of Paris] with our own countrywomen occupied in the tender and tranquil amusements of domestic life, and confess that is a comparison of Americans and angels." Women, he maintained, ought to be excluded from popular assemblies "to prevent depravation of morals and ambiguity of issue."

Mrs. Jefferson was with child less than a month after her marriage, the first of the six children born to her and Jefferson within ten years, of whom only two survived beyond infancy.

At the death of her father, Jefferson's bride inherited one hundred and thirty-five slaves and forty thousand acres of land. Included were Poplar Forest, the beautiful farm in Bedford county which became a favorite refuge and summer home of Jefferson; and smaller properties called Elk Hill, Indian Camp, Angola, Guinea, Bridgequarter and Ligon's. Jefferson, who had inherited nineteen hundred acres from his father and had more than doubled them, and had also made additions to his inherited force of thirty slaves, was now in possession of a princely estate, and was master of two hundred human beings. He could look out on the world from his Monticello eminence and find himself near the summit of human felicity: for besides being a prosperous lawyer and a land, slave and wife owner, he was a member of the Virginia assembly; he was the official surveyor of Albemarle county; and he was the royal lieutenant of the same county and head of its militia by appointment of Lord Botetourt, the royal governor.

An onlooker from above would have said that never was a young colonial Briton more solidly established. An onlooker from below, however, might have seen the foundations of this stately structure already trembling. As for Jefferson, he was a man of neither forebodings nor regrets. His practical mind was intent only on the day's events, and his marriage bells had hardly ceased to ring when he was writing notes like these in his *Garden Book:*

"1772. Jan. 26. The deepest snow we have ever seen. In Albemarle it was about three feet deep.

"Mar. 30. Sowed a patch of later peas.

"July 15. Cucumbers came to table.

"Aug. 20. The wagon with four horses, and the driver without any assistant, brought about 300 yds. wood, which measured 4, 8 and 19½ feet, i.e., nearly 5 cords, calling a cord 4, 4 and 8, in one day. It took 10 loads." [1]

To appear in "the character of a farmer"—that was ever Jefferson's aim and satisfaction. But a note in the *Garden Book* in 1773 is significant: "Mrs. Wythe puts one-tenth very rich superfine Malmesey to a dry Madeira, and makes a fine wine." A farmer Jefferson was, and sometimes a good one; but he was at all times a gentleman-farmer, loving wine and good company.

---

[1] *Jefferson's Garden Book,* ed. Betts.

CHAPTER 6

HOW JEFFERSON BECAME
A REVOLUTIONIST

JEFFERSON HAD BEEN married six months and had settled down into that intimate and beloved routine of farm, books and family when the news reached Virginia that the British government's armed vessel, the *Gaspee,* had been burned in Massachusetts waters; and that the government had decreed all persons accused in connection with the incident might be transported to England for trial on possible treason charges. Loyal subjects of George III in Virginia might have been, and were, anxious and uncertain what to do; but Jefferson showed not the least hesitation. Because of his historical and legal studies of which his *Commonplace Book* had copious notes, his mind was already made up; and he was not slow in joining a group of young fellow-burgesses who wanted to exchange views "on the state of things." Included were the Lees—Richard Henry and Francis Lightfoot; Jefferson's brother-in-law, Dabney Carr and finally Patrick Henry.

Jefferson had already recognized that leadership in the growing intellectual rebellion against England had passed from "the cyphers of the aristocracy" to "the bolder spirits" among the landowners and to plain yeomen like Henry. He had been watching Henry's course ever since 1765, when he, while still a law student at Williamsburg, had stood at the door of the lobby of the house of burgesses and listened to the debate over the resolutions against the Stamp Act. And he had heard Henry thunder: "If this be treason, make the most of it!" or whatever Henry actually said.

This grim conference of young burgesses was now held where lately Jefferson had danced with Rebecca Burwell and the other girls—at the Raleigh Tavern. "We were all sensible that the most urgent of all measures," wrote Jefferson in his *Autobiography*, "was that of coming to an understanding with all the other colonies, to consider the British claims as forming a cause common to all, and to produce a unity of action." And again when in 1774 news of the closing of the port of Boston arrived, Jefferson and the other younger landowning burgesses agreed at once that they "must boldly take an unequivocal stand in the line with Massachusetts"; and this "line," often emphasized by Jefferson, in substance was that America was a commonwealth claiming all the old Anglo-Saxon rights and privileges, and was not a colony to be exploited by, or subjected to, London.

And now came a piece of characteristic Jeffersonian cunning. The chief obstacle to action was the indifference of the American people —lethargy, Jefferson called it. This lethargy probably stemmed from two sources: the natural absorption of the people in their own concerns, and their accustomed loyalty to the British parliament and crown; for although a few of their younger and rasher leaders at this stage had envisaged a possible future rupture with London, a substantial part of the American people regarded with horror the suggestion of a possible separation from Britain; and not a few closed their minds to it as something unthinkable. To awaken the masses and unify their feelings Jefferson and his colleagues took a leaf from the book of the Puritans in their struggle with Charles I; in Jefferson's words, they "cooked up a resolution" setting aside the day on which Boston Port was to be officially closed as a day of fasting, humiliation and prayer. The scheme, exactly suited to the occasion and the psychology of the people, was electrifying, "arousing every man," wrote Jefferson, "and placing him erect and solidly on his centre."

The reply of Governor Dunmore, as the king's agent, was to dissolve the Virginia assembly. The fat now was not only in the fire but was beginning to crackle. On July 26 the freeholders of Albemarle met and named Jefferson as one of their two delegates at a convention to be held in Williamsburg on August 1. The other delegate was Jefferson's neighbor, Thomas Walker. The resolutions passed at this freeholders' meeting were deeply tinged with Jefferson's ideas, particularly when they proclaimed that no legislature other than their own could "rightly exercise authority" over the inhabitants of the several "States" (this word was Jefferson's substitute for colonies) of British America; that they held to certain rights "as the common rights of mankind"; and that they would join others in asserting such rights "when, where, and by whomsoever invaded." It is noteworthy how closely these resolutions, no doubt penned chiefly by Jefferson's own hand, adhered to the line recorded by the notes in his *Commonplace Book*. The view that in resisting Parliament and George III at this period, the American settlers would be upholding ancient British liberties, made a profound impression not only in America but in Britain itself.

It is not strange that Jefferson in his later years was so emphatic in his declarations that the people could be trusted *when informed*. He himself had tested the power that lies in complete and pertinent information.

When the convention met at Williamsburg on August 1 Jefferson was absent because of a sudden illness. Knowing in advance that delegates would be elected to a general congress, he had prepared for their use a set of resolutions of which he sent one copy to Peyton Randolph, the other to Patrick Henry, who ignored it. Randolph, who presided, laid his copy on the table for perusal. Subsequently it appeared in pamphlet form, entitled, *A Summary View of the Rights of British America*. It got to England where it was made use of by Edmund Burke in his support of America, and where it earned Jefferson a place on the government's proscribed list. This paper was an embryo declaration of independence. It was full of startling propositions, not the least of which were these:

1. "His Majesty is no more than the chief officer of the people."

2. "The British Parliament has no right to exercise authority over us."

3. "The God who gave us life, gave us liberty at the same time."

The congress met at Philadelphia in September, 1774, without doing anything of consequence. At the opening of 1775 Albemarle county elected a committee of public safety; Jefferson headed the chosen list, his neighbor John Walker coming second. Jefferson was also a delegate to the second Virginia convention in Richmond on

March 20, 1775, John Walker being again an associate. It was here that Patrick Henry, impatient of any further humble remarks addressed to the throne and fearing delay by the Tidewater conservatives, shouted: "An appeal to arms and the God of hosts is all that is left us!"

When in this spirit a committee was appointed, Jefferson was one of its members. Then came the news of the Battle of Lexington and general recognition that Patrick Henry was right in saying, "We must fight!" Thereafter the more conservative men as well as those most reluctant to give up their attachment to the British crown were swept along until Lord Dunmore, the royal governor, had fled to an armed vessel and most of the natal cords tying America to England were sundered. As for Jefferson, he suffered from none of the qualms and reluctance that had beset the older and more cautious landowners of Virginia and other provinces. He had no internal war of loyalties. He had never wavered from his belief that the colonists, in resisting George III, were acting on their natural, inborn and God-given rights; and it was with a tranquil conscience that in June, 1775, he started from Williamsburg for Philadelphia where the first Continental Congress was to assemble. It took him ten days to make the trip by way of Fredericksburg, Annapolis and Wilmington; he was more than once lost and had to hire guides to get his phaeton back on the right trail.

He was now thirty-two years old, mature, politically seasoned, and already having that prescience and forefeeling that so often served him in later years. But on this solitary journey through tough and primitive country he could have had no conception that the fates had chosen him, and given to him exactly the preparation needed, to carry out at Philadelphia a momentous historical task.

CHAPTER 7

HOW JEFFERSON SPENT
EIGHTEEN DAYS

IN PHILADELPHIA, Jefferson found a room at the house of Ben Randall in Chestnut Street. Learning that his host was a cabinet-maker,
Jefferson employed him to make from his own design a writing
desk with a folding leaf; and this he used for the official writing tasks
assigned him and for his growing correspondence; for although Jefferson sometimes pretended to be burdened by his letter-writing, he
really enjoyed it and kept it up virtually to his last day, so that even
now more than twenty thousand pieces of writing done by his hand
still exist.

In Philadelphia, although Jefferson was the youngest delegate but
one, he found his nascent fame as a writer had already preceded him.
John Adams, who was sometimes Jefferson's friend and sometimes
his harsh critic, wrote of him:

"Mr. Jefferson came into Congress in June, 1775, and brought
with him a reputation for literature, science, and a happy talent of
composition. Writings of his were handed about remarkable for the
peculiar felicity of expression. . . . Though a silent member in Congress, he was so prompt, frank, explicit, and decisive upon com-
mittees and in conversation—not even Samuel Adams was more so—
that he soon seized upon my heart."

Jefferson's first committee was one appointed to declare the causes
of the colonies' having taken up arms. But characteristically he
yielded the forepart of this paper to the conciliatory pen of his friend,
honest John Dickinson of Pennsylvania; for although Dickinson was
a leader among those conservatives who abhorred any disrespect to
the British crown, he was, at this stage, not greatly behind his col-

leagues, including Jefferson; one and all, indeed, they still looked across the Atlantic with a filial if momentarily resentful piety. "With one mind, [we are] resolved to die free men rather than to live slaves" —these words written by Jefferson accurately expressed the sentiments of the more radical Americans; but they were thinking of resistance, not rupture.

Again, when Lord North, George III's minister, made to the colonies an offer known as a "conciliatory proposition," Jefferson was appointed on a committee to examine it. Included were Benjamin Franklin, John Adams and Richard Henry Lee. Jefferson was chosen to draw up the report, which was an American ultimatum in reply to the British one. Congress adopted this report on July 31, 1775, and adjourned. Jefferson took back to Virginia as his passenger Benjamin Harrison, one of the chief Tidewater planters, "an indolent, luxurious, heavy gentleman" (in the words of John Adams), who became the ancestor of two presidents of the United States.

Eleven days later, the Virginia convention again voted to send Jefferson as a delegate to Congress. He wrote a friendly letter to his kinsman, John Randolph, who after succeeding his brother, Peyton Randolph, as attorney general of Virginia, had decided to take refuge in England. Jefferson hinted that John Randolph might make himself useful as a conciliator; but three months later again he wrote to Randolph a letter, which, although it declared his cordial love for the union with Great Britain, used the ominous word "separation."

As one looks back on the events of this period, it appears that a word of sympathy, a measure of generosity, a gesture of kindly feeling, might have re-knit a resentful colony to its mother country. But the British government, in the grasp of mercantilism, was haughty, authoritarian and arrogant, and in trying to hold all, it lost its greatest possession.

The late summer of 1775 Jefferson spent at Monticello with his pregnant and ailing wife. His family was growing. His oldest child, Martha, was three years old. His second, Jane, was about eighteen months old. Besides them, he was taking care of thirty relatives and looking after eighty-three slaves. He passed much of the time in his garden, where he was experimenting with all sorts of European vegetables, especially those recommended to him by his near neighbor, the Italian Philip Mazzei; and he practiced regularly on his violin under the eye of the Italian teacher, Alberti, who came up for the purpose from Williamsburg. On his travels Jefferson often took along in a small case a "kit," a miniature violin on which he could play in solitude without disturbing his neighbors.

Although Congress had reconvened at Philadelphia on September 5, 1775, Jefferson was delayed by the death of his little daughter Jane and his wife's illness. The birth of her second child had so weakened her that her health was a constant anxiety to Jefferson, even in the broils leading up to the break with England; in fact, her failure to recover her strength after the death of this child was the chief cause of Jefferson's dropping out of political life at a time when his pen and counsel were urgently desired.

He did not arrive in Philadelphia until the twenty-fifth; and although the most important events were impending, he remained only until December 28 when again he returned home. Afterward he referred to his "uneasy anxious state" at this period. Three months later he was still at home, and on March 31, 1776, he tersely recorded the fact that his mother had died that morning in her fifty-seventh year.

He did not appear in Congress again until May 13, 1776. By that time North Carolina had, on April 12, empowered her delegates to concur with other delegates "in declaring independency" and the British government had made clear its intention of putting down the rebellion. It had particularly outraged its American subjects by three measures: one was the forcible conscription of American seamen into the British navy; another was the hiring of German soldiers to fight in America; a third was the burning of Norfolk, Virginia and Falmouth, Maine.

On May 16 Jefferson wrote Thomas Nelson that six weeks of his detention had been due to illness; he added: "I am at present in our old lodgings [at Ben Randall's] tho' I think, as the excessive heats of the city are coming on fast, to endeavor to get lodgings in the skirts of the town where I may have the benefit of a freely circulating air. . . . I am here in the same uneasy anxious state in which I was the last fall without Mrs. Jefferson who could not come with me."

And then, just at the right moment to strengthen the wavering inhabitants, there appeared Thomas Paine's propaganda pamphlet, *Common Sense*. Rapidly the movement toward complete separation from Britain began to rise toward a crest. Jefferson noted, however, that the middle colonies of New York, New Jersey, Pennsylvania, Delaware, Maryland and South Carolina still hung back, being "not yet matured for falling from the parent stem."

On June 11, 1776, Congress deemed it safe to choose a committee of five to prepare a declaration of independence. Jefferson received one more vote than any other delegate and hence became head of the committee. The other members were John Adams of Massachusetts, Benjamin Franklin of Pennsylvania, Judge Roger Sherman of Connecticut and Robert R. Livingston of New York.

Jefferson was then living at Graff's lodging house on Market Street near 7th, where he paid thirty-five shillings a week for two rooms, dining as before at the City Tavern where his meals cost from five shillings to eight shillings sixpence. His concern about the crisis with Great Britain and his anxiety about Mrs. Jefferson back home did not prevent him from making careful entries in his memoranda, not only regarding expenses but also the weather. Thus, he recorded on July 4, 1776, that at 1 P.M. the temperature was 76°, having moderated from a high of 81½° on July 1; and that on the same day he had paid out 3 15s. for a thermometer, 27/ for 7 pair of women's gloves and 1/6 for charity.

Since it was recognized that Jefferson was the ablest writer on the committee of five, he was asked to write out a draft. It took him eighteen days to complete the Declaration of Independence. He discussed certain points with his colleagues and submitted to a number of corrections and to interlinear changes made by Franklin and Adams. Jefferson did his work on the folding desk designed by himself. Afterward he gave it to his grandson, Joseph Coolidge, Jr., with this legend pasted on it:

"*Th. Jefferson gives this writing desk to Joseph Coolidge jun., as a memorial of affection. It was made from a drawing of his own, by Ben Randall, cabinet maker of Philadelphia, with whom he first lodged on his arrival in that city in May 1776, and is the identical one*

on which he wrote the Declaration of Independence [sic]. Politics,
as well as Religion, has it's superstitions. These, gaining strength
with time, may, one day, give imaginary value to this relic, for its
association with the birth of the Great charter of our Independence."

To be noted here is Jefferson's reference to the Declaration as
"the Great charter of our Independence." Some years later when
certain critics, among them Timothy Pickering and John Adams of
Massachusetts, charged that the Declaration contained no new ideas
but was only a compilation, Jefferson was able to reply, a year before
his death, that it had been his purpose "not to find out new principles, or new arguments . . . but to place before mankind the common sense of the subject, in terms so plain and firm as to command
their assent. . . . Neither aiming at originality of principles or sentiments, nor yet copied from any particular and previous writing, it
was intended to be an expression of the American mind. . . . All
its authority rests on the harmonizing sentiments of the day, whether
expressed in conversation, in letters, printed essays, or the elementary
books of public right, as Aristotle, Cicero, Locke, Sidney, etc."

"Whether I had gathered my ideas from reading or reflection, I
do not know," Jefferson once wrote Madison. "I know only that I
turned to neither book nor pamphlet while writing it. I did not
consider it as any part of my charge to invent new ideas altogether,
and to offer no sentiment that had never been expressed before."

The Declaration as a whole contains two principal parts, the
body and the preamble. The body recites many grievances and contains much matter which is now of only historical interest. But in
this section omissions were ordered which Jefferson thus explained:

"Those passages which conveyed censures on the people of England were struck out, lest they should give them offence. The clause,
too, reprobating the enslaving of the inhabitants of Africa, was struck
out in complaisance to South Carolina and Georgia, who had never
attempted to restrain the importation of slaves, and who, on the
contrary, still wished to continue it. Our northern brethren also,
I believe, felt a little tender under those censures; for though their
people had very few slaves themselves, yet they had been pretty
considerable carriers of them to others."

The changes suggested by Franklin and Adams, said Jefferson, numbered only two or three and were oral only. Adams, for instance, thought it too strong to call George III a "tyrant." One curious alteration was the striking out of Jefferson's word "States" and the substitution for it of "colonies"; proof that even at that late date there were in Carpenters' Hall delegates who still could not bear to break the link that bound them to Britain.

It is the preamble of the Declaration which has most impressed all generations of men, particularly its first challenging statement:

That all men are created equal. (Jefferson first wrote "equal and independent," but drew a line through the two latter words.) No saying in American political literature has been more hotly debated than this "that all men are created equal." Jefferson meant that they are equal as parties to a compact. It is evident from his other writings he did not mean that all men are created equal in ability, talent or physique; he meant they are equal in the eyes of law and nature, and, when parties to a compact, are born with equal personal rights. Much subsequent misunderstanding would have been obviated if he had not struck out the added words, "and independent." But Jefferson edited and altered his early drafts of the Declaration much more freely than did his colleagues. The second paragraph of the Declaration ran originally as follows:

"We hold these truths to be sacred and undeniable, that all men are created equal and independent; that from that equal creation they derive inherent and inalienable rights, among which are life, liberty, and the pursuit of happiness. . . ."

The second challenging assertion was "that to secure these rights [originally written 'ends'], governments are instituted among men, deriving their just powers from the consent of the governed." This and the preceding assertion are to be compared with this saying by John Locke: "Men being . . . by nature all free, equal and independent, no one can be put out of this estate and subjected to the political power of another without his own consent." [1]

---

[1] See Becker, *The Declaration of Independence, a Study in the History of Political Ideas*, New York, 1922.

The third great challenge in the Declaration's preamble lies in the statement: "Whenever any form of government becomes destructive of these ends [life, liberty and the pursuit of happiness], it is the right of the people to alter or abolish it, and to institute new government . . ."

This was a conclusion drawn not only from Jefferson's copious reading of history, especially that by Stanyan and Sir Walter Raleigh, but it was in line with his firmly held belief in the right of all peoples to sovereignty and independence. And it was in close accord with the Virginia Bill of Rights in which George Mason had written: "When any government shall be found inadequate or contrary to these purposes, a majority of the community has the indubitable, inalienable right to reform, alter or abolish it."

Although Jefferson was so successful in thus embodying an immortal expression of the nascent American spirit, he wrote it with only half his mind present in Philadelphia. The other half was in Monticello where his delicate wife lay prostrate under the weakness of her repeated pregnancies.

"Every letter," he wrote John Page on July 20, "brings me such an account of the state of her health, that it is with great pain I can stay here." And at length he burst out to Edmund Pendleton: "I am sorry that the situation of my domestic affairs, renders it indispensably necessary that I should solicit the substitution of some other person here in my room."

For three days the critics of the Declaration wrangled and argued against it and sought to amend it. Jefferson's phrases did not lack defenders, but he himself, as usual, said nothing. "The pusillanimous idea that we had friends in England worth keeping terms with, still haunted the minds of many," wrote Jefferson later. These appeasers were successful in having some fifteen passages altered or struck out. Finally on the evening of the Fourth of July, 1776, while the stinging flies flew in at the unscreened windows and bit the stockinged legs of the delegates, the amended Declaration was accepted and signed by every member present, except the rich and gentlemanly Dickinson of Pennsylvania. He, however, pledged his loyalty later.

Just after the passage of the Declaration, Jefferson was appointed on a committee with Franklin and John Adams to prepare a device for a United States seal. Jefferson's design, not adopted, was significant. It showed on the one side the children of Israel in the wilderness; on the other appeared, in his own words, *"Hengist and Horsa, the Saxon chiefs, from whom we claim the honor of being descended, and whose political principles and form of government we have assumed."*

To pick up the thread of Anglo-Saxon liberties—that was ever in Jefferson's mind.

"Are we not the better for what we have hitherto abolished of the feudal system?" he asked the tough-minded Edmund Pendleton. *"Has not every restitution of the antient [sic] Saxon laws had happy effects? Is it not better now that we return at once into that happy system of our ancestors, the wisest and most perfect ever yet devised by the wit of man, as it stood before the 8th century?"*

CHAPTER 8

WHAT ARE A MAN'S RIGHTS?

NO MAN KNEW better than Jefferson that the Declaration of Independence was only one step in the process of freeing colonial America from the Old World's feudal systems and ideas. There remained yet the task of freeing it from monarchical and feudal *institutions*. Those institutions were particularly well entrenched in Virginia where English laws and customs had been transplanted with as little change as possible and where they had been crystallized by slavery. Consequently, on September 2, 1776, Jefferson resigned from Congress and a little over a month later took his seat in the Virginia legislature.

"I knew that our legislation, under the regal government, had many vicious points which urgently required reformation," he wrote in his *Autobiography*, "and I thought I could be of more use in forwarding that work."

In returning to Virginia as a legislator, Jefferson revealed that he was still a loyal provincial rather than a nationalist. He wrote and spoke of Virginia as "my country," and it was that country in which he hoped first to make reforms. Yet he recognized that the colonies, to survive, must find some sort of unity or federation. The subject of personal and social rights was still on his mind, but it was Thomas Paine to whom he was indebted for a clear summary of a distinction between these two kinds of rights.

Natural, or personal, rights Paine defined as those "which can be fully exercised by the individual without the aid of exterior assistance," such as "the rights of thinking, speaking, forming and giving opinions . . . in other words, rights of personal competency."

Civil rights, social rights, "or rights of compact," he defined as those that men cannot individually exercise fully and perfectly but only under the guarantee of society, such as the right of acquiring and possessing property, "in the exercise of which the individual natural power is less than the natural right."

"It therefore follows that the more of those imperfect natural rights or rights of imperfect power we give up and thus exchange, the more security we possess . . .

"The word liberty is often mistakenly put for security. . . .

"It does not follow that the more natural rights of *every kind* we resign the more securely we possess,—because if we resign those of the first class we may suffer much by the exchange. . . .

"I consider the individual sovereignty of the States retained under the Act of Confederation to be of the second class of rights. It becomes dangerous because it is defective in the power necessary to support it. It answers the pride and purpose of a few men in each state—but the State collectively is injured by it."

We can see here how Paine was outlining a scheme of social morality and a theory of a collective society in which powers should equal rights, and in which the amount of liberty desired by an individual should be determined by the amount of security he would enjoy. As for the rights of the individual states forming the American republic, Paine showed in the concluding paragraph quoted above how in certain cases they might become not only doubtful but dangerous.

These conclusions have been called [1] "the key to the whole democratic system evolved by Jefferson" and a clear departure from the European theories of Locke and Rousseau: "In forming a social compact" men do not surrender to central power, but "reserve entire a certain class of rights, all those they can exercise fully without the aid of exterior assistance, and they exchange for more security those they cannot exercise themselves."

And at this point it becomes evident why in the Declaration of Independence, Jefferson made the third member of his famous triad of natural rights "the pursuit of happiness" rather than "property" as set forth in the Virginia Bill of Rights; property belonged to the

---

[1] By Professor Gilbert Chinard, who at first thought these definitions were Jefferson's, but it now seems clear the author was Paine.

second class of rights, or rights of compact to be exercised only under the guarantee of society, hence "of defective power." Their statements and actions often revealed the Founding Fathers as highly property-minded; but Jefferson put happiness ahead of property. For it was his conviction, based on long study, that property is not a natural right, but a legal one only; though he never went as far as his preceptor, John Locke, who wrote: *"Where there is no property, there is no injustice."*

In his attack on feudal institutions, Jefferson first questioned the prevailing ownership and use of land. Thus he proved that the American Revolution was a genuine thing. All true revolutions begin with a question involving land; because although all wealth, hence all existence, arises out of and depends on labor, or the exercise of energy, labor must have land to stand on and the land's products to work upon. Under all social systems known to history there are two opposing trends: one is to monopolize the land in the hands of a relatively small group or class; the other is to distribute the land among those who would make it productive. The action and counter-action of these two trends accounts for many of civilization's bitterest conflicts.

Jefferson's attack was quick and blunt. It began with a bill aimed at the English system of entailing land in Virginia which, as noted in his *Commonplace Book,* had subverted the inhabitants' "liberty and independency, with respect to their possessions as well as their persons."

His bill had as its outward purpose, "to enable tenants in taille to convey their land in fee simple," but its inner one was "to strike at the very root of feudalism in Virginia." Jefferson had been convinced by his reading of history that land in England before the coming of the militaristic Normans was an allodial possession (i.e., a personal dominion); and that the entailing system, which he described as "an engine of immense oppression," had been introduced as a measure of military defense. In order to break up the more swollen sort of Virginia estates and get the land into the hands of the yeoman class, it was necessary to break the legal lock that held many thousands of acres out of use. As early as 1701, it was reported to Governor

Nicholson that some landowners "have 20,000, 30,000, or 40,000 acres, the greater part of which is unemployed," while in the latter part of the eighteenth century the Virginia yeoman, who in the previous century had retained his sturdy independence, had, writes one authority, "become an insignificant factor in the life of the colony. . . . The Virginia which had formerly been so largely the land of the little farmer, had become the land of masters and slaves. For aught else there was no room." [2]

And we have Jefferson's own description of the then existing strata of Virginia society in these words:

"Certain families had risen to splendor by wealth and the preservation of it from generation to generation under the law [of] entails. . . . families in general had remained stationary on the grounds of their forefathers."

From the early days of the seventeenth century the huge land grants to favored proprietors were often added to by trading. William Byrd II was so insatiable that although he inherited 23,231 acres from his father, he owned at his death 179,440 acres—the size of a principality if not a kingdom. Robert Carter of Nomini Hall and William Fitzhugh owned 60,000 and 54,000 acres respectively, while even west of the Tidewater, estates of 20,000 to 40,000 acres "were not infrequent." [3] These proprietors left a tradition of carelessness and wastefulness in the use of land that exhausted the soil and produced dwindling crops; so much so that even Jefferson was later crippled by it.

The size, independence and isolation of these great estates produced a strong feeling of dignity and self-esteem, so that a well-knit aristocracy arose, even though many of Virginia's original landed proprietors were the sons of merchants rather than of the English gentry. Jefferson belonged to the landowning aristocracy through his descent from the Randolphs, through his father's acreage which he himself had expanded, and through his wife's possessions; and most of his friends and associates were similarly situated. Why, then, came his attack on the entail system which was one of the foundation stones of this "distinct class of families . . . formed into a patrician

2 Wertenbaker, *Planters of Colonial Virginia*, p. 144.
3 Wertenbaker, *Patrician and Plebeian in Virginia*, pp. 34–35.

order," as Jefferson called it?

There were several reasons. One was Jefferson's perception that an aristocracy of wealth, likely to be "of more harm and danger than benefit to society," as he wrote in his *Autobiography* (note, even at this early stage, his criterion of a social morality), must yield to "an aristocracy of virtue and talent." Another probable reason was that he foresaw the ruin that must overtake a commonwealth resting on a defective agricultural base. A third probable reason was that he was aware of the ground-swell of resentment arising from the class of small farmers—for whom, until he became land-rich himself, Patrick Henry was a chief spokesman—against the stranglehold held on the state's life by the great landed families. One of Jefferson's qualities as a politician lay in his sense of timing; he was striking his main blows now while the iron was still hot, for the Declaration of Independence was scarcely a hundred days old.

Jefferson's sudden blow at the entail system must have taken the opposition spokesmen by surprise; that is the only feasible explanation of their failure to show the expected stubbornness. The only opposing warrior who took the field was Edmund Pendleton, lawyer and dexterous conservative, whom Jefferson, his friend, once called "the ablest man in debate I had ever met." Pendleton fought the bill for eleven days and then, foreseeing defeat, offered a bland amendment—one often used to emasculate formidable measures. It would have allowed proprietors to decide for themselves whether they would keep their lands "in taille" or in fee simple. But the yeoman and small farmer yearning for free land prevailed, and the bill, which allowed slaves as well as lands to be bought and sold and otherwise conveyed, was made law in a thumping but temporary victory. It was temporary because speculation in land afterward nullified what might have been its best effects; and it created for Jefferson a group of bitter enemies who never forgave him for having thus been traitorous to his class. Years later, John Randolph of Roanoke, Jefferson's kinsman and one-time friend, daily denounced in Congress the "leveling" tendencies thus set up.

Jefferson's aims at this period are best summed up in his own words: "I considered four of these bills, passed or reported, as forming a system by which every fibre would be eradicated of ancient or future aristocracy; and a foundation laid for a government truly republican."

The repeal of the laws of entail would prevent the accumulation and perpetuation of wealth in select families and preserve the soil of the country from being daily more and more absorbed in mortmain. The abolition of primogeniture removed the feudal and unnatural distinction "which made one member of every family rich and all the rest poor," substituting equal partition, the best of all agrarian laws. The restoration of the rights of conscience relieved the people from taxation for the support of a religion not theirs; for the establishment was truly of the religion of the rich, the dissenting sects being composed entirely of the less wealthy people.

These, by the bill for a general education, would be qualified to understand their rights, to maintain them, and to exercise with intelligence their parts in self-government; and all this would be effected without the violation of a single natural right of any one individual citizen.

The abolition of the entailing system broke up one half of the foundation of Virginia feudalism; but another half remained. This was primogeniture, by which property in land, in the absence of a will, descended only to the eldest son in each family, disregarding all other sons and entirely ignoring the daughters; "which made one member of every family rich and all the rest poor." The consequence was the locking up of the land and the control of the common wealth by a relatively few families. Jefferson's solution was simple: he proposed an equitable partition of land among all the children of any property-owning father. Here again the doughty Pendleton was the chief objector. Seeing that he could not kill the measure by a frontal attack, he tried to draw its sting by an amendment which would preserve the sacred primacy of the oldest son, to whom he proposed that a double portion be given.

When Jefferson took his political pen in hand he did not always salt his opinions with humor, but on this occasion he knocked out Pendleton's argument with a single appropriate witticism. He would agree, he said to Pendleton, "if the eldest son could eat twice as much and do double work."

The bill passed. Thus sank home another of Jefferson's nails in the coffin of "aristocracy," by which he meant colonial feudalism. If it be wondered why Jefferson at this period was so pressing in his attacks, it was because he believed, as he put it, "the shackles which shall not be knocked off at the conclusion of this war will remain on us long, will be made heavier and heavier, till our rights shall revive, or expire in a convulsion."

Jefferson's epitaph as drawn up by himself showed that among the achievements of which he was proudest was his authorship of the Ordinance for Establishing Religious Freedom. If the relative ease with which entail and primogeniture were swept away had persuaded him that the Virginia assembly was ripe for complete reforms, he was soon disillusioned; for no sooner had he introduced his first resolution to strike the religious shackles off the minds of his countrymen than he found he had brought on himself the most prolonged and rancorous battle of the period.

"Desperate contests," he wrote, "continued almost daily from the 11th of October to the 5th of December." But these, he found out later, were only preliminary skirmishes. Actually he was nearly ten years, with the help of many able men, inducing Virginia to permit full liberty of religious belief and practice. At the moment he began his struggle with this plain, short measure:

"No man shall be compelled to frequent or support any religious worship, ministry, or place whatsoever; nor shall be enforced, restrained, molested, or burdened in his body or goods; nor shall otherwise suffer on account of his religious opinions or belief; but all men shall be free to profess, and by argument to maintain, their opinion in matters of religion; and the same shall in no wise diminish, enlarge, or affect their civil capacities."

Virginia's religious structure at that time was not only feudal; it was medieval. The state regularly lent its powers to the church— the Established Church or Church of England. The church returned the favor by preaching obedience to rulers and respect for great property. The clergy long before had lost the respect of ordinary men. Parsons were sometimes drunkards, loafers or grafters. Dissenters and unorthodox sects were subject to legal or social persecu-

tion. To question the Trinity was to invite death. Quakers were
sent to the pillory; wretched old women were liable to accusation
as witches; Baptist preachers were habitually arrested and often
jailed as disturbers of the peace, and Patrick Henry earned much of
his early fame by defending them. ("Did I hear it distinctly—that
these men are charged with *preaching the gospel of the Son of God?*")
Jefferson himself might have been prosecuted for heresy for uttering
such sentiments as these:

"It is error alone which needs the support of government. Truth
can stand by itself."

"Difference of opinion is advantageous to religion. The several
sects perform the office of *censor morum* over each other."

"What has been the effect of coercion? To make one half the
world fools, and the other half hypocrites."

"Free inquiry must be indulged; and how can we wish others to
indulge it, while we refuse it ourselves?"

"The care of every man's soul belongs to himself."

"The magistrate . . . knows no more the way to heaven than I
do."

It was apparent from the first that the church was going to
receive obstinate support from the Tidewater plantation owners
led by Edmund Pendleton and Robert Carter Nicholas. The dissenters' plea for freedom was reinforced by Presbyterian and Baptist
petitions coming chiefly from the western or Piedmont country
where lay Jefferson's home. Their position was defended by George
Mason of Gunston Hall and by James Madison, a short, apple-
cheeked young legislator fresh from Princeton. The Anglican clergy
brought in a memorial in their own behalf, contending they had a
life contract with the state, on which rested the "sanctity of all
private property."

The first phase of the battle lasted some ninety days, and then
the Anglican conservatives decided to give ground before their flank
should be turned. They agreed to give up those laws punishing
unorthodox opinion and failure to attend church, as well as those
laws taxing dissenters for support of religious societies based on
creeds in which they did not believe. A compromise measure was
brought in. It granted exemptions from taxes for the support of the

church, but it kept all glebes and church properties for the church. So matters stood until 1779 when the Ordinance for Establishing Religious Freedom was introduced. For eloquence and loftiness Jefferson's language here was scarcely second to that of the Declaration of Independence. But it contained several shafts aimed at "ecclesiastical rulers" which brought upon Jefferson the bitter retaliation of the more intolerant portion of the clergy, and from this resentment his reputation suffered for many a day; for they attacked him without mercy. These were some of the chief dicta of the ordinance:

That *"God created the mind free."*

That *"Civil rights have no dependence on religious opinions."*

That *"The opinions of men are not the object of civil government."*

That *"Legal interference is due only when principles break out into civil acts."*

That *"Ideas cease to be dangerous when freely circulated."*

That *"No man should suffer legally for his religious opinions or beliefs."*

Jefferson added one telling clause: that these rights as set forth were "natural (i.e., personal) rights," not to be repealed or narrowed.

At the first stirrings of the rebellion against England, Patrick Henry and Jefferson, as spokesmen for the yeomen and Piedmont farmers, had been often on the same side. But now the religious question parted them. Henry favored a general religious tax; in this he was supported by George Washington. When in 1784–86 the struggle was renewed, Jefferson was far away in France and in the assembly James Madison acted in his stead. Seeing that the ordinance was likely to pass, Pendleton and Nicholas tried to weaken it by ingenious amendments that emphasized the word "Christian." Since a law that gave religious liberty to Christians only would have barred Jews, Moslems, agnostics and other non-Christian citizens from its benefits, Madison had to fight off these amendments. At last the Anglicans were worn down and accepted the bill severing state from church.

Jefferson, hearing the news in Paris, had copies of the ordinance printed for general distribution, and throughout his life he took pride in it as second in importance only to the Declaration of Independence.

In a subsequent review of the stubborn battle over these three measures, Jefferson once wrote that although they had "laid the axe to the foot of pseudo-aristocracy," one other which failed to pass "would have raised the mass of the people to the high ground of moral respectability necessary to their own safety, and to orderly government." It was his bill for "the more general diffusion of learning."

In reflecting upon collegiate education in Virginia in the middle of the eighteenth century, Jefferson decided that laying aside minor criticisms for the moment, it suffered from two chief defects: (1) it was theological at base instead of being scientific, and hence failed to meet the demands of a practical and mercantile age; (2) it existed for the classes and had nothing for the masses. So there arose the question of how to use those talents which, as Jefferson had observed, "nature has sown as liberally among the poor as the rich," and "which perish without use." He concluded that those persons "whom nature hath fitly formed and disposed to become useful instruments for the public" should be sought for and educated "at the common expence of all."

The results of his reflections were contained in his 1779 Bill for the Diffusion of Knowledge. This measure proposed *"three distinct grades of education reaching all classes. 1st, elementary schools for all children generally, rich and poor. 2d, colleges, for a middle degree of instruction calculated for the common purposes of life. . . . and, 3d, an ultimate grade for teaching the sciences generally, in their highest degree."*

This bill was perhaps closer to Jefferson's heart and mind than any other on which he ever labored. He hoped it would be made "the keystone of the arch of our government." For it was ever his dictum that before the masses of the people could be expected to vote and act intelligently, they must be properly educated and informed. That either republicanism or democracy could be safe in the hands of ignorance was never Jefferson's belief.

It was in this bill that Jefferson first publicly introduced his idea of government by wards, or hundreds; an idea all but disregarded by his countrymen. In his own words, his bill "proposed to divide every county into wards of five or six miles square, like your townships; to establish in each ward a free school for reading, writing and common arithmetic; to provide for the annual selection of the best subjects from these schools, who might receive, at the public expense, a higher degree of education at a district school; and from these district schools to select a certain number of the most promising subjects, to be completed at a University, where all the useful sciences should be taught. Worth and genius would thus have been sought out from every condition of life, and completely prepared by education for defeating the competition of wealth and birth for public trusts."

Jefferson alone among American statesmen recognized the need of a political unit lying between the county and the town; and it was a need to which he often recurred. The idea of a ward, or township, corresponding in size to the ancient English "hundred," meaning a hundred people or a hundred families, fascinated him. There was precedent already in the existence in Virginia of hundreds—for example, Bermuda Hundred and Flowerdew Hundred, old plantations on the James—and his studies of old Anglo-Saxon political history had showed him that the hundred was a practical and useful political and educational unit well-nigh indispensable to a functioning democracy.

"It is by division and subdivision of duties alone," he wrote, *"that all matters, great and small, can be managed to perfection. And the whole is cemented by giving to every citizen, personally, a part in the administration of the public affairs."*

He liked to think of these small units as "ward republics." In these areas of five or six square miles would be elementary schools which should "place every householder within three miles of a school." The teacher would be supported by the people of the hundred. All persons in the hundred would be "entitled to send their children three years gratis, and as much longer as they please, paying for it."

The schools would be "under a visitor who is annually to choose the boy of best genius in the school, of those whose parents are too poor to give them further education, and to send him forward to one of the grammar schools."

Twenty of these grammar schools would be "erected in different parts of the country" for teaching Greek, Latin, geography and higher arithmetic.

"The best genius" would be selected from each school at the end of one or two years. These twenty students would be instructed six years longer, the rest dismissed.

"By this means twenty of the best geniuses will be raked from the rubbish annually."

At the end of six years the best ten of these geniuses would be sent to a college or university for three years.

"By that part of our plan which prescribes the selection of the youths of genius from among the classes of the poor," Jefferson summarized, *"we hope to avail the State of those talents which nature has sown as liberally among the poor as the rich, but which perish without use."*

"Where every man is a sharer in the direction of his ward-republic, or some of the higher ones," Jefferson once wrote in further explanation, "and feels that he is a participator in the government of affairs, not merely at an election one day in the year, but every day; when there shall not be a man in the State who will not be a member of some one of its councils, great or small, he will let the heart be torn out of his body sooner than his power be wrested from him by a Caesar or a Bonaparte."

And again he wrote: "Experience has shown that, even under the best forms, those entrusted with power have, in time and by slow operations, perverted it into tyranny; and it is believed that the most effectual means of preventing this would be to illuminate, as far as practical, the minds of the people at large, and more especially to give them knowledge of those facts which history exhibiteth. . . . whence it becomes expedient for promoting the public happiness that those persons, whom Nature hath endowed with genius and virtue, should be rendered, by liberal education, worthy to receive, and able to guard, the sacred deposit of the rights and liberties of their fellow citizens, and that they should be called to that charge without regard to wealth, birth, or other accidental condition or circumstance."

In these and similar statements lie the best refutation of the common accusation that Jefferson was a "leveler" and an equalizer; on the contrary, it is plain that he aimed at government by the best qualified, and that instead of a false aristocracy of "the weak or wicked," he wished a genuine aristocracy of informed and educated men. He was no worshiper of "a heterogenous, incoherent, distracted mass," but the deviser of a severely selective educational system in which genuine talent and energy could rise to the top.

Jefferson would have crowned his educational structure with a college or university governed by visitors "not to be restrained in their legislation by the royal prerogatives, or the laws of the Kingdom of England, or the canons of the Constitution of the English Church, as enjoined in the charter" of William and Mary College. What he thought of the little colonial college at Williamsburg may be guessed from his own words: "The college of William and Mary was an establishment purely of the Church of England; the visitors were required to be all of that church, the professors to subscribe to its 39 articles; its students to learn its catechism; and one of its fundamental objects was declared to be, to raise up ministers for that church." And the report of the legislative committee on revisal, of which Jefferson was a member, in 1779 declared: "The said college, thus amply endorsed by the public, has not answered their expectation, and there is reason to hope, that it would become more useful if certain articles in its constitution were altered and amended."

William and Mary at that time had a school of sacred theology, a school of philosophy, a school of the Latin and Greek languages and a school for Indian boys. Jefferson, with his Renaissance taste for science and mathematics, naturally was not satisfied with such an outmoded curriculum, and he drafted for the Virginia legislature a bill for amending the constitution of the college, so as to convert the institution into a university, in line with his precept that to preserve its own freedom a people must be well informed and instructed. Jefferson also had another word for it: they must be "illuminated."

His bill prescribed eight professorships. One would deal with ethics and the fine arts, divided respectively into the sub-topics of moral philosophy, law of nature and law of nations; under the first head would come sculpture, painting, gardening, music, architecture, poetry, oratory, with criticism under the second. A school of law would teach equity, merchant law, maritime law, ecclesiastical law, politics and commerce. The chair of history would have courses in civil and ecclesiastical history. Courses in "pure" mathematics would be given, comprising arithmetic and geometry; while "mixed" mathematics would include mechanics, optics, acoustics and astronomy. Medical courses would teach anatomy and medicine. There would be a chair of natural philosophy and natural history; another of ancient languages, oriental and northern; and lastly a chair of modern languages, with a "missionary for Indian history" tossed in.

This missionary, it was prescribed, "will be appointed to the several tribes of the Indians, whose instructions will be to investigate their laws, customs, religion, tradition, and more particularly their language, constructing a grammar thereof, as well as may be, and copious vocabularies, and on oath to communicate from time to time, to the said president and professors the material he collects."

In this passage lies a perceptible foretaste of the instructions subsequently given to the Lewis and Clark expedition to the northwest Pacific coast; for Jefferson had an insatiable scientific curiosity and always got a sustaining satisfaction out of what to another temperament would have been a dry collection of dusty and unrelated facts.

Along with this measure for a new kind of state university, Jefferson brought in a bill for a free state library at Richmond. It would have an annual appropriation of two thousand pounds for the purchase of books and maps by three persons "of learning and attention to literary matters." Later he also favored county libraries.

"I always hear with pleasure," he wrote in 1809, "of institutions for the promotion of knowledge among my countrymen. *The people of every country are the only safe guardians of their own rights, and are the only instruments which can be used for their destruction.*[4] And certainly they would never consent to be so used were they not

---

[4] Here Jefferson summed up his political philosophy which he never afterward abandoned.

deceived. To avoid this, they should be instructed to a certain degree. I have often thought that nothing would do more extensive good at small expense than . . . a small circulating library in every county."

No one denied that these bills were carefully designed and would benefit the people of the new republic. But the Virginia conservatives, taken by surprise and routed by Jefferson's earlier bills, now rallied their most stubborn forces, which prevented all action on these measures. It was twenty years from the Declaration of Independence before even the first of them, providing for elementary schools, was reported out of committee hearings.

And then came a nullifying amendment, typical of those so often introduced by the watchful Edmund Pendleton. In Jefferson's words, "In the elementary bill, they inserted a provision which completely defeated it; for they left it to the court of each county to determine for itself when this act should be carried into execution within the county. One provision of the bill was, that the expenses of these schools should be borne by the inhabitants of the county, every one in proportion to his general tax rate. This would throw on wealth the education of the poor; and the justices, being generally of the more wealthy class, were unwilling to incur that burden. I believe it was not suffered to commence in a single county." Thus Jefferson's whole educational plan was quietly strangled at birth by the fears and prejudices "of the more wealthy class."

Not only was Jefferson's educational structure defeated, but down with it went his proposal for the new political unit to be known as the ward or hundred. It was so completely ignored as not to be brought into debate. And yet as late as 1810 Jefferson was writing to Governor Tyler:

"I have indeed two great measures at heart, without which no republic can maintain itself in strength, (1) That of general education, to enable every man to judge for himself what will secure or endanger his freedom, (2) To divide every county into hundreds, of such size that all the children of each will be within reach of a central school."

It is clear that Jefferson first conceived of the hundred in connection with his educational plan, but this germ developed in his mind until imaginatively he saw the hundred function as a miniature

The Wren Building, College of William and Mary, Williamsburg,
Virginia

George Wythe, Jefferson's teacher and host

Photo by Flournoy. Virginia Chamber of Commerce

Poplar Forest, Jefferson's "escape" home

Photo by C. Kiraly

The dining room at Monticello, seen from the tea room. Dumb-waiters
at the ends of the mantle carried wine from the cellar below.

republic, easily fitting itself into his theory of subdivision as a remedy for concentration and centralization of power.

"It is by dividing and subdividing these republics," he said to Joseph C. Cabell, "from the great national one down through all its subordinations, until it ends in the administration of every man's farm by himself; by placing under every one what his own eye may superintend, that all will be done for the best. . . . The elementary republics of the wards, the county republics, the State republics, and the republic of the Union, would form a gradation of authorities, standing each on the basis of law, holding every one its delegated share of powers, and constituting truly a system of fundamental balances and checks for the government."

It can be seen now that the failure to establish, during the early days of the American republic, a political unit to fill the gap between village and county governments was a serious omission that has affected adversely the development of American political democracy. The corruption or inefficiency that so often has beset municipal governments in the United States forms the basis of one of the most searching accusations made against the American political system; while dissatisfaction with the cumbrousness and slackness of county government has increased with the years. Jefferson always had in the back of his mind the vision of a whole democracy in which every competent member would have a function and responsibility, a voice and vote. He recognized, because he felt it as president of the United States, the power of the pressure arising from New England townships and town meetings. He saw that county meetings would not give the same result. He wrote:

"Call a county meeting, and the drunken loungers at and about the court houses would have collected, the distances being too great for the good people and the industrious generally to attend. The character of those who really met would have been the measure of the weight they would have had in the scale of public opinion. As Cato, then, concluded every speech with the words, 'Carthago delenda est,' so do I every opinion, with the injunction, 'Divide the counties into wards.' "

Since pure democracy was difficult to obtain, the next best thing was delegated government kept under constant watch. "I do believe," he said, "that if the Almighty has not decreed that man shall never be free (and it is a blasphemy to believe it), that the secret will be found in the making himself the depository of the powers respecting himself, so far as he is competent to them, and delegating only what is beyond his competence."

CHAPTER 9

THE BOOK OF FATE

ONE OTHER MAJOR measure remained on Jefferson's list: it was designed to put an end to the slave trade. Here one recalls the firmness with which in the Declaration of Independence he attacked George III for the king's alleged encouragement of the slave trade. As regards the Negroes living on his own and other plantations, Jefferson was already convinced, as he wrote in his *Autobiography,* that "nothing is more certainly written in the book of fate than that these people are to be free."

If Jefferson wrote the Declaration of Independence, particularly its preamble, regarding freedom and equality for all men, apparently without a thought as to the slaves who even then were digging out the foundations of his home at Monticello, later he was emphatic enough in his views of slavery and its effects both on owners and owned, for he wrote prophetically: "The whole commerce between master and slave is a perpetual exercise of the most boisterous passions, the most unremitting despotism on the one part, and degrading submissions on the other. . . . Indeed I tremble for my country when I reflect that God is just; that his justice cannot sleep forever. . . . But if something is not done, and soon done, we shall be the murderers of our own children."

As a remedy Jefferson proposed this: all Negroes born of slave parents should be free, but up to a certain age they should remain with their parents; then to be brought up at public expense—to learn tillage, arts or sciences—until, at twenty-one for males and eighteen for females, "they should be colonized to such places as the circumstances of the time should render most proper." The scheme came to naught; for in 1821 Jefferson was obliged to record that "the public mind would not yet bear the proposition"; and he had to content himself with the prophecy that "the day is not distant when it must bear and adopt it, or worse will follow." History bore him out; he had not been dead twenty years when the sectional convulsions that led to the mortal years of 1861–65 began. In 1778, however, he had the satisfaction of seeing his bill to stop the importation of slaves pass without great opposition.

One other effort made by Jefferson and his fellow-revisers likewise succeeded only partly. This was a penal code that tried to get rid of some of the ferocious punishments for crime copied by Virginia from the English medieval system. The old code was founded on the Mosaic law of an eye for an eye, and was full of the rancorous spirit of *lex talionis*. But this spirit, even the wisdom and patience of Jefferson failed to exorcise. The Virginia legal mind retained its medieval tinge.

Two other measures, minor then but important in subsequent results, completed the revisers' task. One of these enabled foreigners to obtain naturalization with relative promptness; this measure was in line with one of Jefferson's favorite tenets—that a good man is a citizen of the world and has a right to move anywhere he believes he can better his lot and further his happiness. The other measure provided for the removal of the Virginia seat of government from tidewater Williamsburg to the more central village of Richmond. It was significant that this move was westward, toward the hills where the upland yeomen and small farmers predominated.

CHAPTER 10

VINES AND PRISONERS

ONE OF JEFFERSON's most devoted supporters in his battle for larger liberties was a newcomer to Virginia and America—Philip Mazzei, an ingenious Italian from Tuscany. Mazzei was one of those Europeans, touched with something romantic or eccentric, with whom Jefferson, despite his occasional reaction against all things European, was often fascinated. Mazzei was a physician, viticulturist, business man and amateur diplomat, but he came to Virginia simply as a grape grower. He landed there in 1773 with a collection of vines and tools, and a small company of workers that included nine Italian *vignerons* and a Mrs. Martin, or Martini, and her young daughter, who were under his protection. Mazzei had an American friend and sponsor, Thomas Adams of Richmond. Adams escorted him to Monticello to meet Jefferson.

As soon as Jefferson learned of Mazzei's far-ranging plans in horticulture, especially vine-growing, he was enraptured; for Mazzei's soaring schemes were of the sort which never failed to stir up the enthusiasm of the proprietor of Monticello. He persuaded Mazzei to remain in Albemarle county and settle on a tract of land which Jefferson offered to give him. Mazzei accepted, bought some additional land, fetched his *vignerons* from the river James, and settled down to make his home on a farm near Jefferson's estate which he called Colle. Here he started buildings which Jefferson helped him to plan and construct. Despite freezes and other accidents, Mazzei's vineyards flourished; by November, 1774, he was encouraged enough to draw up a plan for a company to produce "wine, oil, agriminous plants and silk." Among the subscribers, in addition to Jefferson, were Governor Dunmore, George Washington, John Page, Peyton

Randolph, George Mason, Benjamin Harrison of Brandon, Robert Carter Nicholas, and other Tidewater planters, most of whom were friends of Jefferson.

Mazzei's vines and other plants were swept away by a strange twist in the tide of the Revolutionary War. Mazzei had a weakness for politics and public affairs; and in 1779, at a time when Virginia's war luck was low and her treasury nearly empty, he persuaded the commonwealth authorities to send him to Italy to borrow money from the grand duke of Tuscany. As tenants at Colle, Jefferson brought down the Hessians and other prisoners from the British army who had been captured at Saratoga in the first great American triumph of the war. Included were the Hessian general Baron Riedesel, his formidable wife, and his two daughters. The British commander was Major General William Phillips, who was often haughty and troublesome. The four thousand captured troops were marched down from Saratoga to Charlottesville in the winter of 1779. They built barracks near the town, bought seeds and otherwise went to work to make themselves comfortable. They had almost done so when there arose a sudden demand that they be moved elsewhere, on the ground that they were consuming food needed by patriots. Jefferson sent to Governor Patrick Henry a warm and instant protest.

"Is an enemy so execrable," he wrote, "that, though in captivity, his wishes and comforts are to be disregarded and even crossed? I think not. It is for the benefit of mankind to mitigate the horrors of war as much as possible. The practice, therefore, of modern nations, of treating captive enemies with politeness and generosity, is not only delightful in contemplation, but really interesting to all the world, friends, foes and neutrals."

This magnanimity drew praise and thanks even from the haughty Phillips, to whom in reply Jefferson wrote: "The great cause which divides our countries is not to be decided by individual animosities. The harmony of private societies cannot weaken national efforts. To contribute by neighborly intercourse and attention to make others happy is the shortest and surest way of being happy ourselves. As these sentiments seem to have directed your conduct, we should be unwise as illiberal, were we not to preserve the same temper of mind."

The German officers were effusive in their thanks, they included not only General Riedesel, but General Specht, Baron de Geismer and Lieutenant de Unger. Jefferson often entertained these foreign officers, both British and German, in his home. His hospitalities were warmly returned by Geismer in 1788 when Jefferson was visiting Germany.[1]

As for Mazzei's vineyards, which had given Jefferson romantic dreams of Virginia as a great wine-producing state, General Riedesel's horses ate up in six days what the industrious Italians under Mazzei had taken three years to raise. But an impression had been made on Jefferson which he was never to forget. Throughout his European residence he remained curious about wines and vines, and he never quite gave up his notion that with luck and good weather Albemarle might be made the leading wine-making county of the nation.

---

[1] See Chapter 28.

CHAPTER 11

GOVERNORS vs. DICTATORS

IN 1779 JEFFERSON plunged into a sea of troubles when he succeeded Patrick Henry as governor of Virginia, having won by six votes over his old student confidant and companion in pursuit of the girls, John Page, who was the candidate of the conservatives. Jefferson was then thirty-six years old. Soon after he took office, his friend George Rogers Clark, leader of a colonial force of frontiersmen then operating against British posts in the West, sent back to Virginia a troublesome British captive, ex-Lieutenant Governor Henry Hamilton of Detroit.

Hamilton was charged with various war crimes. He was accused of having offered money to Indians for American scalps, and he was particularly charged with keeping a captured American soldier in irons. As soon as he arrived in Virginia, Jefferson clapped him in jail and in retaliation put him in irons, an action approved both by the Virginia council of state and by General Washington. The general, indeed, hinted that it might help the war effort if the tale of Hamilton's atrocities were well publicized. But the British army made official protests and Washington tossed the whole question back to Jefferson, whereupon he removed the irons from Hamilton, who, after giving a sullen promise that he would neither speak nor act offensively, was allowed to go home to England.

To become a war governor could not have been pleasant to Jefferson. To one of his mind and temperament, war, with its waste, brutality, disorder and hostility to liberty, was bound to be hateful; and yet he may have felt obliged to take the executive power in order to avoid seeing his state resort to something worse. In 1776, Jefferson was a member of the Virginia assembly which had con-

Photo by *Ralph Thompson*

Southwest view of Monticello, showing the gardens restored according to Jefferson's plans

A Declaration by the Representatives of the UNITED STATES OF
AMERICA in General Congress assembled.

When in the course of human events it becomes necessary for one people to
dissolve the political bands which have connected them with another, and to assume
among the powers of the earth, the separate and equal station to which the laws of na-
-ture & of nature's god entitle them, a decent respect to the opinions of mankind re-
-quires that they should declare the causes which impel them to the separation.

We hold these truths to be self evident; that all men are created equal; that
they are endowed by their Creator with inherent & inalienable rights; that among
these are life, liberty, & the pursuit of happiness; that to secure these rights govern-
-ments are instituted among men, deriving their just powers from the consent of the
governed; that whenever any form of government becomes destructive of these ends,
it is the right of the people to alter or to abolish it and to institute new government,
laying it's foundation on such principles & organising it's powers in such form as to
them shall seem most likely to effect their safety & happiness. prudence indeed will
dictate that governments long established should not be changed for light & transient
causes. and accordingly all experience hath shewn that mankind are more disposed to
suffer while evils are sufferable, than ,   themselves by abolishing the form
they are accustomed. but when a long train of abuses & usurpations, begun at a distin-
-guished period, & pursuing invariably the same object, evinces a design to reduce them
under absolute despotism, it is their right, it is their duty, to throw off such government
& to provide new guards for their future security. such has been the patient sufferance
of these colonies; & such is now the necessity which constrains them to expunge their
former systems of government. the history of the present king of Great Britain, is a
history of unremitting injuries & usurpations, among which appears no solitary fact
to contradict the uniform , nor of the rest; but all have in direct object the esta-
-blishment of an absolute tyranny over these states. to prove this let facts be sub-
-mitted to a candid world, for the truth of which we pledge a faith yet unsullied by falsehood
He has refused his assent to laws the most wholesome & necessary for the public good:
he has forbidden his governors to pass laws of immediate & pressing importance, un-
-less suspended in their operation till his assent should be obtained, & when so
suspended, he has neglected utterly to attend to them.
he has refused to pass other laws for the accomodation of large districts of people, unless
those people would relinquish the right of representation in the legislature,
a right inestimable to them & formidable to tyrants only:

Part of a draft of the Declaration of Independence in Jefferson's
handwriting

sidered his code revisions, but after he had returned to Monticello, it had been seriously proposed that what Virginia needed at that stage was a dictator invested, in Jefferson's words, "with any power, legislative, executive and judiciary, civil and military, of life and death over our persons and over our properties."

It was not denied that some persons wished Patrick Henry to be this dictator; but there is no evidence that Henry countenanced the proposal. Wirt, Henry's biographer, declares there was a tradition that Colonel Archibald Cary, speaker of the Virginia senate, threatened to plant a dagger in Henry's heart if he accepted the dictator's post. At any rate, deep and rancorous feelings were stirred up about the subject; and Jefferson was much criticized because he was not sufficiently the ruthless dictator that some political cynics deemed necessary to keep raiding British armies out of Virginia. These political attacks, and perhaps the consciousness that he was not in every case an effective war leader, subsequently made Jefferson feel that this was the most ignoble period of his life. His letters rarely refer to it and it forms no part of his *Memoirs*. Yet his correspondence shows that he labored night and day to defend Virginia while lending all possible help elsewhere, and that in all movements he was constantly consulting General Washington. Even if he had been more successful as a war governor, it is doubtful if any man in his place at that time could have kept the British armies out of Virginia; they were well equipped and supported while the colonial forces were weak.

In his first term, Jefferson got along well enough; but the year 1780 brought on new and threatening situations. The British besieged and took Charleston, South Carolina, beginning a northward movement which Jefferson recognized as full of danger for Virginia. In 1781 the British under Benedict Arnold sent a strong force up the river James. Jefferson acted promptly, but afterward he was accused by those who lost property in the invasion of not acting quickly enough. He ordered out the militia, and sent General Nelson forward, but both men and the money were insufficient. Jefferson took his wife and children out of danger, then rode back to Richmond to supervise removal of stores. He rode his horse to death in so doing.

But Jefferson's utmost efforts as governor could not keep the British back. Cornwallis, checked but not defeated in North Carolina, brought his redcoats across the Virginia border and sent his ace raider, Banastre Tarleton, westward to harass and if possible capture the state lawmakers and officials. The legislature fled Charlottesville for Staunton, but Tarleton's raiders overtook and captured a few, including Daniel Boone.

Tarleton's men pushed on the three miles to Monticello, where Jefferson, having completed his second and last term two days previously, had come home with his wife and children. Warned in time, Jefferson sent his family to safety and himself escaped on horseback only a few minutes before the raiders under Captain McLeod swarmed into Monticello. Two of Jefferson's Negro slaves, Martin and Caesar, were at that moment hiding silver and other valuables in a deep hole under a flank of the front portico, and legend says Caesar remained in that hole eighteen hours rather than make a betraying sound or movement. McLeod withdrew his raiders next day, having had orders from Tarleton to "suffer nothing to be injured"; this was no doubt in part a return for Jefferson's kindness to the captives of Saratoga.

Elsewhere, Jefferson's possessions were not so well treated. Down the river opposite Elk Island lay the plantation Elk Hill. This had been the property of Mrs. Jefferson. Cornwallis moved up to this place, occupied the main house as his headquarters, and spent ten days wrecking the estate. "History," wrote Jefferson later, "will never relate the horrors committed by the British army, in the Southern States of America." He accused the British general at Elk Hill of having destroyed all growing crops, burned all barns, butchered cattle for his army, and carried off all available horses. "Of those too young for service," wrote Jefferson, "he cut the throats; and he burned all the fences on the plantation, so as to leave it an absolute waste. He carried off also about thirty slaves."

Jefferson never forgot this injury by the British; and no doubt it fed the flame of his already kindled resentment. From this time on, he lashed British habits and institutions with the cutting edge of carefully chosen language. He was an aged man when he was still writing of the British in this vein: "They would not lose the sale of a bale of furs for the freedom of the whole world." [1] And again: "I fear nothing for our liberty—from the assaults of force; but I have seen and felt much, and fear more from English books, English prejudices, English manners, and the apes, dupes, and designs among our professional crafts." [2]

Now and again he modified these antagonistic opinions, only to return to them with even harsher epithets. It was from England's government that he feared the undermining of republicanism; by England's rulers that he feared the corruption of democracy. And in some manner his life, from this time on, was a battle against the then existing British influences, either real or imagined.

Concerning his relinquishment of the governorship, Jefferson wrote in his *Autobiography:* "From a belief that, under the pressure of the invasion under which we were then laboring, the public would have more confidence in a military chief, and that the military commander, being invested with the civil power also, both might be wielded with more energy, promptitude and effect for the defence of the State, I resigned the administration at the end of my second year."

The people of Virginia believed they had to make a choice between liberty and security; and Jefferson thought they were of a mind to prefer security. The dilemma is an old one in human history. Once more there was a motion made toward a dictatorship. Of this Jefferson wrote: "The very thought alone was treason against the people; was treason against mankind in general. . . . Those who assume the right of giving away the reins of government in any case, must be sure that the herd, whom they hand on to the rods and hatchet of the dictator, will lay their necks on the block when he shall nod to them."

When the runaway Virginia legislators met at Staunton, George Nicholas, a young man from Jefferson's own county, demanded an inquiry into Jefferson's actions as governor. Jefferson asked for a copy of the intended charges. To answer them, he procured his election to the legislature. On the day set for the hearing, Nicholas

---

[1] Letter to John Jacob Astor, 1813.
[2] Letter to H. S. Spofford, 1814.

failed to appear. Both houses then passed a resolution of thanks to, and praise for, Jefferson as governor. Since Cornwallis had surrendered, the whole matter was dropped. Nicholas afterward was reconciled with Jefferson and became his firm supporter.

After the raid on Monticello, when it appeared that the British had come into Albemarle county to stay, Jefferson retreated with his family to Poplar Forest, near Lynchburg. Here he suffered a bruising fall from his horse and was several weeks recovering. Here, too, he began the preparation of *Notes on Virginia,* an astonishing compound of observation, erudition, science, philosophy and sheer information that acquired for him an immense prestige before he entered upon the new level of life to which he was about to be moved.

CHAPTER 12

BACK ON THE MOUNTAIN TOP

"I HAVE RETIRED to my farm, my family and books from which I think nothing will evermore separate me," so Jefferson wrote to his kinsman Edmund Randolph on September 16, 1781, when he was only thirty-eight years old. More than once Jefferson thus raised his right hand, so to speak, and swore he was done forever with politics and public office. He was never quite able to keep his resolves in this respect; for politics, say what he would, had an undying fascination for him. But there was never any doubt where his thoughts tended to return whenever they were freed from the clutch of public affairs: they flew back to Albemarle county and the little mountain three miles from Charlottesville where perched his home, Monticello. Even during the Revolution, work on Monticello, though relaxed at times, never quite stopped.

"A flower here, a tree there," he wrote to Angelica Church[1] in England. "Yonder a grove, near it a fountain; on this side a hill, on that a river, indeed madam, I know nothing so charming as our own country."

"No occupation," he wrote to Charles Willson Peale, "is so delightful to me as the culture of the earth, and no culture comparable to that of the garden." And finally in his *Notes on Virginia* he proclaimed: "Those who labour in the earth are the chosen people of God."

In 1781, the year that Jefferson ceased to be governor, he made just one entry in his *Garden Book*. This one had to do with orchard terraces; Jefferson noted that each hand could do about twenty feet

---

[1] This sister-in-law of Alexander Hamilton was an admired friend of Jefferson for years.

a day, the terraces being from eight to ten feet wide. He omitted mention of his purchase of a mockingbird for eighteen pounds, but several times in other diaries Jefferson mentioned buying mockingbirds, of whose singing he was very fond. Like a good American, he was convinced their music was superior to that of the nightingales of Europe, which he was later to hear.

We know something of the then appearance of Monticello, still incomplete at this period, from the sketches written by the Marquis de Chastellux, who had been one of the commanders of the French army which had co-operated with Washington in trapping Lord Cornwallis at Yorktown. The marquis visited Jefferson on the latter's mountain top in the spring of 1782. He wrote:

"The house, of which Mr. Jefferson was the architect, and often one of the workmen, is rather elegant, and in the Italian taste, though not without fault; it consists of one large square pavilion, the entrance of which is by two porticoes, ornamented with pillars. The ground floor consists chiefly of a very large, lofty saloon which is to be decorated entirely in the antique style; above it is a library of the same form; two small wings, with only a ground floor and attic story, are joined to this pavilion, and communicate with the kitchen, offices, etc., which will form a kind of basement story, over which runs a terrace. . . . We may safely say, that Mr. Jefferson is the first American who has consulted the fine arts to know how he should shelter himself from the weather. . . . It seemed as if from his youth he had placed his mind, as he had done his house, on an elevated situation, from which he might contemplate the universe."

It is to be noted here that the marquis was impressed by Jefferson's consultation of the fine arts in building his house, particularly the Italian touches in such ornamentations as columns. Indeed, it might be said that Jefferson helped to introduce the Greek column into American architecture. Before his day, colonial America built severely and puritanically. Severe lines carried nothing superfluous or ornamental. But even Jefferson, ordinarily satisfied with mathematical severity, could not brook this bareness. He sought grace— the grace that confers distinction. He found it in the buildings of Greece, and those copied from Greece by Rome; and he got the effect he sought by levying upon ancient Athens for its pillars and columns. Andreas Palladio, the sixteenth-century architect of the Italian Renaissance, was his guide; and Palladio's books and drawings, by way of England, furnished him with his models. The Marquis de Chastellux guessed correctly; Italian taste was indeed visible in Monticello, and it was derived from Palladio, whose love for the classic mode was deeply shared by Jefferson. It was Jefferson who assisted in bringing to the United States the Greek revival that adorned the fronts of planters' houses, and in a later and coarser age the façades of banks, college buildings and gasoline filling-stations.

Jefferson's release from political concerns enabled him to renew his love of work outdoors, and the *Garden Book* for 1782 contained a calendar of the blooming of flowers from March to near the end of June. On May 6 a note that the aurora borealis had been seen at 9 P.M. was joined to an observation that "a quart of currant juice makes 2 blue teacups of jelly, 1 quart of juice to 4 of purée." He saw wild geese flying northwesterly on February 28, and raspberries came to the table on June 10.

But the year 1782 which began so cheerfully was not destined to remain so. On May 8 was born the Jeffersons' sixth child and fifth daughter, Lucy Elizabeth. Child-bearing had exhausted Mrs. Jefferson; she had not the strength to rally from this last birth-giving; and from this moment her life-energy was less each day. Much of the time Jefferson himself waited upon her, fetching her water to drink and medicines to take. For four months he was never far from her bed, at the head of which was a small room he used for writing. At last it became evident she had not long to live.

"A moment before the closing scene," wrote Jefferson's daughter, Martha, "he was led from the room in a state of insensibility by his sister, Mrs. Carr, who with great difficulty, got him into the library, where he fainted, and remained so long insensible that they feared he would never revive." For three weeks Martha witnessed his violent grief, which was scarcely assuaged even when he was so far recovered as to be able to take long horseback rides about the mountain. This is the only time Jefferson is described as having been completely overcome by his feelings.

Neither in this grief, nor in any other, did Jefferson's learning avail; and when his intellect tried to bring him an explanation, it failed. He was an aging man when in the nineteenth century he wrote to John Adams: "There is no degree of affliction, produced by the loss of those dear to us, which experience has not taught me to estimate. I however found time and silence the only medicine, and these but assuage, they never can suppress, the deep drawn sigh which recollection forever brings up until recollection and life are extinguished together." Three years later he was no nearer an answer, and again he wrote to Adams: "There are, I acknowledge, even in the happiest life, some terrible convulsions, heavy set-offs against the opposite page of the account. I have often wondered for what good end the sensations of grief could be intended. . . . I wish the pathologists then would tell us what is the use of grief in the economy, and of what good it is the cause, proximate or remote."

CHAPTER 13

OLD WORLD VISTAS

EVEN WHEN HE was a very young man, Jefferson had in mind a tour of Europe. And twice after his wife's death, Congress offered to send him as a peace envoy to France. But Europe was then not in his plans. When, however, Congress again invited him to become a plenipotentiary to join Benjamin Franklin and John Adams in Paris to make peace with the British government headed by the Marquis of Rockingham, he accepted.

Writing to the Marquis de Chastellux in November, 1782, he apologized for a late answer to a letter. "It found me," he wrote, "a little emerging from the stupor of mind which has rendered me as dead to the world as was she whose loss occasioned it. . . . Before that event my scheme of life had been determined. . . . A single event wiped away all my plans."

In June, 1783, the Virginia assembly again elected him to Congress. Among others elected was his friend James Monroe, whom he always addressed as "Colonel." Jefferson was much at home this year, he wrote few letters, and made few entries in his account book. There was only one note in his *Garden Book;* it concerned an extraordinarily early white frost on September 2 and 3 which killed vines, tobacco and corn. It was evident that he had little heart for any of his usual activities. His affection now turned in double measure to his three surviving children, all girls. Martha ("Patsy") was taken to Mrs. Hopkinson's school in Philadelphia. She was now eleven years old. Yearly she became more like her father—tranquil, sturdy and self-reliant. The younger girl, "Polly," and the infant Lucy Elizabeth, who was too feeble to live long, were placed in the care of Francis Eppes and his wife at their Eppington farm. Polly was unlike

Martha—even as a little thing she was timid, clinging, and completely forgetful of her father's many admonitions respecting work in the garden and the study of nature.

In November, 1783, Jefferson followed Congress to Trenton and in the same month followed it back to Annapolis. During this period he wrote few letters and made almost none of the records, except expense accounts, of which he was ordinarily so fond. His state of mind was mirrored by his admonition to his daughter Martha to obey her teacher and hostess, Mrs. Hopkinson, in all things.

"Consider her, I say," wrote Jefferson, "as your mother, as the only person to whom, since the loss with which Heaven has been pleased to afflict you, you can now look up." Her father then offered to Martha a schedule which would enable her to distribute her time to advantage:

"From 8 to 10, practice music.

"From 10 to 1, dance one day and draw another.

"From 1 to 2, draw on the day you dance, and write a letter next day.

"From 3 to 4, read French.

"From 4 to 5, exercise yourself in music.

"From 5 till bed-time, read English, write, etc."

This rather lame, not to say, vague outline of unexciting duties was obviously in need of reinforcement, and Jefferson, after notifying Martha he expected her to write by every post, added: "Take care that you never spell a word wrong. . . . It produces great praise to a lady to spell well. . . . If you love me, then, strive to be good under every situation, and to all living creatures."

This letter was deemed so suitable not only for republican but royal daughters that the original for a long time was treasured among the private possessions of Queen Victoria of England. It was given to her when as Princess Victoria she asked for an autograph of Jefferson.

A little later Jefferson wrote again to advise Martha against listening to any predictions that the world was about to dissolve or burst. "The Almighty," said Jefferson, "has never made known to anybody, at what time he created it; nor will he tell anybody when he will put an end to it, if he ever means to do it. As to preparations for that event, the best way is for you to be always prepared for it." This was

Jefferson at his driest, most pointed and best; in his next letter, however, he was back in his old didactic vein. In this letter he gravely
lectured Martha on clothes: "I do not wish you to be gaily clothed,
at this time of life, but that what you wear should be fine of its kind.
But above all things, and at all times, let your clothes be clean, whole,
and properly put on."

It was while Jefferson was in the Congress at Annapolis, and room-
ing with James Monroe there, that he drafted the ordinance of the
Northwest Territory, one of the great documents of American democracy, for the government of the territories lying in a wedge shape
west of the Alleghenies, north of the Ohio river and east of the Mississippi. For years settlers from the East, particularly Virginia and
North Carolina, had been moving westward through the mountain
gaps in a search for cheap and fertile land, and ahead of them great
land companies, in which many of the Founding Fathers speculated,
had been formed to make a profit out of this search.[1] Most of the
Western land belonged to Virginia not only by virtue of old royal
grants but by virtue of the conquering strokes delivered by Jefferson's fellow-Albemarlean, George Rogers Clark, against the British
and Indian occupants. New York, Massachusetts and Maryland laid
claim to parts of it. Virginia had offered to cede her territory to the
United States, but the land companies, nervous about their profits
and power, had delayed its acceptance until now.

On the committee which drew up plans for a temporary government with Jefferson were Samuel Chase of Maryland, later an obnoxious judge and enemy of Jefferson, and David Howell of Rhode
Island, who was at one time acting president of Brown University.
They let Jefferson, who as head of the Virginia delegation in Congress had great prestige, do the actual writing. His plan mirrored
his conceptions at that time. It provided for the formation of established states, rather than colonies; for the adoption of written tem-

---

[1] In 1798 Robert Morris, the Philadelphia financier and promoter of the North American Land Company, went to jail for debt and stayed there three and one-half years.
Colonel W. S. Smith, son-in-law of President John Adams, went bankrupt in 1797 because of land speculation. Many of the Founding Fathers were heavy speculators in
land.

porary constitutions; for the setting up of "counties or townships"; and the calling of conventions to establish permanent constitutions and governments when each state had twenty thousand free inhabitants. To these provisions Jefferson attached five articles, the last two of which brought on significant controversies:

1. That the new states should forever remain a part of the United States.

2. That they should be subject to the government of the United States in Congress assembled and to the Articles of Confederation.

3. That they should be subject to pay their duly apportioned part of the federal debt.

4. That they should have governments in republican forms, and should bar from citizenship the holders of hereditary titles.

5. That after 1800 there should be neither slavery nor involuntary servitude in any of the states, except as punishment for crime.

To these proposals Jefferson added his suggestions for the names of ten new states as follows: Sylvania, Michigania, Cherronesus, Assenisipia, Metropotamia, Illinoia, Saratoga, Washington, Polypotamia and Pelisipia. If Jefferson's recommendations had prevailed, the more monstrous of these names today would be engraved on the map of the Middle West. Fortunately Congress quietly struck them all out. They were evidences of Jefferson's deep reading in the classics and of his Greco-Roman leanings, but not much of his tastes. The bar to hereditary titles also was stricken out.

It was the final article relating to slavery in what is now Ohio, Indiana, Illinois and Wisconsin that caused debate and division. The first objection was raised by Richard Dobbs Spaight of North Carolina. When the vote took place, Virginia and Maryland supported the protesting Carolinian, while the seven Northern states stood with Jefferson. Here again was one of those divisions between North and South that indicated a deep, underlying cleavage. Since Jefferson's article against slavery was not supported by a majority, it was finally stricken out.

But at the moment he was busy with other matters, especially preparations for his voyage to France as the American minister succeeding Franklin.

CHAPTER 14

LIFE IN PARIS

In July, 1784, Jefferson sailed from Boston for France to begin an altogether new chapter in his studious life. He took Martha with him. They made the passage from land to land in nineteen days. In Paris they lodged at the Hôtel d'Orléans, Rue des Petits Augustins, before taking a house, the Hôtel Landron, in the Cul-de-sac Têtebout (later extended and named the Rue de Helder). Jefferson and elegance were always found together, and it did not surprise Colonel David Humphreys, secretary of the United States legation, and William Short, Jefferson's personal secretary, when he leased as a permanent residence the handsome house at the northeast corner of the Champs Elysées and the Rue Neuve de Berry (later Rue de Berri) belonging to the Count de l'Avongeac. It was called the Grille de Chaillot. It had a "clever" garden and court, and was considered elegant even in the Paris of that day.

The expense weighed upon Jefferson heavily. "It will take me several years," he confided to Edmund Randolph, "to liquidate the advances for my outfit. . . . Those who hire furniture asked me 40% a year for the use of it." Jefferson's meticulous accounts show that he often spent shillings with caution; but on special occasions he poured out pounds with abandon. In his disregard of expense at such times, he was a typical Southern gentleman of the late eighteenth century.

No period in French history could have been more absorbing to Jefferson than that in which he now found himself immersed; and the Paris of no other age could have furnished a more teeming ground for his observing eyes. France was entering a stage in human history when those three estates of the Old World—the monarchy, nobility and clergy—were giving ground to the middle-class merchant and pragmatic scientist. It was a mercantile world, and Voltaire only lately had sounded its sentiments when he wrote:

"I am not sure that the merchant who enriches his country . . . and contributes to the happiness of the globe is not more useful to a state than the thickly bepowdered lord who knows exactly what time the king rises and what time he goes to bed."

Louis XIV had decreed that the nobles should forsake their country houses and hang around the court at Versailles; and his great-grandson, Louis XVI, now reigning, had followed his pattern to the best of his poor ability. The court was still established at Versailles; but it was chiefly dominated on the feminine side by the queen, Marie Antoinette, and on the masculine by the Count d'Artois, the king's sporting brother.

"A fool"—Jefferson once so described the king; but he was not entirely that. Louis XVI unfortunately had been born into the monarchical profession; he might have been happier in the casual life of an amateur mechanic and hunter; for courts bored him and temperamental queens wearied him.

Marie Antoinette lately had got rid of Benjamin Franklin's friend, Turgot, the physiocrat, who as premier had tried to set up economic reforms. Turgot had been succeeded by Necker, the banker whose task it was to finance France's support of the American Revolution; and now Necker had been succeeded by the spender, Calonne, who was in power when Jefferson reached France. Jefferson rarely saw any of the higher French officials; his chief business was with the foreign minister, Count de Vergennes. Jefferson's terse reply to this minister at their first encounter is famous:

"You replace Dr. Franklin, I hear," said the count.

"I succeed him," said Jefferson. "No one could replace him."

Vergennes was one of the canniest but most effective diplomats of the old regime. Jefferson made no attempt to match wits with this disillusioned but shrewd minister. "As he saw," Jefferson wrote, "that I had no indirect views, practiced no subtleties, meddled in no intrigues, pursued no concealed object, I found him as frank, as honorable, as easy of access to reason, as any man with whom I had ever done business; and I must say the same for his successor, Montmorin, one of the most honest and worthy of human beings."

As Jefferson became better acquainted with the political structure of France under Louis XVI, he was able to see that Vergennes's hands were nearly always tied. The foreign minister, even had he had the will to do so, could make little progress in the face of entrenched interests. For example, Vergennes recognized the merit of Jefferson's proposals regarding the possibility of the direct importation of Virginia tobacco into France. The old way was to import the tobacco through England, that was the way the farmers-general or tax brokers wanted it; and Jefferson wasted much breath and ink before he realized that Vergennes had no taste for breaking up an eighteenth-century monopolistic cartel in the maintenance of which Robert Morris, the American financier, had an interest.

The situation was similar regarding other hallowed French customs and interests; Vergennes preferred to leave them alone. When Jefferson pressed him, he intimated that in case of doubt he always upheld the *status quo*. Hence Jefferson was at length reduced to protracted but often futile negotiations involving American fish, flour, wheat, rice, indigo, hops and peltry. Even this minor mercantile business incurred delay and idle waiting, and Jefferson soon learned to take his major interests elsewhere.

By this time his spirits had revived somewhat from the shock of his wife's death, and his letters home showed he was recovering his ability to observe, collect, criticize and sometimes enjoy. To Mrs. Trist in Philadelphia he wrote referring to the French people: "The roughnesses of the human mind are so thoroughly rubbed off with them, that it seems as if I might glide through a whole life among them without a jostle." But, he had to add, "the people are ground to powder by the vices of the form of government. Of twenty millions of people supposed to be in France, I am of opinion there are nineteen millions more wretched, more accursed, in every circumstance of human existence, than the most conspicuously wretched individual of the whole United States." To James Monroe he wrote in a nationalistic outburst: "My God! how little do my countrymen know what precious blessings they are in possession of, and which no other people on earth enjoy." [1]

---

[1] *Writings*, Memorial Edition, XXI.

At intervals he suffered from loneliness, having placed his daughter Martha in a convent, and once he wrote to Francis Hopkinson at Philadelphia: "I am here burning the candle of life without present pleasure or future object. . . . I envy your Wednesday evening entertainments with Rittenhouse and Dr. Franklin. They would be more valued by me than the whole week at Paris."

At first he wrote very little beyond business and diplomatic communications, and since few of his letters written in his first year in France survive, we can look to the able pen of Abigail Adams, wife of John Adams, for intimate detail of life in Paris in Jefferson's time. Of attending a party at Jefferson's house she wrote:

"A pretty large company—the Lafayettes, Commodore Jones, Mr. Jarvis, an American, a Mr. Bowdoin, Chevalier de la Luzerne, Mr. Williams and Mr. Short. . . . They have some customs very curious here—gentlemen seldom or never sit, stand or walk with their swords on, and *chapeau de bras*, small silk hat, always worn under the arm. . . . In winter it shuts out all the fire from the ladies; I know, I have suffered from it many times. . . . Conversation is never general, but tête-a-tête. . . . Mr. Jefferson is one of the choice ones of the earth."

Further reflections on French customs appear in a letter from Mrs. Adams to Mercy Warren back home in Massachusetts: "If you ask me what is the Business of Life here, I answer, Pleasure. . . .

"What idea, my dear Madam, can you form of the manners of a nation one city of which furnishes (Blush, O my sex, when I name it) 52,000 unmarried females so lost to a sense of honor and shame as publicly to enroll their names in a notary's office for the most abandoned purposes and to commit iniquity with impunity?" She had to admit that in Paris "the greatest decency and respect is shown by all orders to the female character, but vice is supposed to walk at large soliciting the unwary. . . ."

Jefferson himself never mentioned such matters. His interests led him to observe another kind of woman, on whom he commented in a letter to the Reverend James Madison, president of William and Mary College and cousin of the secular James Madison. At Fontainebleau, Jefferson wrote, "I fell in with a poor woman. . . . She told me she was a day laborer at eight sous or four pence sterling the day;

Mrs. William Bingham (Anne Willing), friend and correspondent of Jefferson, by Gilbert Stuart

Robert R. Livingston, participant in the Louisiana Purchase, by John Vanderlyn

Maria Cosway (self-portrait), Jefferson's admirer and his correspondent
for more than 30 years

that she had two children to maintain, and to pay a rent of thirty livres for her house (which would consume the hire of seventy-five days) and that often she could get no employment and of course was without bread." He gave her twenty-four sous, which caused her to burst into tears. He then added to his letter a few sentences in which he summed up the heart of his own doctrines:

"Whenever there are in any country uncultivated lands and unemployed poor, it is clear that the laws of property have been so far extended as to violate natural right. The earth is given as a common stock for men to labor and live on. . . . The small landholders are the most precious part of a state."

On the departure of Benjamin Franklin for home, Jefferson assumed the full duties of minister plenipotentiary at the court of Versailles. While waiting there on the cautious movements of Count de Vergennes, Jefferson sounded the Emperor Frederic II of Prussia, "Old Fritz," about an amicable commercial treaty, and was delighted to be cordially received and to see a treaty promptly concluded. He also opened negotiations with Denmark and Tuscany (the latter being the native heath of his vine-growing friend, Philip Mazzei), but other powers showed indifference.

"They seemed, in fact," wrote Jefferson, "to know little about us but as rebels who had been successful in throwing off the yoke of the mother country. They were ignorant of our commerce, which had been always monopolized by England, and of the exchange of articles it might offer advantageously to both parties."

Jefferson could not occupy his whole time with the business of whale oil and salted fish, and finding that printing costs were substantially lower in France than in the States, he ordered two hundred copies of his *Notes on Virginia* done by a Paris printer. Part of these he sent to learned men in Europe and America, accompanied by a caution against publication.

"My reason is," he wrote James Monroe, "that I fear the terms in which I speak of slavery, and of our Constitution, may produce an irritation which will revolt the minds of our countrymen against reformation in these two articles, and thus do more harm than good."

This passage gives a hint of that caution which was ever characteristic of Jefferson; it reveals also his knowledge of human psychology—the human mind, when irritated by excess, easily works in reverse.

Notes on Virginia was the first American book to be received with respect in Europe. It revealed Jefferson as a naturalist, philosopher, scientist, statistician and observer of men and things. It brought him to the notice of France's foremost men in science, art and letters. It was originally written as information to help François Barbé-Marbois, the French chargé at Philadelphia, become acquainted with the New World.

CHAPTER 15

JEFFERSON'S FEMININE FRIENDS

JUDGING BY HINTS made in letters to his closest friends, James Monroe and James Madison, Jefferson, during his first few months in France as the American minister, was often homesick; but by the middle of 1785 he was able to write gaily to Abigail Adams in London:

"I would not give the polite, self-denying, feeling, hospitable, good-humored people of this country & their amability [sic] in every point of view (tho' it must be confessed our streets are somewhat dirty, & our fiacres rather indifferent) for ten such races of rich, proud, hectoring, screaming, squibbing, carnivorous animals as those among whom you are; and that I do love this people with all my heart, & think that with a better religion, a better form of government & their present governors their condition & country would be most enviable."

No doubt this fondness for the French people had been influenced somewhat by his first reception into that circle of literati, dominated by clever French women, which he had often dreamed of from a distance. The door had been opened for him by the Countess d'Houdetot, who was admired by academicians, who was an old friend of Benjamin Franklin, and who had been loved by J. J. Rousseau. She had been the wife of an officer of gendarmes who was much older than she. He had left her much alone. She invited Jefferson to her home at Sannois, in the valley of Montmorency near Paris, on June 20, 1785; and it was from this date that Jefferson began to look upon things French with new and admiring eyes; for Jefferson, beneath his outward diffidence and occasional coldness to strangers, secretly and strongly craved affection.

"I took a trip yesterday to Sannois & commenced an acquaintance with the old Countess d'Hocquetot [sic]," he wrote triumphantly to

81

Abigail Adams. "I received much pleasure from it and hope it has opened a door of admission to the circle of literati with which she is environed."

(It was here, incidentally, that Jefferson for the first time heard the nightingale. He was disappointed, and as a steady patriot and an occasionally homesick Virginian, he told Mrs. Adams: "In America it would be deemed a bird of the third rank only, our mocking bird and fox-coloured thrush being unquestionably superior to it.")

Sophie de la Live, Countess d'Houdetot, no longer owned the mass of curly black hair and the sparkling black eyes that once had brought her the devotion of many admirers including, in addition to Rousseau, Saint Lambert; but she still had the sympathy and charm that once had made Rousseau describe her as *douce et vive,* "sweet and lively." She was a patron of St. John de Crèvecœur, the emigrant Frenchman who came to America and wrote *Letters of an American Farmer.* Her adoration of Franklin was due not only to his roguish way with the ladies, but to her view of him as the greatest living representative of a country that was the world's new beacon and hope.

With Franklin's successor she was never on such good terms, owing not only to Jefferson's cloak of occasional aloofness, but to his preoccupation with the business of his office and with feminine friends who lived nearer. However, "la bonne comtesse," as she was often called, had one thing strongly in common with Jefferson: that was a love for trees. She had at her country home at Sannois a park in which she wanted to have an American section; and, learning that the Virginian was trying valiantly to give an American aspect to the European landscape through imported plants, she gave him a list of American trees and shrubs to procure for her.

Another French great lady with whom Jefferson was on friendly, even affectionate, terms and for whom he ransacked American botany, was the Countess Noailles de Tessé, an aunt of Lafayette but by him called "cousin." Every autumn for several years after his return to Virginia from France, Jefferson sent her at Chaville, her country house, a box of seeds or plants. Jefferson was a frequent visitor at her houses at Chaville and Versailles; and since she had a love of architecture only second to that of nature, she may have had some influence on Jefferson's knowledge of that art, which was so greatly stimulated during his stay in France. She was an ardent supporter of a constitution for France, and next to architecture and gardens, she loved to talk about politics.

"She was a little woman," wrote Brand Whitlock in his biography of Lafayette,[1] "with piercing dark eyes, her face showing the marks of smallpox, her small mouth, as she talked, constantly twitching into a queer grimace with a nervous *tic;* and yet she had a grace and nobility of manner, a rare charm and a wit that made her irresistible. . . . She was of a delightful inconsistency; an atheist who ridiculed all pious practices, she always made the sign of the cross whenever she took medicine; she detested priests, and helped all the poor clerics in Paris; she had no faith in mankind, and believed in democracy."

It was to this lively Frenchwoman that Jefferson addressed one of the gayest and happiest letters he wrote while living in Europe. It was sent from Nîmes (Nismes as it was then spelled) while he was on a tour in southern France, and it chronicled some of the architectural discoveries whose influence he later carried to America. These are passages:

"Here I am, Madame, gazing whole hours at the Maison Quarrée, like a lover at his mistress. . . . This is the second time I have been in love since I left Paris. The first was with the Diana at the Chateau de Laye-Epinaye in Beaujolais, a delicious morsel of sculpture by M. A. Slodtz.[2] This, you will say, was in rule, to fall in love with a female beauty; but with a house it is out of all precedent. No, Madame, it is not without a precedent in my own history. While in Paris, I was violently smitten with the Hotel de Salm, and used to go to the Tuileries almost daily to look at it. . . . From Lyons to Nismes I have been nourished with the remains of Roman grandeur. They have always brought you to my mind, because I know your affection for whatever is Roman and noble. . . . I am immersed in antiquities from morning to night. . . . If I am sometimes induced to look forward to the 18th century, it is only when recalled to it by the recol-

---

[1] New York, 1929.

[2] The name is spelled this way in Jefferson's printed papers, but undoubtedly he meant the sculptor Stoldtz, who was one of the teachers of Houdon.

lection of your goodness and friendship."

This letter is noteworthy for two other passages. In one, Jefferson referred to Louis XVI as "a good and young King"; in the other he proposed that the Assembly of Notables, then in session at Paris, consist of no more than two houses under the said king: revealing that as a trusting American, he was not yet abreast with French history.

Jefferson corresponded with Madame de Tessé at intervals long after he had returned to America. He last wrote her in 1813. For reply he received these somber lines written in English by Lafayette:

"She *Has Not* lived to *Enjoy* this token of your remembrance—M. de Tessé who Had Been declining Rapidly was the first of the two for whom we Had to Mourn—She assisted Him to the Last Hour . . . ten days after Her Husband's death She was no More—Her illness was Slight—Her departure Gentle." [3]

Still another woman in whom Jefferson showed marked interest and who seems to have been often a guest of Madame de Tessé, was Madame de Tott, a portrait painter who, although of Greek blood herself, was the wife of a Hungarian diplomatic official. Preserved among Jefferson's papers in the Library of Congress is a long and sprightly letter written to Madame de Tott by Jefferson from Marseilles in April, 1787. Earlier he had written to her for her opinion of what seemed to him to be a "superb picture" at the house of Madame Drounay in Paris done by the latter's son "much in David's manner" (Jefferson was a solid admirer of the painter David). "Really it appears to me to have extraordinary merit," said Jefferson. "Write me your judgment on it. It will serve to rectify my own, which, as I told you, is a bad one, and needs a guide. It will multiply too the occasions of my hearing from you."

Her reply found fault with the picture for various reasons. Jefferson wrote to thank her and added:

"I should go on, Madam, detailing to you my dreams & speculations, but that my present situation is most unfriendly to speculation. 4350 market women (I have counted them) brawling, squabbling, jabbering patois, 300 asses braying & bewailing to each other, and to

---

[3] Chinard, *Trois Amitiés Françaises de Jefferson,* Paris, 1927.

the world, their cruel oppressions, 4 files of mule carts passing in constant succession, with as many bells to every mule as can be hung about him, all this in the street under my window, & the weather too hot to shut it. Judge whether in such a situation it is easy to hang one's ideas together. Besides, writing from a colony of your own country, you would rather I should say less of myself and more of that. But, just dropped among them, how can I pretend to judge the legitimacy of their descent? Of beauty, you will say, one may judge on a single coup d'oeil. Of beauty, then, Madam, they have a good share, as far as the public walks, the Spectacles, & the assemblée of Mademlle Conil enable me to decide. But it is not a legitimate Grecian beauty. It is not such as yours. The reason I suppose is that yours is genuine & brought from the spot, whereas, theirs has been made here, &, like all fabricated wares, is sophisticated with foreign mixtures."

Jefferson's letters to men were usually on serious topics and were written in a serious tone; but his letters to women were nearly always sprightly and often sparkled with a humor which he did not always reveal except to intimates. He closed this letter to Madame de Tott with a typical paragraph saying: "Perhaps you would rather I should write you news?—Any thing to obey you.—Oil is 10. dols the cwt. almonds 2#. cacao 19". caffe 31'. rice 21#, etc. This is not in the stile of Paris news; but I write from Marseilles and it is the news of the place."

Previously he had given to Madame de Tott a copy of Homer, accompanying it with a note saying:

"To so perfect an edition then of so charming a poet, allow me to add so charming a reader."

A fourth Frenchwoman with whom Jefferson kept up a friendship and correspondence for many years was Madame de Corny. She lived not far from Jefferson in the Rue Chaussée d'Antin, and was often Jefferson's companion on his regular daily walks in the Bois de Boulogne. Like the Countess d'Houdetot, she was somewhat younger than her husband. He was Louis-Dominique Ethis de Corny, author, economist and municipal officer. Having no children of her own, Madame de Corny was delighted with Jefferson's daughter Martha, and often entertained her and later the younger daughter Polly, whom she called "Polie." That she and Jefferson were on terms of friendship is evidenced by this portion of a note by him dispatched to her by messenger one day in October, 1787:

"How do you do this morning? I have feared you exerted and exposed yourself too much yesterday. I ask you the question, though I shall not await its answer. The sky is clearing, and I shall away to my hermitage. God bless you, my dear Madam, now and always. Adieu."

Jefferson was at Madame de Corny's house on July 14, 1789, when her husband came in and broke the news that on that day the Bastille had been attacked; in fact, it was Corny himself who called on De Launay, the custodian, to hand over the key of the Bastille. That De Corny's house must have been a handsome one is proved by a note from Jefferson to Madame de Corny in which he thanked her for the gift of a drinking glass: "The beauty of the former had struck me at your house, where all is beautiful," he said. His gifts to her were more practical, and in one case took the form of a book, the *Memoir* of Louis XVI's minister Calonne, of which Jefferson wrote:

"Do not injure yourself in hurrying its perusal. Only when you shall have read it at your leisure be so good as to send it back that it may be returned to the Duke of Dorset." [4] [This was the British minister to France, with whom Jefferson, despite his dislike of the duke's government, was on good terms.]

When Jefferson left Paris to return to America, he did not call on Madame de Corny to take leave, but instead wrote her a note of farewell; his excuse was that partings were too painful. Although he intended, after attending to his affairs in Virginia, to return to Paris, Madame de Corny recognized this leave-taking for what it proved to be—a final departure. Her anguished little note, which did not reach Jefferson till long after he was back home in Virginia, said just one thing: *"I know that you will never return and that I shall never see you again."* She was right in her foreboding: the revolution, which came so soon, tossed her about like a bit of wreckage; and in a matter of months she was alone, ill and all but destitute. Though silenced

---

[4] Chinard, *Trois Amitiés.*

London 15 July 1788

Is it possible that I write another letter before I have any
any answer from my two last! what can be the reason? it is
either obstinacy, or constancy in me: but what does your
silence mean my dear friend! it seems that opportunities
absolutely force themselves on you to recal me to your
remembrance, should I have otherwise so much courage
or should I be so bold as to insist a correspondence!
Mr. d'André is coming to Paris & asks me particularly
for a letter to you, when I think of you I forget all formality
I only remember your kindness, your friendship, you cannot
change; it is only by chance (& that is seldom) if I don't think
of you that I suppose I could not write to anybody that
does not think of me; then a string of punctilios & formalities
stand frowning before me waiting for the happy time, which
brings me letters to answer. Such is the situation of your
                                 Most affte. Maria Cosway in waiting

An impatient letter to Jefferson from Maria Cosway, "in waiting"

Saint-Lambert and Mme. D'Houdetot, by
J. F. Gigoux, Musée des Beaux-Arts, Besançon.
The latter was Jefferson's first hostess in France

Madame la Baronne de Staël-Holstein, one of Jefferson's brilliant
women friends. Engraving after a painting from life by P. L. Bouvier.

for a time, she clung despairingly to her friendship with the strong man of Monticello, wrote to him persistently for years, and drew what comfort she could from his cordial but preoccupied replies.

"When I went to your house after your departure," exclaimed one of her letters, "extreme sadness was a very true presentiment. Well, be happy as you understand it in your way, very far from me. . . . It is true that I shall never see you again. I can only lose and regret my friends. My memory of you is certain, but yours—ah, how doubtful it is! I am going to foretell your future. You will marry again, yes, it is certain, and your wife will be happy." And then she added, "And you, also, I hope." [5]

The French Revolution silenced this correspondence for several years, and then Madame de Corny's name again was brought to Jefferson's notice by Angelica Church, sister-in-law of Alexander Hamilton. She let Jefferson know that this once gay hostess to his daughters was living alone in Rouen in a hired lodging where she had been in "extreme distress"; and Madame de Corny herself confessed that at one time she had been able to keep a little green plant in the window, but had not been able to afford the cost of the water to keep it flourishing, and so it had died.

Jefferson was president of the United States when after a long lapse he resumed their correspondence and sent her some tea. Thanking him, she wrote: "I think of you every morning and this habit is truly sweet to me." Years passed and Jefferson was an aging man when one day he wrote to John Trumbull about the old days in Paris and the "charming coterie" there.

"And Madame de Corny?" he asked. "What has become of her? Is she living or dead?"

He heard about her again through the Monroes, and in 1817, when he was seventy-four years old, he wrote her:

"Thro' what scenes, my dear friend, have we passed since those endeared to us by the society of Mrs. Church, Cosway, Trumbull, etc. What transitions from those to the tyrannies of Robespierre, of the Directories, of Bonaparte, and now of the Allies. . . . My oldest daughter, who was just old enough to be a little known to you, has rendered that a circle of no small compass among ten grandchildren

---

[5] Chinard, *Trois Amitiés*.

and four great grand-children, we are in no solitude. . . . Give me
another letter, my friend, and tell me all about this [a fall which
injured her severely], and a great deal more about yourself, and be
assured of my unabated sentiments of affection and respect."

CHAPTER 16

JEFFERSON AND MADAME DE STAËL

THERE EXISTS no written record of how Jefferson met the most formidable woman in Europe in her day; yet he must have done so
many times, for her mother's salon in Paris often attracted men who
were friends of Jefferson, such as Buffon, Grimm, and the Abbés
Raynal and Morellet; while her own salon drew the patronage of the
Constitutionnels, with whom Jefferson, at least at one stage, often
agreed. These men hoped to preserve the French monarchy while
enlarging the liberties of the people under a written constitution.
This woman whose brilliant gatherings made even so confident an
American as Gouverneur Morris "feel very stupid," was Madame de
Staël-Holstein, daughter of Necker, the financier. She was the wife of
the Swedish minister to France. Morris first saw her when she was
barely twenty-three in the Necker salon in Paris in 1789 and wrote
of her:

"She seems to be a woman of sense and somewhat masculine in her
character, but has very much the appearance of a chambermaid." [1]
Another American, James Gallatin, secretary to Albert Gallatin,
Jefferson's cabinet treasurer, wrote she "is not handsome, but such a
great charm of manner. . . . She is not tall, rather fat, and has
coarse features, but splendid eyes." [2]

To have splendid eyes was not all that Madame de Staël wished of
life. She would have loved to be physically enchanting, but since the
gods had denied her beauty, she made what she could of her mind;
for she was of an omnivorous disposition—omnivorous of literary
fame, of notice and of male attention. A year after their first meeting

---

[1] *Diary and Letters of Gouverneur Morris,* ed. Anne Cary Morris, New York, 1888.
[2] Hawkins, *Mme. de Staël and the United States,* Cambridge, 1930, p. 8.

Morris wrote of her:

"She is a woman of wonderful wit, and above vulgar prejudices of every kind. Her house is a kind of Temple of Apollo." A year later he wrote of dining in this house again and witnessing "a fine scene of vociferous argumentation between her and an abbé," and in still another year he was calling her "a devilish woman."

Jefferson does not mention her in his Paris letters, but since he and her father were friends, it may be assumed he met her in the Necker salon, which was avid of all celebrities. The first letter from her to him is written in a tone that indicates Jefferson was no stranger to her. "When shall we see each other again?" she asked. This letter was dated April 25, 1807, from Coppet, her father's Swiss estate, to which she had retreated when Napoleon forbade her to remain in Paris. She assured him "your name is sacred" in France, and mentioned she was sending him "an evidence of my interest and respect." This may have been a copy of her novel, *Corinne,* which had just been published.[3] She hinted that her son might be going to America the next year and added the whole family might join him there. In France, she said, "neither the governors nor the governed are happy."

In his reply from Washington in July, 1807, Jefferson wrote not only to her but to Europe and especially England; for he seems to have believed that she would be useful as a publicity channel.

"Unmeddling [*sic*] with the affairs of other nations," he said with an emphasis on isolation that must have been plain not only to her but to anyone who opened his letter, "we presume not to proscribe or censure their course. Happy could we be permitted to pursue our own in peace, and to employ all our means in improving the conditions of our citizens."

As to her son, he thus advised: "In our cities he will find distant imitations of the cities of Europe. But if he wishes to know the nation, its occupations, manners and principles, they reside not in the cities; he must travel through the country, accept the hospitalities of the country gentlemen, and visit with them the school of the people."

Not often was Jefferson's agrarian philosophy made clearer than in this letter to Madame de Staël: the true guides to the nation's economy were the country people, and the way to see the people was

---

[3] *Revue de Littérature Comparée,* II, 1922.

to visit them in their homes. Such a passage goes far to explain why Jefferson, although no better than Satan to some parts of the country, never lost the friendship of his fellow-Virginians, even the wealthier planters of the Tidewater area.

The next letter from Madame de Staël of which we have record was written in French in Stockholm in November, 1812, five months after war had been opened between Great Britain and the United States. She began by saying: "You saw the first days of the French revolution and I recall that at my father's house you used to say to over-eager men that their demagogic principles would lead to despotism in France; your prediction has come true."

Then she came to her main point—a defense of England. If by some misfortune, she wrote, England's navy fell into the hands of "the conqueror of the world [Napoleon], it is against you that he would turn it." And then she rose to a climax in terms that subsequent events have made familiar: "You say America has nothing to do with the continent of Europe. But has she nothing to do with the human species? . . . For ten years England has been the sole dike against this singular despotism. . . . When one nation of twelve million men must struggle against a hundred million in the grip of one man, is it surprising that certain abuses occur in the means she must employ in order to resist?" She ended with the exclamation in English: "God bless you and deliver Europe. Farewell."

Jefferson answered in a long letter dated United States of America, May, 1813, which was evidently carefully composed and certainly intended to reach a larger public than that group of intellectuals who constantly circled about Madame de Staël.

Napoleon, he granted, would have only one pre-eminence—"that of having been the greatest of the destroyers of the human race." But the ocean also has a tyrant no less unprincipled. "Bonaparte will die," he exclaimed, "and his tyrannies with him. But . . . the English Government and its pyratical principles and practices have no fixed term of duration. . . . England is, in principle, the enemy of all maritime nations, as Bonaparte is of the continental. . . . Peace is in her hand whenever she will renounce the practice of aggression on the persons of our citizens. If she thinks it worth eternal war, eternal war she must have." He closed this letter, which he did not

sign for reasons he said she would understand, by regretting the
French constitution of 1789 which "would have ensured" liberty, "if
wisdom could have staid at that point the fervid but imprudent zeal
of men who did not know the character of their own countrymen."

In July, 1815, he sent Madame de Staël from Monticello a pamphlet
sustaining these views regarding the international situation. She
replied from Pisa saying that his previous letter had been kept in an
iron chest, where lay her father's will, that she might often reread his
prophecy of Bonaparte's fall.

"If only slavery were destroyed in the South," she wrote, "there
would at least be in the world one government as perfect as human
reason could conceive of." She closed by asking for news of Latin
America where various countries were fighting for their independence.

He answered in September, 1816, saying Spain was in a fair way
of "conquering" herself out of the southern continent. He gave some
details of rebel successes, but declared, "In the meantime everything is at the mercy of military leaders," of "factionists" and of
"ignorance and bigotry." His hope was that in time the rebels would
"form some canons of freedom" and "restrain their leaders to an
observance of them." As for France, that "such a country and such a
people can never be kept permanently prostrate on the earth is a
decree of heaven."

CHAPTER 17

JEFFERSON AND HOUDON

As IF JEFFERSON as plenipotentiary in Paris had not enough to do, the Virginia assembly in 1784 voted to place in his hands the matter of procuring a satisfactory statue of George Washington. Jefferson promptly replied to Governor Patrick Henry that "there could be no question raised as to the sculptor who should be employed; the reputation of Mons. Houdon of this city being unrivalled in Europe." When approached, Houdon assented readily, even eagerly, as if aware that a satisfactory figure would immortalize the sculptor as well as the subject. In fact, Jefferson reported that the artist "was so anxious to be the person who should hand down the figure of the General to future ages, that without hesitating a moment he offered to abandon his business here, to leave the statues of kings unfinished, and to go to America to take the true figure by actual inspection and mensuration. . . . We are agreed in one circumstance, that the size shall be precisely that of life."

Houdon sailed to America with Benjamin Franklin in July, 1785, and Jefferson gave him a letter to Richard Henry Lee requesting him to render to the sculptor "such civilities as may be convenient." To Governor Henry he had to break the uncomfortable news that Houdon's terms were "vastly more" than expected: twenty-five thousand livres or one thousand English guineas, his hosts to pay his expenses going and coming. Also it would be necessary to assure Houdon's family of ten thousand livres if the sculptor died while absent on this mission. Jefferson confessed he did not like this provision, but he admitted Houdon had a father, mother and sisters wholly dependent on him, "and he himself one of the best men in the world." The intricate financial arrangements that made the whole project possible finally had to be shouldered by Jefferson himself.

To prepare George Washington for Houdon's coming, Jefferson wrote concerning the sculptor: "He is disinterested, generous, candid, and panting after glory . . . his eminence and merit gives him admission into genteel societies here . . . he brings with him a subordinate workman or two, who of course will associate with their own class only."

When Jefferson wrote of "genteel societies" in Paris, he was perhaps thinking of the literary and artistic set which later gave a welcome to Maria Cosway. She was a friend of Houdon's, and that fact no doubt created a bond between the sculptor and Jefferson. Houdon was a little older than Jefferson and died two years later. As a youth he studied under Stoldtz and Pigalle, and then spent some years in Italy, where he leaned strongly toward the classical in art. As a sculptor of portraits his chief gifts were a rare fidelity of resemblance added to an innate grace touched with idealism. He made busts of some of the great personages of the day, including the Americans Benjamin Franklin, John Paul Jones, and Jefferson himself. His bust of Jefferson, strongly emphasizing the Virginian's masculinity and intellectual power, is still considered by Jefferson's followers to be the best portrait ever done of him. Houdon's statue of Washington at Richmond is regarded as one of his greatest works. From his heads of Franklin, Washington and John Paul Jones the United States Post Office for years has drawn the models for the illustrations on its postage stamps.

CHAPTER 18

JEFFERSON AND CONDORCET

AMONG THE INTELLECTUALS of that period in France who became friends of Jefferson, one of the foremost was the philosopher, Marie-Jean-Antoine-Nicolas Caritat, Marquis de Condorcet. He was the last of the *philosophes,* that circle of writers, teachers, economists and historians who in the eighteenth century gave France the leadership of the Enlightenment, which hoped to rescue Europe from absolute monarchy, from inertia and from superstition, and guide it toward reason, intelligence and humanitarianism. Included at various stages were Voltaire, Rousseau, Diderot, Montesquieu, Turgot, Quesnay, D'Alembert, Helvétius, and the Abbés Raynal and Mably. When Benjamin Franklin, dressed in his cap of marten's fur and his woolen stockings, arrived in France as the representative of the newborn republic across the sea, the *philosophes* had greeted him with boundless enthusiasm; and when the aging and tired Franklin left Paris, they, or their survivors, transferred their admiration to his successor, Jefferson.

When after five years, Jefferson returned to America and at the request of George Washington re-entered political life, his enemies filled press and pulpit with accusations that he had brought back with him foul French notions and was trying to poison American political life with ideas hatched by French revolutionaries. On the contrary, it is clear from the French writings of the period that whatever were the political novelties entertained, they passed oftener from America to France than vice versa. The Founding Fathers of the infant American republic were the teachers and the French intellectuals of Jefferson's day were the admiring pupils. Particularly is this clear in the writings of Condorcet, who in 1787 even went to the length of publishing a series of letters supposed to have been written by a citizen of New Haven in which he recommended woman suffrage and a one-house legislature.

Condorcet no doubt became acquainted with Jefferson through his admiration for Benjamin Franklin, who was a close friend of Turgot, the physiocrat and minister, who was Condorcet's mentor and model. Both Condorcet and Franklin belonged to the Masonic lodge "of the Nine Sisters," which had as members such figures as Voltaire, Sieyès, Brissot and Danton, and which strongly influenced educated opinion toward change and reform in government.

Jefferson became a member of the circle of distinguished men who gathered regularly in Condorcet's home not only to listen to the philosopher but to enjoy the hospitality of his intellectual young wife, the former Sophie de Grouchy, who was later the translator of Adam Smith and Thomas Paine. And here at her table Jefferson met such rising publicists and writers as Beaumarchais, Chénier, Volney, the Abbé Morellet and Melchior Grimm, the German who was agent and correspondent in Paris for Catherine II of Russia.

Jefferson and Condorcet were of almost exactly the same age. Soon they found they had other things in common. The French philosopher and the Virginian had temperaments much the same: both were inclined to be aloof and shy except among intimates; both had a boundless faith in the future and in people; and both had as salient traits a serene goodness of heart and manner. "Goodness was the most distinctive characteristic of his soul," said Julie de Lespinasse of Condorcet. He and Jefferson also held similar social and political opinions: at this stage both believed a constitutional monarchy was best suited to French conditions; and as friends of the physiocrats both believed that in land lay the true and only source of wealth, and that the possession of land formed the best qualification for citizenship.

By nature Condorcet was far more ardent and emotional than Jefferson, who knew so well how to hold himself in check; and when Americans set up a republic and began to man it with great men, the Frenchman believed the New Jerusalem and the end of human woes were almost in sight. The philosophic tone with which Wythe and Jefferson had imbued the Virginia Declaration of Rights and the

American Declaration of Independence filled him with delight and convinced him that ships of state in future must be steered by philosophers alone. Of the Virginia Declaration Condorcet wrote that "its author is entitled to the eternal gratitude of mankind," while he praised the Philadelphia document as "an exposition, simple and sublime, of rights that have been sacred, though long forgotten."

Condorcet may have influenced Jefferson by his emphasis on self-government and his belief in history of the past as a yardstick for the future, but the American's influence on the Frenchman was evident in the latter's pamphlet, *The Influence of the American Revolution on Europe,* written in 1786. Condorcet, however, could not understand America's retention of slavery, and he strongly criticized the American separation of the three powers of government which Jefferson advocated. The French Revolution, which came so soon after Condorcet's pamphlet, was not kind to idealists, and Condorcet was one of its leading victims. In an attempted flight he was arrested and jailed. Next day he was found dead. Exhaustion, said one rumor. Poison, said another. All such tragedies Jefferson escaped by going home. At one time Condorcet hid himself in the house of the widow Vernet. To while away the slow hours here he wrote his brilliant *Historical View of the Progress of the Human Mind.* This passage, owing to its accord with Jefferson's own thought, must have been of particular interest to Jefferson:

"The invention of the bow was the work of a single man of genius; the formation of a language that of the whole society. The two kinds of progress belong equally to the human species." Individual progress and social progress—Jefferson was for both.

CHAPTER 19

LAFAYETTE HELPS

JEFFERSON'S OCCASIONAL homesick yearnings for the Virginia country-side lessened a little as soon as he began to gain entrance to a circle of Frenchmen who like himself loved philosophy, science or the arts. Naturally the chief figure among his French friends was Lafayette, with whom Jefferson had become well acquainted when governor of Virginia. (Lafayette had named his youngest child Virginia, born about two years before Jefferson's arrival in France.)

The marquis was the owner of an elegant Paris house in the Rue de Bourbon, where Jefferson was often a visitor. Here Lafayette had hung in a double frame on a wall a copy of the American Declaration of Independence. But the space beside it was empty (says a legend).

"Why?" asked a friend.

"It is waiting for a copy of the French Declaration of Rights," said Lafayette.

With the French intellectuals, and indeed with the French intelligentsia as a whole, Jefferson found himself at home and at ease. "Here it seems," he wrote Charles Bellini, professor at William and Mary College who had come over from Italy with Philip Mazzei, "that a man might pass a life without encountering a single rudeness." And then recalling the roughness of frontier and plantation manners in America, he added: "In the pleasures of the table they are far before us, because with good taste they unite temperance. They do not terminate the most sociable meals by transforming themselves into brutes. I have never seen a man drunk in France, even among the lowest of the people. Were I to proceed to tell you how much I enjoy their architecture, sculpture, painting, music, I should want words."

Social life in France he praised in the fondest terms; it was the political and economic life of the people that revolted him. He saw the truth of Voltaire's remark that in Europe a man was "either the hammer or the anvil," and for the first time in his life he saw governments as partners in the exploitation of peoples, and could look on while peoples were "ground to powder by the vices of their form of government."

"The Marquis de Lafayette is a most valuable auxiliary to me," wrote Jefferson to Madison. "His zeal is unbounded, and his weight with those in power great. His education having been merely military, commerce was an unknown field to him. But his good sense enabling him to comprehend perfectly whatever is explained to him, his agency has been very efficacious. He has a great deal of sound genius, is well remarked by the King, and rising in popularity. He has nothing against him but the suspicion of republican principles. I think he will one day be of the ministry. His foible is a canine appetite for popularity and fame; but he will get above this."

Jefferson often found that Lafayette could help him out where, because of diplomatic usages or his ignorance of French customs, his own hands were tied. One example occurred early in Jefferson's Paris career when he got into a battle with the tobacco monopoly, the French end of which was sustained by the farmers-general while the American end was supported by Robert Morris, the Philadelphia financier. Lafayette induced Count de Vergennes, the French foreign minister, to appoint a committee, with himself as a member, to study the whole question of tobacco handling. This caused a useful delay, but in the end the monopoly and Morris won a new contract which stopped the free exchange of French products for American tobacco, much to Jefferson's disgust. He could only write to James Monroe about the battle without naming the "powerful person in Philadelphia who was profiting by that abuse."

It was also Lafayette who helped Jefferson obtain the recall of the undesirable Count de Moustier as French minister to the United States. No doubt influenced by the haughty attitude of his companion, the Marquise de Bréhan, the count had made himself obnoxious not only in social intercourse, but by taking an arrogant tone in pressing for the repayment of the debts owed to France. Jefferson, in

doubt as to what he could properly do, went to Lafayette, and Lafayette went to Montmorin, the foreign minister who had succeeded
Count de Vergennes. Two results followed: it was agreed that notes
about debt questions thereafter should be prepared by the foreign
ministry and not by Moustier; and Montmorin remembered a sentence in one of Moustier's dispatches which could be construed as a
request for leave of absence. Consequently Moustier was transferred
to Berlin.

When in 1787 a meeting of the Assembly of Notables, of which
Lafayette was a member, was called, Jefferson wrote him this screened
advice:

"I wish you success in your meeting. I should form better hopes
of it, if it were divided into two Houses instead of seven. Keeping
the good model of your neighboring country before your eyes, you
may get on, step by step, towards a good constitution. Though that
model is not perfect, yet, as it would unite more suffrages than any
new one which could be proposed, it is better to make that the object. If every advance is to be purchased by filling the royal coffers
with gold, it will be gold well employed. The King, who means so
well, should be encouraged to repeat these Assemblies. You see how
we republicans are apt to preach when we get on politics."

It is to be noted here how Jefferson numbered himself among
republicans; that is, as upholders of republics. At this stage he was
identifying a republic as a form of government having two houses
of legislature and a constitution, but no king. As he saw the shadow
of political upheavals approaching, he became ever more apprehen-
sive that revolt would outrun the habits of the French people. As
he wrote to the Countess de Tessé, Lafayette's aunt, almost at the
same time: "Should they [the deputies of the Assembly of Notables]
attempt more than the established habits of the people are ripe for,
they may lose all, and retard indefinitely the ultimate object of their
aim."

These sentiments reveal to what extent Jefferson's critics in America, who regarded him as poisoned by subversive French influences,
overlooked his basic sub-stratum of conservatism and gradualism.

Jefferson's personal fondness for Lafayette was not hidden—"I
have often wished for you," he wrote to the marquis when he was

in the south of France; but there came a time when Lafayette's political conduct made him anxious.

"As it becomes more and more possible that the Noblesse will go wrong," he wrote Lafayette on May 6, 1789, "I become uneasy for you." This uneasiness was due to his discovery that Lafayette owed his election from his home province of Auvergne to the aristocrats and that they expected him to act according to their instructions. Jefferson feared this would cause Lafayette to try to balance himself between the Third Estate (the rising middle class) on the one hand and the aristocracy on the other, and would cause him to be called a trimmer. This is just what happened; Lafayette was later called by the revolutionists not only a trimmer but a traitor, and was forced into exile. In the Assembly of Notables, the marquis became a tongue-locked member, although privately he was disposed to take the liberal view, or rather, what was then known as the side of the physiocrats, including Jefferson's friends Condorcet, the Duke de la Rochefoucauld and Du Pont de Nemours. The part played here and later by the marquis was undoubtedly due not only to the new ideas he had learned in America but to the influence of Jefferson, who wrote him constantly suggesting what course he might pursue and also often visited Lafayette's house in the Rue de Bourbon. These hints were given not only directly to the marquis but indirectly through notes to his aunt, the Countess de Tessé, who, being a lover of politics, did not fail to pass them on.

Incidentally, Lafayette's presence in the Assembly of Notables led to the perpetration of one of Jefferson's few known puns. He wrote the marquis from the south of France: "Your head, my dear friend, is full of Notable Things." Lafayette's reply, also a pun, was that they might better be called "not ables."

CHAPTER 20

JEFFERSON AS MONK

JEFFERSON AS THE American minister to France had to be, and enjoyed being, a bountiful host, but he remained at heart the solitary student; and there were days when routine business of diplomacy irked him. At such times he sought the poultice of solitude, and in order to enjoy perfect quiet he engaged rooms at the Carthusian monastery on Mont Calvaire where the inmates were forbidden to converse outside their own cells. This institution accepted laymen as paying guests, of which it had about forty. They were permitted certain privileges such as having their own servants, breakfasting in their own rooms and walking in the gardens. They could assemble at dinner but they had to observe the rule of silence.

Here Jefferson found peace as often as he had concentrated work or thinking to do. In resorting to this hermitage he was obeying the same instinct that had led him to build the solitary house on the mountain of Monticello. The monastery brothers occasionally visited him in Paris, and the Superior once showed his friendship by presenting him with an ivory broom made in the monastery shop.

Although by temperament and upbringing Jefferson was a Protestant—he was sometimes suspected of Unitarian and again of Baptist leanings—he also unhesitatingly patronized a Catholic institution when he placed his daughter Martha, then thirteen years old, in a convent school at the Abbaye Royale de Panthemont, or Pentemont, in the Rue de Greñelle. "It is a house of education altogether the best in France," he once described it. "There are in it as many Protestants as Catholics, and not a word is ever spoken to them on . . . religion." He was still proceeding on the plan by which he considered Martha "as the head of a little family of her own"; he also had to envisage

102

an eventuality he summed up so: "The chance that in marriage she will draw a blockhead I calculate at about fourteen to one." Martha was now growing up into a sturdy, healthy girl with no little of her father's character in her face and nature: like him, she was poised, self-contained and gracious; and Jefferson came to lean upon her more and more.

"To your sister and yourself," he once wrote her, "I look to render the evening of my life serene and contented. Its morning has been clouded by loss after loss, till I have nothing left but you."

Once when Martha owned up to hard bouts with Latin and confessed she could not manage Livy except with a master's help, Jefferson wrote her an admonition in which he revealed no little of the American frontiersman's psychology:

"It is part of the American character to consider nothing as desperate, to surmount every difficulty by resolution and contrivance."

CHAPTER 21

SNUBBED IN ENGLAND

IN THE SPRING of 1786 Jefferson went over from Paris to England and there encountered several humiliations. There were also several pleasures. The humiliations came from rancorous old George III and his ministers. The pleasures came from what Jefferson had long wanted to see and study—English gardens; for, as he wrote his friend John Page, "the gardening in that country is the article in which it surpasses all the earth."

John Adams, then the American minister in England, had long desired Jefferson to come to London and assist him in negotiations which might settle treaty questions involving Tripoli, Portugal, and Great Britain herself. "His real errand," wrote Adams to John Jay, secretary of state at Washington, "will be concealed from the public here."

After a week of relaxation, Jefferson joined Adams in facing George III and Queen Charlotte at a reception. England's king was then within two years of the madness that led his doctors, replete with pomposity and ignorance, to wrap him in a strait jacket and have him whipped. At the moment he was lucid enough, but as he grew older he manifested more and more of the bullheadedness that had cost him his once loyal American colonies. "He has a pleasure in his own will and way," wrote John Adams to John Jay, "without which he would be miserable."

When at the reception, Jefferson and Adams came up, their majesties barely nodded and then turned their backs on the two commissioners. No one was deceived as to the reason for this discourtesy; John Adams had been getting nowhere in his pressure for a treaty, but he had received no outright rudeness; the courtiers knew this

104

snub was aimed at Jefferson. Jefferson has left in his *Autobiography* an account of his cold reception.

"On my presentation, as usual, to the King and Queen, at their levées, it was impossible for anything to be more ungracious, than their notice of Mr. Adams and myself. I saw, at once, that the ulcerations of mind in that quarter left nothing to be expected on the subject of my attendance."

Their next call was on the Marquis of Caermarthen, the foreign minister, but he soon showed he wore King George's collar. He had nothing to offer except "vagueness and evasions." The commissioners left with him their proposals and later asked for an appointment, but the minister never granted it. For seven weeks he made excuses of "pressing occupations," and then Jefferson, recognizing that the rebuffs were intentional, stopped fooling with King George's henchmen.

Later from his desk in Paris he wrote his tried friend in Virginia, John Page, burning words about England that showed how near he was to breaking through his own precepts:

"This nation hates us, their Ministers hate us, and their King more than all other men. They have the impudence to avow this, tho' they acknowledge our trade important to them. But they think we cannot prevent our countrymen bringing it into their lap." He could not help letting be seen his spleen against other English institutions, though he made a manly effort to be fair. Incidentally he revealed the cancer in France's land system:

"I traversed that country [England] much, and own, both town and country fell short of my expectations. Comparing it with this, I found a much greater proportion of barrens, a soil, in other parts, not naturally so good as this, not better cultivated, but better manured, and therefore more productive. This proceeds from the practice of long leases there, and short ones here. The laboring people here are poorer than in England. They pay about one-half their produce in rent; the English, in general, about a third. The gardening in that country is the article in which it surpasses all the earth. I mean their pleasure in gardening. This, indeed, went far beyond my ideas. The city of London, though handsomer than Paris, is not so handsome as Philadelphia. Their architecture is in the most wretched style I ever saw, not meaning to except America, where it is bad, nor even Virginia, where it is worse than in any other part of America which I have seen. The mechanical arts in London are carried to a wonderful perfection."

To George Wythe, his old preceptor at Williamsburg, Virginia, Jefferson sent from Paris these additional observations regarding the English people:

"The people of England, I think, are less oppressed than here. But it needs but half an eye to see, when among them, that the foundation is laid in their dispositions for the establishment of a despotism. Nobility, wealth, and pomp, are the objects of their admiration. They are by no means the free minded people we suppose them in America. Their learned men, too, are few in number, and are less learned, and infinitely less emancipated from prejudice, than those of this country."

As for the other diplomatic negotiations attempted in London, neither that with Tripoli nor that with Portugal turned out satisfactorily. The envoy representing the Tripolitan pirates wanted thirty thousand guineas to ensure the safety of American ships entering the Mediterranean, and he hinted that Algiers and Morocco would want the same sum. No deal was made.

Conversations about a treaty with Portugal on a most-favored-nation basis were carried on for weeks. The Chevalier Pinto, the Portuguese ambassador, was friendly; but when a point was raised as to the free entry of American flour into Portugal, the envoy confessed "several nobles of great influence" at the Portuguese court owned windmills near Lisbon, and he hinted they would not like any threat to their profits in grinding wheat. And with this lesson in economic determinism, the Portuguese treaty was placed on the shelf for further, much further, reference.

Before he had done with England, Jefferson cast off diplomatic cares and, accompanied occasionally by John Adams and by Adams' son-in-law, William Stephen Smith, began what was far more enjoyable to him, a study of England's gardens, which were then at their eighteenth-century best. He carried as his guide Thomas Whately's *Observations on Modern Gardening*, published in 1770; meantime making careful entries, with a view to use them at Monticello, in his notebook and account book. First he visited the Duke of Devonshire's garden at Chiswick, then Hampton Court; he dismissed them respectively as showing "too much art" and as "old fashioned." The poet Pope's three and one-half acre garden at Twickenham on the Thames he noticed particularly because of the obelisk planted as a monument to the poet's mother. Lady Frances Pelham's vast garden—forty-five acres—at Esher Place pleased him because of its "lovely mixture" of trees. He gave the servants here six shillings and stopped to record the sum in his account book. Rapidly he visited Claremont, Paynshill, Woburn, Caversham, Wotton and Stowe, which last he noted required fifteen men and eighteen boys for its upkeep. At Leasowes in Shropshire he noted that Shenstone "ruined himself by what he did to this farm."

And then he came to Hagley and Blenheim, which really detained him. The former had one thousand acres, a blend of park and garden, with two to three hundred deer at large in it. He noticed the recesses built for statuary. In one was a *Vénus pudique,* "turned half around as if inviting you with her into the recess." On this John Adams's comment was: "The temples to Bacchus and Venus are quite unnecessary, as mankind have no need of artificial incitement to such amusements." . . . "The beauty, convenience and utility of these country seats are not enjoyed by the owners. They are mere ostentations of vanity; races, cocking, gambling, draw away their attention."

At Blenheim, seat of the Dukes of Marlborough, Jefferson noted that two hundred people were employed on the twenty-five-hundred-acre estate, but "art appears too much." He gave the Blenheim servants seven shillings. He concluded his garden tour with visits to Enfield Chase, Moor Park and Kew. At the last place he paid sixpence for lemonade. At Moor Park, once the property of Sir Thomas Dundas, the house made a deep impression on him. In front was a Corinthian portico of four columns. The wings each had a colonnade in front. At the back were a terrace and four Corinthian pilasters. Did Monticello and other houses designed by Jefferson receive something from Moor Park?

We should never know that on this tour Jefferson visited Stratford-on-Avon and Shakespeare's tomb except for items put down in his account book. His notebook contains no word about the bard, though Adams's records say, "We cut a chip, according to custom," from Shakespeare's chair. There are only the bare entries among Jefferson's itemized accounts: "For seeing house where Shakespeare was born, 1s; seeing his tombstone, 1s; entertainment 4s. 2d; servants, 2s; horses to Hackley, 12s."

Other entries make it plain that on this tour Jefferson was not interested in history, literature, drama or art, or in emotional associations; he had a mind only for those utilitarian objects and methods that might be useful to him at Monticello, or interesting to his farming countrymen back home. At times Jefferson's mind was singularly one-tracked. It had a gift for excluding whatever was not in the immediate foreground of his interest. Jefferson at no time was a dreamer in aught but practical matters, and he was never a mystic. A primrose by the river's brim, to him, was simply something to get seeds from. But such a practical operation would be relieved of sordidness by the pains he would take to distribute the seed among all his friends.

One matter which struck Jefferson during his stay in England was the bad impression being made by American laggardness in paying overseas debts while in American cities there was much spending and speculation. A gambling fever had arisen in the United States following the peace made at the end of the Revolutionary War, and there was much mad trading done on a loose credit basis. His sharp comment was:

"American reputation, in Europe, is not such as to be flattering to its citizens. Two circumstances are particularly objected to us; the non-payment of our debts, and the want of energy in our government. These discourage a connection with us. I own it to be my opinion, that good will arise from the destruction of our credit. I see nothing else which can restrain our disposition to luxury, and to the change of those manners which alone can preserve republican government. As it is impossible to prevent credit, the best way would be to cure its ill effects, by giving an instantaneous recovery to the creditor. This would be reducing purchases on credit, to purchases for ready money. A man would then see a prison painted on everything he wished, but had not ready money to pay for."

Jefferson's visit to England opened his eyes in other respects, altered some of his views, and confirmed others. The effect on his actions and writings soon became visible.

CHAPTER 22

BACK IN PRE-REVOLUTIONARY
FRANCE

BACK IN PARIS, Jefferson found a lull had taken place in political life and he was so glad to be where he was and not in England that he wrote gaily to Mrs. John Adams in London:

"Here, we have singing, dancing, laughter and merriment, no assassinations, no treasons, rebellions, nor other dark deeds. When our King goes out, they fall down and kiss the earth where he has trodden; and then they go on kissing one another, and this is the truest wisdom. They have as much happiness in a year as an Englishman in ten."

An odd thing about this period was the nearness with which Jefferson at first, despite his eager interest in science, came to missing the meaning of that improved invention, the steam engine, or its relation to the power age, which was about to come into being. In 1785 he wrote to James Madison (the president of William and Mary College, not the statesman), referring to a letter of his:

"You therein speak of a new method of raising water by steam, which you suppose will come into general use. I know of no new method of that kind."

Yet in a later letter, written in April, 1786, to Charles Thomson, scholar, scientist and secretary of the Continental Congress, Jefferson revealed that not only he realized something of the portent of steam power but that in the course of his London visit he had had a talk with Matthew Boulton, partner of James Watt in developing the first effective steam engines, a fact he had failed to mention elsewhere.

"One [improvement] deserves particular notice," he wrote, "because it is simple, great, and likely to have extensive consequences.

110

It is the application of steam as an agent for working grist mills. . . . I hear you are applying the same agent in America to navigate boats." Again in the same year he wrote Thomson:

"You say you have not been able to learn whether, in the new mills of London, steam is the immediate mover of the machinery, or raises water to move it. It is the immediate mover. The power of the agent, though long known, is but now beginning to be applied to the various purposes of which it is susceptible." He then mentions learning from Boulton that the London steam mills made "a peck and a half of coal perform exactly as much as a horse in one day can perform."

To Jefferson whatever was new in science or invention was always fascinating, and when a Paris gunsmith devised a weapon with standardized parts—a preliminary symptom of the mass production to come—Jefferson sought him out and sent a description of his gun to Patrick Henry in Virginia.

To Charles Thomson he also described the workings of a cylinder oil lamp and the "beautiful discovery" of phosphoric matches. "Very useful," he wrote, "to heads which like yours and mine cannot at all times be got to sleep. The convenience of lighting a candle without getting out of bed, of sealing letters without calling a servant, of kindling a fire without flint, steel, punk, &c, are of value."

For James Madison, who was always alert to scientific novelties, he procured a pocket telescope, a walking stick, a "chemical box" and a portable copying press which Jefferson designed himself and had made to order.

When he learned that plans for a capitol building at Richmond had been made, he hastily wrote to Edmund Randolph begging him to have the work held up until his own plan, on which an architect was busy, could be finished. He explained that it was designed after the Maison Carrée of Nîmes, "built by Caius and Lucius Caesar and repaired by Louis XIV, which, in the opinion of all who have seen it, yields in beauty to no piece of architecture on earth." He added that his building "will be more convenient, give more room, and cost but two-thirds" of the other. It is that building which is Virginia's capitol today.

Despite all these interests and distractions, Jefferson kept up a constant pressure on the French government for a relaxation of restrictions that affected imports from the United States, and despite the monopolistic alliance between the farmers-general and Robert Morris of Philadelphia, at last he was able to obtain a customs concession called "the order of Bernis," and won promise that no more restrictive contracts on tobacco would be made with Morris. This order granted, besides improved regulations governing duty payments, four free ports in France instead of the previous two. "As far as I am able to see," reported Jefferson, "the friendship of the people of this country toward us is cordial and general."

Much of this cordiality came from the foreign minister, the Count de Vergennes, whom Jefferson greatly respected although the count had "very imperfect ideas of our institutions and no confidence in them" and his age had "chilled his heart." Within a year the count was dead; but his successor, Montmorin, though he had not Vergennes's head, was friendly and simple, and Jefferson liked him.

In France the year 1786 passed off without disturbance, but in the United States it produced Shays's Rebellion. The comment on this that reached Jefferson was so excited that he was moved to write several letters about it, and these have been among the most quoted of his papers.

The uprising in western Massachusetts led by Daniel Shays, who had been an officer in the Revolutionary War and a participant at Bunker Hill, produced hysteria, fright and violent reaction in upper American circles. It was a populist movement that grew directly out of the speculation, credit splurges and unequal taxation that distinguished the post-war period in the thirteen American states; for the Revolutionary War was like others in producing economic and social disturbances that fell most heavily on the weakest strata of the population. And as in all post-war periods, the farmers were first economically elevated and then suddenly dashed down. It was they, combining with the neglected war veterans, who fell in behind Shays and urged him on when he would have preferred to go slow. Shays's forces were finally scattered by militia led by General Benjamin Lincoln.

But the fact that such an uprising should have occurred at all in young America gave rise to the most dismal forebodings about the future of the republic and to head-shakings about the endurance of democracy. Particularly in New England was there an alarm and a reaction not far short of convulsion. With the emotional extremism that since the earliest days has characterized some Americans, liberty-lovers suddenly became doubters and Tories, while property-owners everywhere imagined their possessions being attacked and their security menaced. In Massachusetts and Connecticut there occurred such a revulsion that the foundation was laid for a political counter-movement which Alexander Hamilton later headed and which developed such an opposition to Jeffersonian "leveling" that secession from the United States was openly proposed. But Shays's Rebellion had no such effect on Jefferson. After receiving the first few reports of it late in 1786, he wrote:

"It is believed this incident will strengthen our government. Those people are not entirely without excuse." A little later he extended his comment:

"I am persuaded myself that the good sense of the people will always be found to be the best army. They may be led astray for a moment, but will soon correct themselves. The people are the only censors of their governors: and even their errors will tend to keep these to the true principles of their institution. To punish these errors too severely would be to suppress the only safeguard of the public liberty. The way to prevent these irregular interpositions of the people is to give them full information of their affairs thro' the channel of the public papers, and to contrive that those papers should penetrate the whole mass of the people. The basis of our government being the opinion of the people, the very first object should be to keep that right; and were it left to me to decide whether we should have a government without newspapers or newspapers without a government, I should not hesitate a moment to prefer the latter." [1]

Jefferson's next comment on Shays came a few days later in a letter to James Madison saying, "I am impatient to learn your sentiments on the late troubles in the Eastern States."

"Those characters wherein fear predominates over hope . . ." he added, "may conclude too hastily that nature has formed man insusceptible of any other government but that of force, a conclusion

[1] Letter to Edward Carrington, January 16, 1787.

not founded in truth, nor experience." A government of force, he went on, "is a government of wolves over sheep . . . I hold it that a little rebellion now and then is a good thing, and as necessary in the political world as storms in the physical."

This thought he repeated in a letter to Mrs. Adams on February 22, 1787 (the day the Assembly of Notables convened in Paris):

"The spirit of resistance to government is so valuable on certain occasions, that I wish it to be always kept alive. It will often be exercised when wrong, but better so than not to be exercised at all. I like a little rebellion now and then. It is like a storm in the atmosphere."

And again he voiced the same idea in a letter to Mrs. Adams's son-in-law, Colonel W. S. Smith, but in terms much more emphatic:

"God forbid we should even be 20 years without such a rebellion. . . . The tree of liberty must be refreshed from time to time with the blood of patriots and tyrants. It is its natural manure."

These sayings indicate to what extent Jefferson's philosophy of society was shaping itself. In substance he was proclaiming that sovereignty resides in peoples and not in governments. Although he was insistent that ultimate power belongs to and is derived from the people, he was still calling himself a republic-man. At this period he never used the word "democrat." In fact, we do not find the word in his writings until 1816 when he declared to Du Pont de Nemours, the French physiocrat, that "we of the United States . . . are constitutionally and conscientiously Democrats."

But it was plain that he was thinking of government through delegates rather than a collectivity; for to Du Pont he also wrote: "We think experience has proved it safer, for the mass of individuals composing the society, to reserve to themselves personally the exercise of all rightful powers to which they are competent, and to delegate those to which they are not competent to deputies named, and removable for unfaithful conduct, by themselves immediately." He maintained that "the people" are competent as judges of human character, but not necessarily as managers of public affairs. "We believe," he wrote, "that this proximate choice and power of removal is the best security which experience has sanctioned for ensuring an honest conduct in the functionaries of society," for "human character, we believe, requires in general constant and immediate controul [sic] to prevent its being biased from right by the seductions of self-love."

In brief, Jefferson viewed men as having on the one hand an egotistic or centripetal instinct, and, on the other, a social or centrifugal instinct; of the two the former was stronger. But this could be held in check by reason and proper information.

Jefferson's observations of English gardens had the effect of whetting his appetite for seeds, plants and horticultural experiments; and after his return to Paris, probably because of his heightened social instinct, he became much more active than before in promoting an exchange of American for European plants. To William Drayton, chairman of the South Carolina Society for Promoting Agriculture, he wrote accepting membership and forwarding seeds of sanfoin grass and of the cork oak. He wrote also to his kinsman, Richard Cary, in Virginia, asking for American plants and seedlings and giving detailed directions for packing. Occasionally he added pungent comments, for example:

"Mushmelons [sic], such as are here, are worse than the worst in Virginia. There is not sun enough to ripen them, and give them flavor . . . the only garden vegetable I find here better than ours is the turnep [sic]." He also showed a curious interest in importing pecan nuts to France, nearly always spelling it "paccan."

"The Paccan nut," he wrote Francis Hopkinson in Philadelphia, "is, as you can conjecture the Illinois nut, the former is the vulgar name South of the Potomac as also with the Indians & Spaniards, and enters also into the Botanical name which is Jugglans Paccan." [2]

Another vegetable that agitated his interest was rice. It disturbed him that more Carolina rice was not sold in France, and that it was not brought in directly instead of through England.

---

[2] *Garden Book*, ed. Betts, pp. 118–119.

CHAPTER 23

QUEEN OF ALL

NONE OF THE women with whom Jefferson was friendly in France could compare with the graceful and gifted Anglo-Italian artist, Maria Hadfield Cosway. Here was a woman who had virtually every attribute that Jefferson most admired: she was personally attractive; she was musical; she was an artist with pencil and brush; and she occupied, as to the manner born, the very center of a circle of talent such as Jefferson, when he first came to Paris, hoped to belong to. Moreover, she liked Jefferson with a continuity and devotion that might, it would seem from this distance, have grown, had he cared to foster it, into a more ardent feeling. At their very first meeting she all but took possession of him, and she showed in a thousand ways that even when they both had long ago left their youth behind, and when an ocean and many miles lay between them, her regard for him had no whit waned.

The manner of their first meeting was odd and unlooked for. It took place through John Trumbull, the American painter. Jefferson had invited Trumbull to come over to Paris from London and stay in his house at the Grille de Chaillot, where he helped him complete his ambitious canvases depicting scenes from the American Revolution, particularly the signing of the Declaration of Independence (for which Jefferson patiently posed). Jefferson also helped Trumbull obtain appointments in Paris with some of the French officers who had taken part in the trapping of Cornwallis at Yorktown, such as Rochambeau, Chastellux and La Luzerne.

Trumbull had come thus far toward success by a long hard road but at one leap, thanks to Jefferson, he landed in a European capital where art and artists received more attention than anywhere else in

116

the world. He accepted eagerly Jefferson's invitation to come to Paris, where, he later wrote in his autobiography, "I was most kindly received by him. My two paintings, the first fruits of my national enterprise, met his warm approbation, and during my visit I began the composition of the Declaration of Independence with the assistance of his information and advice."

Trumbull had a gift for meeting gay and interesting people, and soon he was friends with such celebrities as Houdon the sculptor, David the painter, Belessaire the architect and Madame Vigée-Lebrun, the portrait painter, who showed him the celebrated portrait, not yet finished, of herself and her young daughter. Trumbull was much taken by this young and talented Frenchwoman.

"One of the most charming women I ever saw," he wrote. "Among female names, Angelica [Church] alone can come in any competition with Madame Le Brun."

August, 1786, was one of Trumbull's particularly active months. On Sunday, the fifth, he recorded that he went with Jefferson and others to see the ceremony of the crowning of the *rosière* of Sarennes, a village near St. Cloud, four miles from Jefferson's house; and on the thirteenth he went with Jefferson to Passy to dine with the Abbés Chassé and Arnout. "Mr. Jefferson," says his August diary, "joined our party almost daily, and here commenced his acquaintance with Mrs. Cosway, of whom very respectful mention is made in his published correspondence."

Mrs. Cosway lately had come to Paris with her husband, Richard Cosway, the London miniature painter, who had been engaged by the Duke of Orleans, the eccentric "Philippe Egalité," to paint the duchess and her children. Trumbull does not say so, but perhaps it was he who introduced Jefferson to Mrs. Cosway and it was certainly he who subsequently carried many messages between them.

Like several other women who were attracted to Jefferson, Mrs. Cosway was much younger than her husband, had become bored with him, and finally had lost respect for him; for Cosway, although near the top as an English miniaturist, in person was an affected and self-concentrated little fop with a simian face. In addition, Maria hated British weather and despised the fashionable but brutish London life of the late eighteenth century.

She had been born in Italy near Florence, and all her life she spoke and wrote English with a bit of Italian flavor; the Latin arts and the Latin outlook on the world—these she loved best. Her father was Charles Hadfield, a Manchester man who kept a boarding-house for English travelers in Florence. She was brought up in convents and never ceased to love the life of cloisters; but her talents in the arts, especially drawing and music, brought her such attention that when her father died in 1778, she was taken to London and introduced by Angelica Kauffman, the painter, to a fashionable circle of people who loved to talk about and sometimes to practice the finer arts. Since a young woman alone in London would have had a poor time making a living in the arts, her friends pushed her in the path of Richard Cosway, who under royal patronage was becoming prosperous and sought after; and these friends were successful in marrying her to him. He was then forty, she twenty-two. They believed she could not fail to be happy. Her concerts and "evenings" in Pall Mall indeed were often crowded with notables, but she had to confess later: "The climate did not agree with me—in the midst of so much happiness I never enjoy'd health."

Picture a lonely and talented young woman, large-eyed and light-haired, whose heart is at war with her life; inwardly adrift; and despising most of the denizens of her circle. She meets, probably in David's studio, the tall and talked-of minister from exotic America. He is poised and dignified but courtly, with an awkward sincerity. His hazel eyes and homely-handsome, freckled face kindles when he finds she knows music—knows it better than he—and is versed in all the arts of which he has only a book knowledge. His speech shows he is gentle and unaffectedly kind. It is not strange that this young woman reaches out to him and even clings to him.

Jefferson at first draws back slightly; it is the natural reaction of a man who is prone to be constrained with strangers, even attractive ones. Trumbull has already told him about the Cosways, particularly Maria—her chestnut-blond hair piled in masses around her head; her large, blue eyes.

"Yes," Trumbull insists, "you must meet the Cosways. When may I arrange for an introduction?"

But Jefferson fails to show any interest: he has no time now, he

Marquis de Lafayette by Charles C. Ingham

I am glad to hear that our new constitution is pretty sure of being accepted by states enough to secure the good it contains, & to meet such opposition in some others as to give us hopes it will be accommodated to them by the amendment of it's most glaring faults, particularly the want of a declaration of rights. — the long expected edict for the protestants at length appears here. it's analysis is this. it is an acknolegement (hitherto withheld by the laws) that protestants can beget children and that they can die & be offensive unless buried. it does not give them permission to think, to speak, nor to worship. it enumerates the humiliations to which they shall remain subject, & the burthens to which they shall continue to be unjustly exposed. what are we to think of the condition of the human mind in a country where such a wretched thing as this has thrown the state into convulsions, and how must we bless our own situation in a country the most illiterate peasant of which is a Solon compared with the authors of this law. there is a modesty often which does itself injury. our countrymen profess this. they do not know their own superiority. you see it; you are young, you have time & talents to correct them. study the subject while in Europe in all the instances which will present themselves to you, and profit. your countrymen of them by making them to know & value themselves. Adieu, my dear Sir, & be assured of the esteem with which I am
your friend & servt   Th:Jefferson

Page of a letter from Jefferson to John Rutledge of South Carolina on the new U.S. Constitution

pleads, for new acquaintances; besides, he tells himself, people of charm and talent would be all the more dangerous to a tranquillity attained only after long emotional stress; he cannot bear the pain of unnecessary partings; moreover, there is never out of his mind the day when he is to return home.

And then one day Trumbull accompanies him on a visit to Legrand and Molino's, the architects, and then to the Halle aux Blés, the grain market, for a look at its domes and arches. For Jefferson's interest in architecture has become keener than at any time since as a young man trying to find a design for Monticello he studied Morris's *Select Architecture,* Gibbs's *Rules for Drawing* and Leoni's *Palladio;* he is particularly interested in a possible design for a central market at Richmond, Virginia. Afterward there is an adjournment to a studio—there is a hint it was David's. Here occurs the long-planned (by Trumbull), long-avoided (by Jefferson) introduction to the Cosways. A discussion ensues; time runs on. Watches are consulted. It is found that every person has an engagement. Jefferson himself is due to dine with the Duchess d'Anville, one of the great ladies of France.

In chorus it is proposed that, regardless of invitations, all remain together for the rest of the day: Jefferson hesitates. Mrs. Cosway pleads. She sees Jefferson yield slightly. She grasps her advantage and sends off a messenger who is to inform the duchess that owing to urgent dispatches, etc., the American minister cannot come to dinner today.

From that moment, the tall and dignified American minister was much devoted to the energetic little Anglo-Italienne. Not since his student days at Williamsburg when he was running after Belinda and the other girls, had he cast off mundane care and surrendered himself so giddily to the iridescent hour. Without further thought for engagements, "with cheerful nonchalance," as Jefferson himself afterward described it, he, Trumbull and the Cosways called a carriage and bounced off on a round of restaurants, cafés and sights. First they dined, and then drove down the Seine to St. Cloud, on whose slopes and river banks many generations of pleasure-hunting Parisians have relaxed and diverted themselves. Then they visited a picture gallery. They returned to Paris and went to see a fireworks exhibition offered by one of the famous showmen of the day, Ruggieri.

Then, no doubt at Maria's urging, they deserted fireworks for music and went to call on Johann Baptiste Krumpholz, music master and composer. Though born in Bohemia and trained under Haydn at Vienna, Krumpholz had reached his greatest popularity in Paris and had added to his fame by inventing several mechanical music devices. His favorite instrument (also Maria's) was the harp. To this he had attached a double pedal and made other improvements which fascinated Jefferson and formed the subject of letters to Francis Hopkinson, the Declaration signer, musician and science-minded Philadelphian whose mother had been hostess to Martha Jefferson.

"I have lately," Jefferson wrote Hopkinson with that attention to detail which often amazed his friends, "examined a foot-bass invented here, by the celebrated Krumfoltz [sic]. It is precisely a piano-forte, about ten feet long, eighteen inches broad, and nine inches deep. It is of one octave only, from fa to fa. The part where the keys are, projects at the side in order to lengthen the levers of the keys. It is placed on the floor, and the harpsichord or other piano-forte is set over it, the foot acting in concert on that, while the fingers play on this. There are three unison cords to every note, of strong brass wire, and the lowest have wire wrapped on them as the lowest in the piano-forte. The chords give a fine, clear, deep tone, almost like the pipe of an organ."

So Jefferson's letter ran on in a visible enjoyment, making it easy to realize the truth of what he had once said about himself: "Music is the passion of my soul."

Next to this day Jefferson remembered that on which he and Mrs. Cosway had visited St. Germain, old resort of Parisians and once the seat of Henry IV.

"How beautiful was every object!" he wrote to Maria later. "The Port de Neuilly, the hills along the Seine, the rainbows of the Machine of Marly, the terras of St. Germains, the chateaux, the gardens, the statues of Marly, the pavillion of Lucienne.[1] Recollected, too, Madrid, Bagatelle, the King's garden, the *Dessert*. How grand the idea excited by the remains of such a column! The spiral stair-

---

[1] *Louvechienne* was the name. Jefferson, like many other eighteenth-century writers, spelled by ear.

case too was beautiful. Every moment was filled with something agreeable. The wheels of time moved on with a rapidity of which those of our carriage gave but a faint idea. And yet in the evening when one took a retrospect of the day, what a mass of happiness had we travelled over!"

We know of no other letter written by Jefferson, addressed either to man or woman, suffused with such a glow as this. Rarely did the sage of Monticello permit himself to approach such raptures as he expressed here in a communication intended for Mrs. Cosway alone.

Almost every day for more than a month Jefferson was in Maria's company. Sometimes Trumbull went along, sometimes Jefferson's secretary, William Short, who had learned to become a devoted swain to some of the Parisian ladies. But there is some evidence that Maria and her Virginian beau went on several excursions unescorted. At such times, delighted though Jefferson was, an interior voice, which never fell quite silent, would not permit him an unclouded enjoyment. As he later confessed to Maria, his heart gave one counsel, his head another. Indeed, he quotes his head as saying to his heart:

"I often told you during the course that you were imprudently engaging your affections under circumstances that must cost you a great deal of pain; that the persons [i.e., Mr. and Mrs. Cosway] indeed were of the greatest merit, possessing good sense, good humor, honest hearts, honest manners, and eminence in a lovely art; that the lady had moreover qualities and accomplishments belonging to her sex, which might form a chapter apart for her; such as music, modesty, beauty, and that softness of disposition, which is the ornament of her sex and charm of ours. But that all these considerations would increase the pang of separation; that their stay here was to be short; that you rock our whole system when you are parted from those you love, complaining that such a separation is worse than death, inasmuch as this ends our sufferings; whereas that only begins them: and that the separation would in this instance be the more severe as you would probably never see them again."

Most of this took place in August, 1786. One day in September Jefferson suffered an odd and highly painful accident. He was out walking with Mrs. Cosway, probably in that Bois de Boulogne of which he was so fond, when he fell and fractured a bone in his right wrist. Just how the mishap occurred he would never tell. The most he would say was what he wrote to Colonel W. S. Smith, son-in-law of John Adams in London:

"How the right hand became disabled would be a long story for the left to tell. It was by one of those follies from which good cannot come, but ill may."

The legend is that after the accident Jefferson walked all the way home, gripping his injured wrist with his other hand but saying nothing about the injury to his companion. As soon as possible he took the fractured wrist to a supposedly competent Paris surgeon who, ignorant and pompous, bungled the treatment and failed to give the patient even temporary relief. The result was that Jefferson suffered grievously, never recovered the full and normal use of his right hand, and even three weeks later was unable to attend the presentation by Virginia to the city of Paris of Houdon's bust of La-fayette. Moreover, he was compelled in the midst of much diplomatic correspondence, to which he often had to attend personally, to learn to write with his left hand. In consequence, his penmanship under-went a grim and sudden change. It was still legible, but it no longer had smoothness or grace.

Although Jefferson could write more eloquently, Mrs. Cosway was far more personal and less formal in her letters, as the following, ap-parently written soon after Jefferson injured his wrist, testifies:

"You don't always judge by appearance or it would be much to my disadvantage this day, without deserving it; it has been a day of con-tradictions. I meant to have seen you twice, and I have appeared a monster for not having sent to know how you were the whole day. I have been more uneasy than I can express. This morning my husband killed my project I had proposed to him, by burying himself among pictures and forgetting the hours. Though we were near your house, coming to see you, we were obliged to come back, the time being much past that we were to be at St. Cloud to dine with the Duchess of Kingston. . . . Oh, I wish you were well enough to come to us tomorrow to dinner, and stay the evening . . . I would save you and help you at dinner and divert your pain after with good music." [2]

Early in October Richard Cosway finished a portrait of the

2 Randolph, *Domestic Life of Thomas Jefferson.*

Duchess of Chartres (she who called Jefferson "Monsieur the Clever")
and her children, and prepared to return with his wife to London
by way of Antwerp. The happy days were over; there would remain
to the solitary American minister only the task of trying to sell leaf
tobacco and fish oil to the French merchants.

Just before the Cosways' departure for London, Maria sent this
mournful little note to Jefferson by messenger:

"I am very sorry indeed, and blame myself for having been the
cause of your pains in the wrist. Why would you go, and why was I
not more friendly to you, and less so to myself by preventing your
giving me the pleasure of your company? You repeatedly said it would
do you no harm. I felt interested and did not insist. We shall go, I
believe, this morning. Nothing seems ready, but Mr. Cosway seems
more disposed than I have seen him all this time. I shall write to you
from England; it is impossible to be wanting to a person who has
been so exclusively obliging. I don't attempt to make compliments—
there can be none for you, but I beg you will think us sensible to
your kindness, and that it will be with exquisite pleasure I shall
remember the charming days we have passed together, and shall long
for next spring. You will make me very happy if you would send a
line to the *poste restante* at Antwerp, that I may know how you are.
Believe me, dear sir, your most obliged, affectionate servant, Maria
Cosway."

Jefferson accompanied the Cosways to the Porte St. Denis, whence
there was a road north, and handed them into their carriage. With
them was Trumbull. Jefferson said good-by and, "more dead than
alive," as he afterward confessed to Mrs. Cosway, returned to his fireside, "solitary and sad"; and there he dipped a quill in ink and wrote
two things: one was a methodical entry in his account book, "pd
expences at St. Denis 55f"; the other, despite his aching wrist, covered "three mortal sheets of paper." It is preserved today in all the
major collections of Jefferson's writings as the *Dialogue Between
My Head and My Heart*. He himself, when he sent it to Mrs. Cosway,
labeled it a dialogue; but anyone with half an eye can see that it is
really a love letter. It is also a confession: it admits that since Belinda's time temperamentally he has not made much advance, that he
remains the suffering victim of war between the two halves of his

character, the one urging him to plunge forward and take chances, the other warning him to go slow and look ahead.

In the letter he pretends to be thinking of both Mr. and Mrs. Cosway—"these good people" who have "good sense, good humor, honest hearts, honest manners, and eminence in a lovely art"; but the lady deserves "a chapter apart" for her "music, modesty, beauty, and that softness of disposition, which is the ornament of her sex and the charm of ours." His dilemma is that he cannot see a future for their friendship; if she and he remain in Europe where they may meet at intervals, "God only knows," he confesses, "what is to happen." He hints that his eventual return to his "own dear Monticello" is never long out of his thoughts; and that raises the question: "Where could they [the Cosways] find such subjects as in America for the exercise of their enchanting art? Especially the lady, who paints landscapes so inimitably?" And then he suggests these American subjects for her brush: the Falling Spring in Virginia, Niagara Falls, the passage of the Potomac River through the Blue Ridge Mountains, and finally, Natural Bridge!

Then he lays down what are undoubtedly his own intellectual standards of judgment and philosophy of life:

"Everything in this world is a matter of calculation. Advance then with caution, the balance in your hand. Put into one scale the pleasures which any object may offer; but put fairly into the other the pains which are to follow, and see which preponderates. . . . Do not bite at the bait of pleasure till you know there is no hook beneath it. The art of life is the art of avoiding pain. . . . The most effectual means of being secure against pain is to retire within ourselves, and to suffice for our own happiness. . . . Hence the inestimable value of intellectual pleasures."

On the other hand (here the Heart makes reply): "Assuredly nobody will care for him who cares for nobody. . . . Friendship is precious, not only in the shade but in the sunshine of life. . . . I will recur for proof to the days we have lately passed. On these, indeed, the sun shone brightly. How gay did the face of nature appear! Hills, valleys, chateaux, gardens, rivers, every object wore its liveliest hue! Whence did they borrow it? From the presence of our charming companion. They were pleasing, because [you] seemed pleased. Alone, the scene would have been dull and insipid: the participation of it with [you] gave it relish."

And then he separates the offices of Head and Heart. "When nature assigned us the same habitation, she gave us over to a divided empire." To the Head she gave the field of science, to the Heart that of morals. "Morals were too essential to the happiness of man to be risked on the uncertain combinations of the head. . . . I do not know that I ever did a good thing on the suggestion of the Head, or a dirty one without it."

He then returns to a statement of a Stoic philosophy not greatly different in essence from that which he proclaimed when he was a youth at William and Mary College: "We have no rose without its thorn; no pleasure without alloy. It is the law of our existence; and we must acquiesce. It is the condition annexed to all our pleasures, not by us who receive, but by him who gives them."

And then comes this outburst of personal confession:

"True, this condition is pressing cruelly on me at this moment. I feel more fit for death than life. But, when I look back on the pleasures of which it is the consequence, I am conscious they were worth the price I am paying."

At this point Jefferson tries to veil his meaning by referring to the Cosways together; but it is perfectly evident that where he says "they" he means "you":

"I comfort myself with expectations of their promised return. Hope is sweeter than despair; and they were too good to mean to deceive me. In the summer, said the gentleman; but in the spring, said the lady: and I should love her forever, were it only for that! Know then . . . that I have taken these good people into my bosom; that I have lodged them in the warmest cell I could find: that I love them, and will continue to love them thro' life."

Finally he comes to a conclusion which, though conventional, begs for "partiality and warmth":

"Present me in the most friendly terms to Mr. Cosway, and receive me into your own recollection with a partiality and warmth, proportioned not to my own poor merit, but to the sentiments of sincere affection and esteem, with which I have the honor to be, dear Madam, your most obedient humble servant."

Who can deny this dialogue was a love letter? It was the beginning of a correspondence with Madame Cosway that lasted more than thirty years.

Maria's first letter was from Antwerp, and to Jefferson it was disappointingly short: "I prepared myself for a feast," he answered. "I read two or three sentences; looked again at the signature to see if I had not mistaken it. It was visibly yours. Read a sentence or two more. *Diable!* Spelt your name distinctly. There was not a letter of it omitted. Began to read again. In fine, after reading a little and examining the signature, alternately half a dozen times, I found your name was to four lines only, instead of four pages. I thank you for the four lines, however, because they prove you think of me; a little, indeed, but better a little than none." [3]

Then came Maria's turn to be impatient.

"What does this silence mean?" she demanded. "I await the post with so much anxiety and when each time it arrives without bringing me a single letter from Paris, I am truly uneasy. I suppose that you must be ill, and that your arm is worse." [She continued in Italian, confessing that in her state of mind she hardly knew what she was saying.]

"When I began this letter," she wrote, "I thought but to say three words; unconsciously I have reached this point without even knowing what I have said. When women begin to talk it is difficult to restrain them, even though they be aware that they are talking nonsense. I have several times seen Mr. and Mrs. Paradise and I have the pleasure of talking often about you with them." [4]

It was Mrs. Paradise who wrote to Jefferson from London, with the claws scarcely sheathed:

"I have not seen Mrs. Cosway since my return, but I have been told that your Excellencies Verses, you sent her, and your Letters were like yourself well done— Indeed She shows your Letters to every body. I feel myself greatly honored and flattered whenever I receive a Letter from you, but, I do not make them a show to any person."

[3] *Writings of Jefferson,* ed. Ford, IV, 323.
[4] Bullock, *My Head and My Heart,* New York, 1945.

Whether this feline hint had an immediate effect on Jefferson's letters to Maria is not known, but his longer and more intimate letters to her, after this, were often sent unsigned. He explained that his letters were regularly opened by both the French and English secret services, and when he could, he entrusted his missives to Trumbull, to Colonel W. S. Smith or other travelers between England and France. He wrote Mrs. Cosway on November 29, 1786:

"My letters which pass thro' the post offices either of this country or of England being all opened, I send thro' that channel only such as are very indifferent in their nature. This is not the character, my dear madam, of those I write you. The breathings of a pure affection would be profaned by the eye of a Commis of the post. I am obliged then to wait for private conveiances. . . . Could I write by the post I should trouble you too often: for I am never happier than when I commit myself into dialogue with you, tho' but in imagination. . . .

"I am determined when you come next not to admit the idea we are ever to part again. But are you to come again? I dread the answer to this question, & that my poor heart has been duped by the fondness of its wishes. What a triumph for the head! God bless you! May your days be many & filled with sunshine! May your heart glow with warm affections & all of them be gratified! Write to me often, write affectionately & freely, as I do to you. Say many kind things, and say them without reserve. They will be food for my soul."

By the next courier from London she sent him a roll of her own songs in Italian. Jefferson replied saying: "The first words which met my eyes on opening them, are, I fear, ominous. *'Qua l'attendo e mai non viene.'* " [I wait but he does not come.] They were indeed ominous, as we shall see later.

Mrs. Cosway did not return to Paris either in the spring or summer. But she did come in the early winter of 1787. And she left her husband behind. She remained four months, but was not satisfied with the development of her friendship with Jefferson. "If my inclination had been your law I should have had the pleasure of seeing you more than I have," she wrote. And she scolded him further after her return to London because he wrote so little and seldom.

Jefferson's first letter on the Heart and Head had set a precedent in length that spoiled her, Maria confessed in a letter of February 15,

1788, which was very long and which she admitted she would have liked to carry to infinity:

". . . I shall never learn to be reasonable in my expectations, and shall feel disappointed whenever your letters are not as long as the first was; thus you are the occasion of a continual reproaching disposition in me. . . . I feel at present an inclination to make you an endless letter, but have not yet determined what subject to begin with. . . . Of all torments, temptations, and wearinesses, the female has always been the principal and most powerful, and this is to be felt by you at present from my pen. . . . I have written this *in memoria* of the many pages of scrawls addressed to you by one whose good intentions repay you for your beautiful allegories with such long, insipid chit-chat. . . ." Then she switched to Jefferson's recently published *Notes on Virginia:*

"It is written by *you,* but Nature represents all the scenes to me in reality, therefore do not take anything to yourself. . . . Oh! how I wish myself in those delightful places! those enchanted grottoes! those magnificent mountains, rivers, etc., etc., etc.! Why am I not a man, that I might set out immediately, satisfy my curiosity, and indulge my sight with wonders?"

Maria sought Trumbull's help, and the artist wrote in her behalf:

"Mrs. Cosway's love to you and his too. She is angry yet she teases me every day for a copy of your little portrait—that she may scold it no doubt." [5]

This miniature hangs today in the convent at Lodi, Italy, founded by Mrs. Cosway. A copy was given to Angelica Church, taken from Trumbull's panoramic picture of the signing of the Declaration of Independence; it is not a flattering likeness, the painter, who had strong Federalist opinions, having failed to give it the care and distinction he bestowed on his portraits of Washington. Toward Jefferson, Trumbull later cooled off and finally ended his friendship with him, for reasons which Trumbull thus described in his autobiography:

"As the French revolution advanced, my whole soul revolted from the atrocities of France, while he approved or apologized for all. He opposed Washington—I revered him—and a coldness gradually suc-

[5] See frontispiece of this volume.

ceeded until in 1793, he invited me to dine."

On entering Jefferson's house, then in Maiden Lane, New York City, Trumbull says he found several men there, including the red-faced and sporting senator from Virginia, W. B. Giles, who annoyed Trumbull by a "railling of New England." There was already a soreness between the two, because, says Trumbull, he had rendered Giles "ridiculous in the eyes of a lady to whose favorable opinion he had aspired." The discussion led to an argument on religion which "proceeded so far at last as to ridicule the character, conduct, and doctrines of the divine founder of our religion—Jefferson in the meantime smiling and nodding approbation on Mr. Giles." Trumbull says he later wrote Giles breaking off all relations and adds:

"From this time my acquaintance with Mr. Jefferson became cold and distant."

CHAPTER 24

THE JOURNEY SOUTH

OWING TO JEFFERSON's meticulous habit of recording in his account book every item of expense, even the smallest and most intimate, we know the exact date, September 4, 1786, on which, in the course of a walk with Maria Cosway, he fell and dislocated his right wrist. Up to that day his entries were firm and legible in his usual cursive hand; we can easily read that on September 2 he paid out four sums of twenty-four francs each and two of twenty-three francs for the nineteenth volume of the Encyclopedia around which a circle of French intellectuals had gathered so devotedly as to coin the name of Encyclopedists. These books were for his first and second lieutenants, James Madison and James Monroe; also for Benjamin Franklin, for Francis Hopkinson and for Dr. James Currie.

On the next day he paid six francs for seeing the gallery at St. Cloud; this was also probably in the company of Mrs. Cosway. And then on September 4 his handwriting suddenly altered, becoming ragged and almost vertical, though still legible. This was the day on which he had to shift the burden of writing duty from his right to his left hand. And on this left hand he had to rely for weeks and even months following; in fact, because of the incompetence of his Paris surgeons, he never recovered the full and easy use of his right hand. His record shows that on September 18 he paid two surgeons twelve francs; if they were the guilty ones, this was twelve francs too much.

In that day, both in France and England, the fashionable doctors, when they ran out of ideas otherwise, were accustomed to prescribe for unhealed patients a course of "waters," hence watering places arose all over Europe. When after several months Jefferson's wrist was still disabled, his surgeons suggested he go to bathe his wrist

130

in the warm springs at Aix, the old capital of Provence, just above
Marseilles. Jefferson consented eagerly; in fact, so eagerly that we can
surmise that wrist-bathing was not the only object he had in mind.
He told James Monroe he would use the journey to "acquire knowledge of that species of navigation which may be useful hereafter" and
to discover the improvements that might be made in commerce between France and America. It is possible that he also wanted to
wrench himself free from his attachment to Mrs. Cosway, from whom
he had parted seven months before "more dead than alive" and
whose warm letters he was still receiving.

But when the year 1787 came, there were still several matters to
be disposed of before he could leave Paris for southern France. One
thing that oppressed him was the mortal illness of Vergennes, the
foreign minister. Jefferson had learned to value Vergennes for his
"clear, well organized head" and his personal geniality, but he
lamented in the great Frenchman his "imperfect ideas of our institutions" and his devotion to despotism. Another Paris event that fascinated Jefferson was Louis XVI's desperate calling of the Assembly
of Notables and Lafayette's participation in it. After Jefferson had
attended its first sitting and called on Montmorin, Vergennes's successor, he was at last free to go south.

First he went up the Seine and then down the Rhone through
Lyons, Avignon and Nîmes, studying vineyards, orchards, soils, seed
and agricultural methods. He also gave some attention to the arts,
especially architecture, as his letter to Madame de Tessé, quoted elsewhere, testifies. His touring methods he thus described to Lafayette:

"In the great cities I go to see what travellers think alone worthy
of being seen; but I make a job of it, and generally gulp it all down
in a day. On the other hand, I am never satiated with rambling
through the fields and farms, examining the culture and cultivators,
with a degree of curiosity which makes some take me to be a fool,
and others to be much wiser than I am." That he was enjoying himself was evident from this exclamation to Lafayette: "From the first
olive fields of Pierrelatte, to the orangeries of Hieres, has been continued rapture to me."

Jefferson's knowledge of botany and horticulture was a constant
amazement to those persons who considered him an aloof philoso-

pher or desk-bound diplomat. For example, he wrote about French fruits:

"Of fruits, the pears & apricots alone are better than ours . . . the fruits of the peach-class do not degenerate from the stone so much as is imagined here."

His anxiety to have South Carolina and Georgia establish upland rice, olive and caper plantations was almost pathetic, and his unsparing exertions on this journey to obtain suitable seed led him far from the usual paths. He even resorted to severely prohibited forms of smuggling to get desired varieties of rice from Italy, showing that persons who intend to do good to their fellow-men are nearly as determined as those who do evil. He corresponded at length with such plant specialists as John Bartram and Peter Legaux of Philadelphia; amateur botanists like Dr. Ramsay, the South Carolina historian, and Benjamin Hawkins of North Carolina; and he wrote to William Drayton of the South Carolina Society for Promoting Agriculture tremendous letters about olives, almonds, capers, figs, mulberries and, above all, rice, "which sows life and death with almost equal hand." As regards the olive tree, Jefferson showed how slavery was always in the background of his thought when he exclaimed to Drayton:

"Would the owner of slaves to view it only as a means of bettering their condition, how much would he better that by planting one of those trees for every slave he possessed!"

To Nicholas Lewis, his manager at Monticello, he wrote asking for corn seed to replace the hard and dry French-bred corn and revealing that he raised Indian corn in his own garden in Paris. "I had at Monticello," he wrote, "a species of small white rare ripe corn which we called Homony-corn . . . Great George [a servant] will know well what I mean."

In Languedoc, after visiting the fountain of Vaucluse, he paused to write eloquently to his daughter Martha:

"I arrived somewhat fatigued and sat down by the fountain to repose myself. It gushes, of the size of a river, from a secluded valley of the mountains, the ruins of Petrarch's chateau being perched on a rock 200 feet perpendicular above. To add to the enchantment of the scene, every tree and bush was filled with nightingales in full song. . . . Endeavor, my dear, to make yourself acquainted with the music of this bird, that when you return to your own country, you may be able to estimate its merit in comparison with that of the mockingbird."

He now reminded Martha that Polly could be expected from Virginia soon and that Polly would become her charge.

"Teach her above all things to be good," he urged, "because without that we can neither be valued by others nor set any value on ourselves. Teach her to be always true; no vice is so mean as the want of truth, and at the same time so useless. Teach her never to be angry; anger only seems to torment ourselves, to divert others, and alienate their esteem."

At Marseilles Jefferson was told that if he wished to learn the merits of the "Piedmont" rice which France imported in quantity he must go beyond the Alps to Lombardy, so he traversed the rice country from Vercelli to Pavia in Italy, about sixty miles. Finding the Italian threshing machine to be almost the same as that used in South Carolina, he asked for some of the unhusked seed, but was told its exportation was illegal. He wrote that he took "such measures as he could" to bring it out anyhow. These measures were smuggling in two forms—by himself and by bribing another man as carrier. He confessed to Edward Rutledge of South Carolina that he filled his coat and surtout pockets with the forbidden seed, and went back to France guiltily leaking rice like a bridegroom; and that at Poggio he had hired a muleteer to smuggle a sack of rough rice to Genoa, although the penalty for being caught was death. He sent this rice to South Carolina and Georgia, but only in the latter did it take hold.

Although he regarded the olive tree of Aix, yielding sixty pounds of olives and fifty of oil, as the richest gift of heaven, scarcely excepting bread, and although he shipped to South Carolina friends at least five hundred plants in two lots, he had to admit twenty-five years later that "it is merely a curiosity in their gardens; not a single orchard of them has been planted." The same thing happened to a shipment of caper plants.

The third matter of extra interest to him on this journey was the vineyards of the famous wine-making ridge called the Côte. Here he packed his notebook with those statistical facts which Jefferson loved. "A farmer of ten arpents has about three labourers engaged by the year. He pays four louis to a man, and half as much to a woman, and feeds them. He kills one hog and salts it, which is all the meat used in the family during the year.

.   .   .   .   .

"The wines which have given such celebrity to Burgundy grow only on the Côte, an extent of about five leagues long and half a league wide. They begin at Chambertin, and go through Vougeau, Romanie, Veaune, Nuys, Beaune, Pommard, Voulenay, Meursault, and end at Mon[t]rachet . . . It is remarkable that the best of each kind, that is, of the red and white, is made at the extremities of the line, to wit, at Chambertin and Monrachet.

.   .   .   .   .

"The best wines are carried to Paris by land. The transportation costs thirty-six livres the piece. The more indifferent go by water. Bottles cost four and a half sous each."

These are samples of entries that went on, page after page. Jefferson's passion for details was never satiated. At Marseilles he even measured a mule and found it to be five feet, two inches high. At the locks of the canal of Languedoc he estimated that five minutes were lost at each basin because of archaic and cumbrous mechanisms. At Lyons he put it down that the nine arches of a bridge measured forty feet from center to center. Two spots he remembered long afterward: the Col de Tende, between Nice and Turin; and the whole Italian Riviera and its villages "where air, water and earth concur to offer what each has most precious."

Of the Château de Saorgio he wrote to Maria Cosway in London: "Imagine to yourself, Madam, a castle and village hanging to a cloud in front . . . a mountain . . . a river . . . the whole formed into a bason, it's sides shagged with rocks, olive trees, vines, herds, &c."

Her reply, partly in Italian and not a little indignant, said: "How long do you like to keep your friends in anxiety! . . . I was glad to know you was well . . . & had only to lament I was not a castle hanging to a cloud, a stream, a village, a stone on the pavement of

Turin, Milan, & Genoa, &c." And then she reminded him that Italy was her cradle and she had little need to be told of its beauties.

Among the other things noted in the course of this journey was climate, its varieties and effects on plants. For instance, in the Alps he found an ascending scale of hardiness of which he wrote to Drayton: "Their order, proceeding from the tenderest to the hardiest, is as follows: caper, orange, palm, aloe, olive, pomegranate, walnut, fig, almond. But this must be understood of the plant only; for as to the fruit, the order is somewhat different. The caper, for example, is the tenderest plant, yet, being so easily protected, it is among the most certain in its fruit. The almond, the hardiest, loses its fruit the oftenest, on account of its forwardness."

The trouble he took in obtaining rice seed from Italy no doubt left him open to shock when later in the year he got a letter from Ralph Izard of South Bay, Charleston, South Carolina, disparaging the foreign product:

"The Seed which you have sent, & which you say is of the best kind, will bear no comparison with ours; & I am surprised to learn that the price is nearly equal."

Jefferson's visit to Nîmes, whence he wrote the memorable letter to Madame de Tessé quoted elsewhere, had a concealed purpose which he disclosed to John Jay, secretary of state, in a letter from Marseilles dated May 4, 1787. It was to give an interview to a man who wished to discuss the possibility of a revolution in Brazil; this approach was the first of two he had had recently from men dreaming of Latin American independence. Jefferson told Jay he had had a confidential letter dated Montpellier, October 2, 1786, from a writer who called himself a Brazilian, saying his country was ripe for revolt against Portuguese oppression but it would need help. His people, said the writer, had "decided to follow the guiding light which you have held out to us" and would look to the United States for assistance.

In the interview at Nîmes, the Brazilian, Jose de Maia, said his people would need "cannon, ammunition, ships, sailors, soldiers and officers." Jefferson replied that he could answer, only as an individual, that the United States "were not in a condition at present to meddle nationally in any war"; that "we wished particularly to cultivate the friendship of Portugal, with whom we have an advantageous commerce"; and that at the same time "a successful revolution in Brazil could not be uninteresting to us."

Jefferson later informed Jay he had also recently received in Paris a personal call from a Mexican, thirty-three or thirty-four years old, who wished his opinion on the chances of a revolution in Mexico against Spain. Jefferson reported he had offered his private opinion for Mexicans that "a successful revolution was still at a distance with them" that he "feared they must begin by enlightening and emancipating the minds of their people"; that as regards Spain, it was not likely the United States would risk present advantages in commerce for "uncertain and future ones." Thus did Latin America, in the opening stages of its long fight for freedom from European control, make its first overtures to Jefferson.

On his return to Paris he wrote that he had "never passed three months and a half more delightfully," and added, "I was alone through the whole, and think one travels more usefully when alone, because he reflects more." What he was to witness in Paris gave him extra food for reflection.

CHAPTER 25

THE COURTING OF A
VIRGINIA LADY

OF ALL THE WOMEN whose names are associated with Jefferson's in France, none had to be courted so persistently, or for a time so unsuccessfully, as Polly, the great man's own daughter. Jacob twice had to serve seven years to win his two wives; but Jefferson had to plead two years with his younger surviving child before she would even say yes to his pressing invitation to join him in Paris. Jefferson urgently wanted her to come; but Polly positively didn't want to go —that, simply put, was the gist of the situation.

When Jefferson sailed for France with his older daughter, Martha (Patsy), he left behind his younger daughter, Mary (Polly), with her aunt Elizabeth Eppes at the Virginia farm in Chesterfield county called Eppington. It has been noted that as Martha grew older she became more and more like her father in her independent character and gracious nature; but Mary, who was called Polly, Maria and Marie too, was of softer fiber. Polly could not endure independence or solitude; she must lean on and cling to whatever she loved. And though she was so gentle and pliable, she could cling with a tenacity that often baffled Jefferson and sometimes upset him. Martha was his own child and natural helper; but Polly, he never quite knew how to manage.

The battle which for years was secretly waged between them began soon after Jefferson arrived in Paris. He then strongly hinted to Mr. and Mrs. Eppes that ere long he would want Polly with him because he wanted to hold his little family together. If these hints ever reached Polly, she gave no sign. In fact, she withdrew so far into the silences of her being that her father complained in September, 1785,

137

that since reaching France he had not had a line from her.

"If you knew how much I love you," he added reproachfully, ". . . you would have written to me. . . . I wish so much to see you, that I have desired your uncle and aunt to send you to me."

Anticipating some of Polly's alarms, he hastened to meet her objections to forsaking the family at Eppington: "I know, my dear Polly, how sorry you will be, to leave them and your cousins; but your sister and myself cannot live without you, and after a while we will carry you back again to see your friends in Virginia. In the meantime you shall be taught here to play on the harpsichord, to draw, to dance, to read and talk French, and such other things as will make you more worthy of the love of your friends; but above all things, by our care and love of you, we will teach you to love us more than you will do if you stay so far from us. . . . When you come here you shall have as many dolls and playthings as you want for yourself, or to send to your cousins whenever you shall have opportunities."

Polly's answer from Eppington wasted few words:

"Dear Papa—I long to see you, and hope that you and sister Patsy are well; give my love to her and tell her that I long to see her, and hope that you and she will come very soon to see us. I hope that you will send me a doll. I am very sorry that you have sent for me. I don't want to go to France, I had rather stay with Aunt Eppes. Aunt Carr, Aunt Nancy and Cousin Polly Carr are here. Your most happy and dutiful daughter, Polly Jefferson."

Father Jefferson's instructions became more detailed and grim. To Mr. Eppes he wrote: "I must now repeat my wish to have Polly sent to me next summer." And then in his detailed instructions he gave evidence of his gift of factual observation: "The vessel should have performed one voyage at least, but not be more than five years old. We do not attend to this circumstance till we have been to sea, but there the consequence of it is felt. I think it will be found that all the vessels which are lost are either on their first voyage or after they are five years old." He also mentioned the necessity for someone to go along to take care of Polly: "A careful negro woman, as Isabel, for instance, if she has had the small-pox, would suffice under the patronage of a gentleman. . . . I commit to Mrs. Eppes my

kisses for dear Poll, who hangs on my mind night and day." Later
he wrote again to Mr. Eppes to urge that he confide Polly "only to
a French or English vessel having a Mediterranean *pass*"—this, no
doubt, in fear of Algerian pirates.

Polly's own sentiments remained brief and pointed. "Dear Papa,"
she wrote, "I should be very happy to see you, but I can not go to
France, and hope that you and sister Patsy are well. Your affectionate
daughter. Adieu. Mary Jefferson."

Jefferson, on his part, remained firm. "Would to God," he wrote
Mrs. Eppes, "the great step was taken and taken safely; I mean that
which is to place her on this side of the Atlantic." A year later little
Polly was still safe with her aunt and uncle, but the latter wrote in
July, 1786, that she would surely start for France the next summer.
She, however, only wrote two lines to signify that the mountain must
come to Virginia:

"Dear Papa—I want to see you and sister Patsy, but you must come
to Uncle Eppes's house. Polly Jefferson."

But her strong-willed father went ahead to make plans for her
arrival, and he wrote Martha to be ready to take charge of her
younger sister, saying: "Teach her . . . to be good . . . Teach her
to be always true . . . Teach her never to be angry . . . And teach
her industry, and application to useful pursuits."

The faithful Martha, still immured at the convent of Panthemont,
answered dutifully: "I wish she would write to me; but as I shall
enjoy her presence very soon, it will make up for a neglect that I
own gives me the greatest pain."

It must have been disconcerting to Jefferson to discover that persons other than Polly were secretly in sympathy with her and were
hoping his plans would be brought to naught. In March, 1787, Mrs.
Eppes felt compelled to say openly to him:

"I never was more anxious to hear from you than at present, in
hopes of your countermanding your orders with regard to dear Polly.
We have made use of every stratagem to prevail on her to consent to
visit you without effect. She is more averse to it than I could have
supposed."

No countermanding order came from Jefferson, and at length Mrs.
Eppes with a heavy heart broke the news to a frightened Polly that

a ship was ready—the captain was a kind man named Ramsay—and a sailing date had been set. To induce Polly to set foot on the ship, Mrs. Eppes had to send her own children on board to play with her and divert her. And then to avoid a final rending scene, the children were quietly removed and the ship sailed while Polly was asleep in care of the young Negro woman who was to be her companion on the voyage. We can only imagine the terror of eight-year-old Polly when she awoke and heard the ship's timbers creaking and found herself far at sea with only a dark hand to hold to. Luckily Captain Ramsay was a jovial and ingratiating sailor, who knew how to chase horrors away with laughter and games, and the voyage was not yet old before he had won the young girl's heart.

On July 2, 1787, there started from Paris a note to Francis Eppes from Jefferson saying: "The present is merely to inform you of the safe arrival of Polly in London, in good health. I have this moment dispatched a servant for her [Petit, his French steward]. . . . She was in the best hands possible, those of Captain Ramsay."

In London Polly was met and taken home by Abigail Adams. The Adamses had a son, John Quincy Adams; but a little girl in the house was a novelty, and Mrs. Adams at first did not know what to do with her. Polly settled all questions of this kind. She looked up at Abigail Adams with large eyes and told her how hard it had been for her to leave her Aunt Eppes in Virginia, and what fun she used to have with her little cousins at Eppington, including Jack (Jack Eppes, who was one day to be her husband); and did Mrs. Adams think her father would want her to go on to France? Abigail melted and gathered her up, and thereafter Polly Jefferson had a new adorer and a friend for life. Polly was comforted and at once transferred her trusting affections from Captain Ramsay to Mrs. Adams, who afterward wrote to her sister:

"A finer child of her age I never saw. So mature and understanding, so womanly a behavior, and so much sensibility united, are rarely to be met with. I grew so fond of her, and she was so much attached to me, that, when Mr. Jefferson sent for her, they were obliged to force the little creature away. . . . She clung round me so that I could not help shedding a tear at parting with her."

Indeed, when Petit came from Paris to the Adams house to fetch

Polly, he had to take hold of the child's convulsed body as she clung
to Mrs. Adams and bear her off while both she and her hostess wept
in anguish. But there was a still more trying scene in Paris when,
after a successful crossing of the Channel, Polly was brought face to
face with her father and sister. She did not know either of them and
refused to recognize them as having any claim on her. Jefferson had
to lay aside the business of state and win his daughter back again. It
took him a week to make any impression on her, helped by Martha
who had been granted a leave of absence from the convent. In order
to forestall any further anguished scenes, Martha also escorted Polly
several times to the convent, where she was introduced to the nuns,
including Martha's favorite, Madame Taubenheim, and the pupils,
and was made much of; so that at last she was reconciled and entered
the convent life quite readily. Later she was also taken to Madame
de Corny's house, where Martha was already a favorite, and Madame
at once fell in love with her and called her "Mademoiselle Polie."
Polly's other French friends called her Marie, and this name when
she returned to Virginia became Maria; and it was as Maria that she
finished her life, which was not long. Maria, indeed, is the name we
find on her gravestone at Monticello.

Polly's arrival made her father radiant, and he wrote happily to
her Aunt Eppes: "A parent may be permitted to speak of his own
child when it involves an act of justice to another. The attentions
which your goodness has induced you to pay her prove themselves
by the fruits of them. Her reading, her writing, her manners in
general, show what everlasting obligations we are all under to you.
. . . It is impossible for a child to prove a more sincere affection to
an absent person, than she does to you." And a little later he could
add the news that in French "she begins to speak easily enough, and
to read as well as English. She will begin Spanish in a few days, and
has lately begun the harpsichord and drawing." In writing letters he
confessed Polly was not so good. "She gets all the apparatus, places
herself very formally with pen in hand, and it is not till after all this
and rummaging her head thoroughly that she calls out, 'Indeed,
papa, I do not know what to say; you must help me,' and, as I obsti-
nately refuse this, her good resolutions have always proved abortive,
and her letters ended before they were begun. Her face kindles with

love whenever she hears your name."

Polly and Martha were both suddenly removed from the convent because of a strange incident. Matters were apparently proceeding according to the usual routine when one day Jefferson was astounded to receive without warning a note from Martha saying that she wished to remain permanently at the convent as a nun. His reply was to call at the convent and ask for his daughters. The abbess made no objections and gave him leave to take the two girls home at once. This Jefferson did, and never referred in the presence of either to Martha's note.

Martha was then just over sixteen. She was becoming tall like her father, and daily she resembled him more and more in feature and manner. Jefferson soon made friends for her. One was the young Countess Tufton, daughter of the Duke of Dorset, the British ambassador to France. In remembrance of this friendship Martha easily persuaded her father to name one of his farms Tufton.

Jefferson never explained what had turned Martha's thoughts to holy orders. Certain friends surmised it was the natural fruit of her close association with Catholic sisters and students, but others thought it had something to do with the visit to Paris about this time of her distant cousin, Thomas Mann Randolph of Tuckahoe, who had been a student at the University of Edinburgh. It was known that she and he were much interested in each other, and he eventually became her husband. Was there a tiff or some misunderstanding that made Martha wish to hide her tears beneath a nun's veil? No one ever knew, but the incident may have caused Jefferson to make up his mind that he must soon return home and take his daughters with him. He wrote to President George Washington in the spring of 1789: "In a letter of November 19th to Mr. Jay, I asked a leave of absence to carry my children back to their own country, and to settle various matters of a private nature."

CHAPTER 26

WATCHER OF REVOLUTION

WHEN JEFFERSON RETURNED to Paris from the south of France in the early summer of 1787 his first concern was not with the slow stirrings of the revolutionary sentiment around him, but with the news of uneasy developments in his own country. Most alarming were reports of separation, and even secession, of parts of what was not yet a tight union of states but only a loose confederacy. Already he had written that though he could not help endorsing Kentucky's move for independence from Virginia, its separation from the American confederacy would frighten him.

"Our confederacy," he wrote Archibald Stuart of Virginia, "must be viewed as the nest from which all America, North and South, is to be peopled."

How to save the West for the embryo union that was constantly on his mind. To Madison he now wrote of his fear that a dilatory Congress would sacrifice the Western territories to the maritime states of the East. And here we see a plain foreshadowing of what was soon to come—the sectional focusing which played its part in the War of 1812 and the Mexican War, and rose to an eruption in the Civil War of 1861–65. This separatist spirit, which caused New England first to propose the secession which the South later actually adopted, was to Jefferson a recurring nightmare.

"I am uneasy," he wrote Madison, "at seeing the sale of our western lands is not yet commenced . . . When we consider the temper of the people of that country . . . we must suppose their separation possible, at every moment."

Another of his latent worries was betrayed in the same letter to Madison—the final adoption of a framework of government which could be fixed in a constitution.

"The idea of separating the executive business of the confederacy from Congress," he said to Madison, "as the judiciary is already, in some degree, is just and necessary."

A third subject which, he confessed to John Adams, often preyed on his spirits and which in France made "more noise against us than all our other debts put together" was the money owed to French officers who had served in the American Revolution. Jefferson mentioned that the interest was about two thousand guineas, from which he estimated that the principal was between thirty and forty thousand guineas.

As to the strife in France between the king and parliament, he now had few good words to say of Louis XVI. To Secretary of State John Jay he reported that the king said to a deputation which had waited on him at Versailles: "I will acquaint you with my intentions. Now get out. Let the door be closed."

Jefferson previously had hoped that compromise would allay the irritation between people and monarchy, but now he began to lose confidence in the king and wrote to Madison:

"The King loves business, economy, order, and justice, and wishes sincerely the good of his people; but he is irascible, rude, very limited in his understanding, and religious, bordering on bigotry. He has no mistress, loves his queen, and is too much governed by her. She is capricious like her brother, and governed by him; devoted to pleasure and expense; and not remarkable for any other vices or virtues. Unhappily the King shows a propensity for pleasures of the table. That for drink has increased lately, or, at least, it has become more known."

He still had some hope in the intelligence of the ministers, but even that fell low when in the late summer of 1787 he received a hint from the French government "that it would be agreeable not to press our commercial regulations at that moment, the ministry being too much occupied with the difficulties surrounding them to spare a moment on any subject that would admit of delay."

This was a cortical blow. Nullified now were all his struggles against monopolies and his battles for the fish oils and salted fish of New England, the tobacco of Virginia and the rice of South Carolina.

However, there was no time for depressed feelings. There were other matters to be dealt with—the possibility of inducing Holland bankers to take over all American debts in Europe, including the sums due to the French government and to French officers; assistance to Commodore John Paul Jones in his private tangles; the curbing of the Barbary States; the rescue of American seamen and other stranded citizens.

In the midst of all these distractions and despite his injured wrist, he sat down and wrote to his nephew in Virginia, Peter Carr, son of his sister Martha and of his beloved friend, Dabney Carr, a long letter which contained controversial passages that kept him busy defending himself for years afterward. These are a few extracts:

1. "Man was destined for society. His morality, therefore, was to be formed to this object. He was endowed with a sense of right and wrong merely relative to this. This sense is as much a part of his nature as the sense of hearing, seeing, feeling. . . . The moral sense, or conscience, is as much a part of man as his leg or arm."

2. "State a moral case to a ploughman and a professor. The former will decide it as well, and often better than the latter, because he has not been led astray by artificial rules."

3. "Question with boldness even the existence of a god; because if there be one, he must more approve of the homage of reason than that of blindfolded fear . . . If it ends in a belief that there is no god, you will find incitements to virtue in the comfort and pleasantness you feel in its exercise and the love of others which it will procure you. If you find reason to believe there is a god, a consciousness that you are acting under his eye, and that he approves you, will be a vast additional incitement."

4. "Travelling. This makes men wiser, but less happy."

But the principal part of his correspondence at this time dealt with the efforts in Philadelphia to agree on a constitution.

"My own general idea," he wrote to his old teacher, George Wythe, in Williamsburg, "was that the states should severally preserve their sovereignty in whatever concerns themselves alone, and that whatever may concern another state, or any foreign nation, should be made a part of the general sovereignty. That the exercise of the federal sovereignty should be divided among three several bodies, legislative, executive, and judiciary, as the state sovereignties are: and that some peaceable means should be contrived for the federal head to enforce compliance on the part of the states."

To W. S. Smith, son-in-law of John Adams, he wrote: "Our [Constitutional] Convention has been too much impressed by the [Shays] insurrection of Massachusetts: and in the spur of the moment they are setting up a kite to keep the henyard in order."

To John Adams he wrote: "How do you like our new constitution? I confess there are things in it which stagger all my dispositions to subscribe to what such an Assembly has proposed. . . . Indeed, I think all the good of this new constitution might have been couched in three or four new articles, to be added to the good, old and venerable fabric, which should have been preserved even as a religious relique."

To James Madison he wrote his approval of several provisions contained in the proposed new Constitution, but said: "There are other good things of less moment. I will now add what I do not like:

1. "The omission of a bill of rights providing clearly and without the aid of sophisms for freedom of religion, freedom of the press, protection against standing armies, restriction against monopolies, the eternal and unremitting force of the habeas corpus laws, and trials by jury in all matters of fact triable by the laws of the land and not by the law of nations. . . . Let me add that a bill of rights is what the people are entitled to against every government on earth, general or particular, and what no just government should refuse, or rest on inferences."

2. "The second feature I dislike, and greatly dislike, is the abandonment in every instance of the necessity of rotation in office, and most particularly in the case of the President. . . . The election of a President of America some years hence will be much more interesting to certain nations of Europe than ever the election of a King of Poland was."

3. "Smaller objections are the appeal in fact as well as law, and the binding all persons Legislative, Executive and Judicial by oath to maintain that constitution."

4. "I own I am not a friend to a very energetic government. It is always oppressive. The late rebellion in Massachusetts has given more

alarm than I think it should have done. Calculate that one rebellion in 13 states in the course of 11 years, is but one for each state in a century and a half."

Then followed a passage often quoted:

"After all, it is my principle that the will of the majority should always prevail. . . . I think our governments will remain virtuous for many centuries; as long as they are chiefly agricultural; and this will be as long as there shall be vacant lands in any part of America. When they get piled upon one another in large cities, as in Europe, they will become corrupt as in Europe. Above all things I hope the education of the common people will be attended to; convinced that on their good sense we may rely with the most security for the preservation of a due degree of liberty."

To William Carmichael, minister to Spain, he wrote the same sort of sentiments, summing up criticism of the framers of the Constitution by saying that "proposing to melt all down into one general government, they have fenced the people by no declaration of rights." It was characteristic of Jefferson that at the end of this letter he should append a paragraph containing a prophetic hint of things to come:

"I have been told, that the cutting through the Isthmus of Panama, which the world has so often wished, and supposed practicable, has at times been thought of by the government of Spain, and that they once proceeded so far, as to have a survey and examination made of the ground. . . . I should be exceedingly pleased to get as minute details as possible on it, and even copies of the survey, report, etc."

A few months later Jefferson again addressed James Madison on the draft of the United States Constitution and the defects in it. And again he returned to his insistence on a bill of rights to be attached to the Constitution, to guard against abuses of power. He particularly answered the objection that a bill or declaration of rights would be ineffective.

"Though it is not absolutely efficacious under all circumstances, it is of great potency always, and rarely inefficacious," he wrote. "A brace the more will often keep up the building which would have fallen. . . . The inconveniences of the declaration are, that it may cramp government in its useful exertions. But the evil of this is short-lived, moderate and reparable. The inconveniences of the want of a declaration are permanent, afflicting and irreparable. . . . The tyranny of the legislatures is the most formidable dread at present, and will be for many years. That of the executive will come in its turn, but it will be at a remote period." He added in a letter to Colonel Humphreys: "There are rights which it is useless to surrender to the government, and which governments have yet always been found to invade."

In Jefferson this distrust of governments was characteristic and basic. It had been sharpened by his observations in the Old World where he noticed that governments were always ready to strengthen the hammer but rarely cared for the anvil. And this distrust led to the Bill of Rights in the United States Constitution.

In these opinions of Jefferson on the United States Constitution, two of the lessons he had learned by studying the history of European peoples stand out: that an aggressive central government was to be feared; and that the common people, when properly educated and informed, could be relied on to do essential justice. He was now strengthening his own long-held opinion that just government could not rest on force, but only on reason and persuasion, and on the consent of the governed. How a government of force is likely to conduct itself in the face of pressure he was soon to observe in France. As he wrote to the Count de Moustier: "The public mind is manifestly advancing on the abusive prerogatives of their governors, and bearing them down. No force in the government can withstand this, in the long run." That belief was to be put to the test sooner than he supposed.

In a letter to George Washington dated December 4, 1788, Jefferson recorded his recognition of the fact that American life had entered a new and significant phase, and that the United States in future was to be one of the nations competing for a footing in the markets of the world.

"The produce of the United States," he wrote, "will soon exceed the European demand; what is to be done with the surplus, when there shall be one?" Thus did Jefferson signalize the birth in America of the era of the salesman; for surpluses, to be disposed of, require salesmen, and salesmen require backing. What that backing was to be was implied by Jefferson in his further remarks:

"It [the surplus] will be employed, without question, to open, by force, a market for itself, with those placed on the same continent with us, and who wish nothing better. Other causes, too, are obvious, which may involve us in war. . . . In the meantime, I have laid my shoulder to the opening the markets of this country to our produce, and rendering its transportation a necessity for our seamen."

In this letter Jefferson disclosed that soon he hoped to return home for six months and that he was looking forward to "the pleasure of personal conferences" with Washington. Those conferences, when they took place, led to consequences probably not dreamed of by either.

CHAPTER 27

ENEMY IN THE HOUSE

JUST AS JEFFERSON began to arrange his affairs with a view to this visit home, there arrived in Paris an American who very soon revealed himself as Jefferson's opposite in virtually every respect. This was Gouverneur Morris of New York and Pennsylvania, who was acting as agent for Robert Morris (no relation), financier and partner of the monopolistic French farmers-general in handling American tobacco. Morris came over with a letter of introduction from George Washington, who said of him in a note to the Marquis de Chastellux, an old comrade of the Yorktown campaign:

"Only let him be once fairly presented to your French Ladies, and I answer for it, he will not leave the worst impression in the world of the American character for taciturnity and proper reserve. I rely upon it he will make his way good."

Morris lived well up to this introduction. He kept a diary and his first entry, April 20, 1787, regarding Jefferson was a signpost of what his subsequent attitude was to be:

"Call on Mr. Jefferson, and sit an hour with him, which is, at least, fifty minutes too long, for his daughters left the room on my approach, and waited only my departure to return. At least I think so."

At the same time Morris wrote prophetically to the Count de Moustier in America: "I find on this side the Atlantic a strong resemblance to what I left on the other—a nation which exists in hopes, prospects, and expectations—the reverence for ancient establishments gone, existing forms shaken to the foundation, and a new order of things about to take place, in which, perhaps even to the very names, all former institutions will be disregarded." [1]

---
[1] *Diary and Letters of Gouverneur Morris.*

Martha Jefferson Randolph, Jefferson's daughter, by Thomas Sully

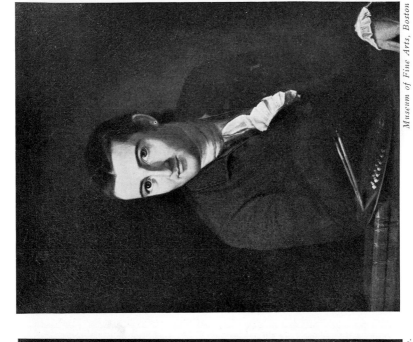

John Trumbull (self-portrait), Jefferson's
guest in Paris

Edmond Charles Genêt, French envoy who annoyed Jefferson, by Ezra Ames

Morris was nine years younger than Jefferson and, like him, belonged to the landed gentry of his native state. He had attended King's College, which became Columbia, and delivered two orations there which were symptomatic of his maturing tastes: one was entitled "Wit and Beauty," the other "Love." In time Morris became a lawyer and real estate agent. He and Jefferson previously had been linked in an endeavor to bring order into the chaotic early-American coinage system. Morris proposed a new currency unit based on the 440th part of a dollar. Jefferson objected to this unit as being cumbrous, and proposed that the unit be the dollar with decimal divisions. Morris wanted the smallest coin to be a "doit," about equal to a mill. Jefferson suggested the smallest coin be a penny or cent, as the hundredth part of a dollar. Congress accepted his simpler system; hence Jefferson became known as the "Father of the Dollar."

Before coming to France, Morris had been prominent in the Constitutional Convention at Philadelphia, where he had lost a leg in a carriage accident. He also enjoyed a close friendship with George Washington, who often employed him as an observer. Washington admired in Morris what he himself lacked—wit, flexibility and social ease. Though Morris had cleverness and executive ability, his usefulness to the infant American republic was often vitiated by what Theodore Roosevelt, his admirer and biographer, called his "incurable cynicism and deep-rooted distrust of mankind."

Morris represented the Federalist aspect of the American class-conscious character, believing in a strong central government, despising common men and advocating rule by the wealthy and well-born. Soon after his arrival in France, he took a position with the Right and from there he graduated into support of monarchy; he even went to the help of Louis XVI and Marie Antoinette and tried to check, or at least abort, the progress of the French Revolution. His personality, habits and opinions could not fail to be repellent to Jefferson, who, however, was characteristically polite and showed him all due attention.

Morris revealed very early that indeed he had those attractions attributed to him by George Washington—"this is a woman's country," he wrote in his diary—and he became a regular visitor at the most fashionable salons and centers in Paris, his wooden leg not interfering with his social activities. He enjoyed the particular favors of Madame de Flahaut, who was a friend of Jefferson's friend, Madame de Corny. Madame de Flahaut also enjoyed the protection of Talleyrand, then the bishop of Autun. Morris thus quoted her in his diary regarding Jefferson: "She told me some days ago, after seeing Mr. Jefferson's countenance, '*Cet homme est faux et emporté.*'" [That man is false and irritable.] Morris's writings of this period contain not a few digs at Jefferson, showing that if the Virginian secretly disliked him, Morris fully returned the feeling. He criticized Jefferson for not forming "just estimates of character but rather assigning too many to the rank of fools," and satirized him as belonging to "these literary people." He wrote: "The literary people here, observing the abuses of the monarchical form, imagine that everything must go the better in proportion as it recedes from the present establishment, and in their closets they make men exactly suited to their systems; but unluckily they are such men as exist nowhere else, and least of all in France."

After Jefferson had returned to the United States and become a political candidate, he was often accused of having imbibed dangerous French ideas. That not a few of the ideas which shaped the French Revolution came by a channel just the reverse is indicated by this passage from a letter by Morris to Washington: "The leaders here are our friends. Many of them have imbibed their principles in America, and all have been fired by our example."

The sum of Morris's advice to the French government was that "at present nothing should be done." This course, so contrary to that being urged by Jefferson, was followed by the king only too well. The end of it was the guillotine.

Jefferson's ideas of what Louis XVI should do at this stage took a far different direction. On the evening of June 2, 1789, he took part in a discussion of a proposal that the king offer the people a Charter of Rights. Others present were Lafayette, who had probably arranged the meeting, and Saint Etienne, a member of the States-General who belonged to the moderate party of "patriots" which would be satisfied with a constitutional government. It was these moderates or *Constitutionnels* whom Jefferson consistently favored and whose positions he often helped to define. After this discussion

Jefferson sent both to Lafayette and Saint Etienne an outline of what he thought this Charter should contain. To the latter he offered the excuse of "an unreasonable love for your nation, and a painful anxiety lest despotism, after an unaccepted offer to bind its own hands, should seize you again with ten-fold fury."

Jefferson's own position was that the States-General should be content with basic reforms without resorting to violence or risking reaction. In brief, Jefferson suggested that the proposed Charter of Rights, to be signed by the king, and by members of the three orders of nobles, clergy and middle class, should give the States-General control over elections, taxes, the military, money, and the laws. These five points having been won, he would wait until the public mind should "ripen and be informed," in all cases stopping "where violence would otherwise begin."

Jefferson himself found fault with this outline of government because it had no provision for trial by jury; and he considered that provision, as he wrote to Thomas Paine, "the only anchor ever yet imagined by man, by which a government can be held to the principles of its constitution." (The people, he wrote the Abbé Arnoud, "are not qualified" to judge questions of law—only of fact.) However, he found some comfort in the draft of the new French constitution which began with "a declaration of the natural and imprescriptible rights of man." This Declaration of Rights was proposed by the Marquis de Lafayette, who for material drew heavily on the Declaration of Independence as written by Jefferson. Lafayette's draft, however, had one important alteration. Where Jefferson wrote "the pursuit of happiness," Lafayette wrote "the right of property." The opening portion of the French Declaration therefore ran as follows:

"Nature has made men free and equal; the necessary distinctions in the social order are based only on general utility.

"Every man is born with inalienable and imprescriptible rights; these are the freedom of his opinions, the care for his honor and his life, the right of property, the entire disposition of his person, his industry, and all his faculties, the communication of his thoughts by every possible means, the pursuit of well-being, and resistance to oppression.

"The individual's exercise of his natural rights has no limits save those which assure the enjoyment of the same rights to the other members of society."

Jefferson had hoped William Short, his faithful secretary, would succeed him in France, but instead his successor was Morris. Jefferson's sympathies were on the side of the French people in their struggle with those three social strata which he denounced so often: kings, nobles and priests. Morris, on the other hand, was an active though cynical adviser and supporter of the whole trio.

Although the political atmosphere of France was sultry, Jefferson's letters at this period were almost always cheerful. The reason, no doubt, lay in the inspiriting arrival in France of Polly, his winsome daughter from Virginia. With Martha and Polly both at hand, Jefferson now had something like a family around him. That being so, he was almost happy. No one looking through Jefferson's many letters can doubt that although externally he was often dignified and even aloof, his emotional temperament was deep and strong. Affection he must have, and it must be warm and constant. Just as he sought to draw ever closer to him men like Madison, Monroe and Short, so constantly he reached out, though more cautiously, for the friendship of women, and his daughters were his first reliance. With two adolescents now in his charge, his attitude was like that of the male bobwhite who has lost his mate—strongly maternal as well as paternal. He watched over the details as well as the principles of their lives.

Polly's arrival now made the Grille de Chaillot a home as well as an office, and it moved him to have at his side the younger daughter who so lately had been a stranger. He wrote to Francis Hopkinson, who shortly before had sent him a book of songs and ballads, a touching little incident concerning her. Martha was playing on the harpsichord, one made to order in London "with a celestine stop," one of these very songs. Polly sat near the fire. Her father noticed her secretly wiping away tears.

"I asked her if she was sick," wrote Jefferson. "She said 'no; but the tune was so mournful.'"

CHAPTER 28

RESCUE FROM THE BANKERS

"OUR AFFAIRS at Amsterdam press on my mind like a mountain." This exclamation in a letter from Jefferson in Paris to John Adams at The Hague, late in the winter of 1787–88, reveals to what extent the failure of the infant American republic to pay its debts, particularly to the French officers who had served the American cause, had worried the minister at the Grille de Chaillot. Hearing that Adams, who formerly had been the United States agent in Holland, was about to take leave at The Hague and go home, Jefferson resolved to meet him there, try to pull financial affairs into order and save the credit of the United States.

While in Holland Adams had been authorized to borrow enough money from Dutch bankers to pay interest and to meet the running expenses of the various American envoys in Europe. This he had done, but now that Adams was about to sail for Boston, Jefferson saw himself as left without money or instructions or authority. Hence hastily he ordered repairs to his carriage and set out for The Hague, hoping to reach it in four days. He traveled through Senlis, Roye, Péronne, Cambrai, Valenciennes, Mons, Brussels, Malines, Antwerp and Rotterdam. He just caught Adams at The Hague, agreed with him to borrow a million florins, and the next day went with him to Amsterdam to face the bankers, Willincks and Van Staphorsts. These gentlemen purred and demurred. The season was late, they had not received due notice, and they doubted that any new American bonds would sell on the European market. This dismal reception frightened Jefferson; he saw the name and fame of the United States lowered and humiliated. Adams was less disturbed; he had spent several years twisting money out of doubting Dutch bankers, and he

thought they were now staging an act. He told Jefferson it was un-
true that American credit was slipping, but that United States paper
was being freely bought by all sorts of bankers and brokers. "Depend upon it," he said, "the Amsterdammers love money too well
to execute their threats. They expect to get too much by American
credit to destroy it."

The bankers balked, boggled and deplored, but eventually they
gave in and advanced the million florins. This sum would pay off the
most pressing obligations in Europe, would restore and enhance the
credit of the United States, would keep up the American diplomatic
establishment for at least two years, and, best of all in Jefferson's
eyes, it would relieve him "from the torment of incessant duns," the
most trying of which had come from French veterans of the American Revolution who really needed the money. He wrote: "Though
much an enemy to the system of borrowing, yet I feel strongly the
necessity of preserving the power to borrow."

In his elation, as soon as the last papers were signed and Adams
had departed, Jefferson packed his bags for a holiday tour of Germany. Even while at his hotel, Het Wapen van Amsterdam (The
Arms of Amsterdam), which is still standing,[1] Jefferson made his
characteristic utilitarian notes, most of them evidently for use when
he should return to Virginia. He itemized:

"Joists of houses, placed, not with their sides horizontally, but
diamond wise.

"Windows opening so that they admit air and not rain.

"A machine for drawing light empty boats over a dam.

"A lantern over the street door, which gives light equally into
the antechamber and the street.

"A bridge over a canal turning on a swivel."

Where another tourist might have lingered over art or quaintness,
Jefferson fell in love with a Dutch wheelbarrow and made a careful
sketch of it.

On leaving Holland, Jefferson set out for the Rhine country by
way of Utrecht and Nyjmegen. He wrote Secretary Short at Paris that
he would call at the Frankfort and Strasbourg post offices for letters

---

[1] Dumbauld, *Thomas Jefferson, American Tourist*, Norman, Okla., 1946.

and "be happy to find news from you relative to yourself, my daughters and America." On crossing the border between Holland and Prussia he noticed "the transition from ease and opulence to extreme poverty. . . . The soil and climate are the same; the governments alone differ. With the poverty, the fear also of slaves is visible in the faces of the Prussian subjects." He was reminded of what he had written to Edward Rutledge: "On this side of the Atlantic, the blood of the people is become an inheritance, and those who fatten on it will not relinquish it easily."

At Düsseldorf he became more cheerful when he discovered "the best tavern I saw in my whole journey"; also the art gallery to which he had been directed by Trumbull where he found a "sublime" collection of paintings—he was particularly impressed by those of Vanderwerff. Then by way of Langveld, Cologne, Bonn, Remagen and Andernach, he reached Coblenz. In the Elector of Treves's palace he was excited by a central heating system warmed by air tubes extending from an oven beneath.

From there he rode through Nassau and Wiesbaden to Frankfort on the Main, which was one of his chief objectives because near here at Hanau lived his staunch friend, Baron de Geismer, who had been among the Hessians in Burgoyne's captured army and had spent some time as a prisoner of war in Albemarle county under Jefferson's protection. Jefferson had written in advance that one of his motives in returning to Paris by this route was the desire to see him and renew "sentiments of sincere attachment and esteem." Geismer did not fail to meet Jefferson at the Rothen Haus and eagerly took him to his home in Hanau where the American, though glad to accompany the German, was depressed by the military atmosphere and the incessant "drum and fife." Militarism and evil government he thought were much responsible for the condition of the German peasant women who "dig the earth, plough, saw, cut and split wood."

"Here is so heavy a military establishment," he wrote, "that the civil part of the population is reduced to women only. But this is a barbarous perversion of the natural destination of the two sexes. Women are formed by nature for attentions and not hard labor. A woman never forgets one of the numerous train of little offices which belong to her. A man forgets often."

But for other reasons he had a special interest in this part of the Rhine country. "The neighborhood of this place," he wrote William Short, "has been to us a second mother country. It is from the Palatinate on this part of the Rhine that those swarms of Germans have gone who next to the descendants of the English, form the greatest body of our people. I have been continually amazed by seeing here the origin of whatever is not English among us. I have fancied myself often in the upper parts of Maryland and Pennsylvania."

From Frankfort Jefferson went to Mainz, and thence plunged into the vineyards where he filled his notebooks with information about the famous Rhine wines; at this stage Jefferson was still interested in wine-making, though later he called the vine "the mother of misery." He wrote:

"It is only from Rudesheim to Hocheim that wines of the very first quality are made. The river happens there to run due east and west, so as to give its hills on that side a southern aspect. And even in this canton it is only Hocheim, Johansberg, and Rudesheim that are considered of the very first quality. . . . On the road between Mayence and Oppenheim are three cantons, which are also esteemed as yielding wines of the second quality. These are Laubenheim, Bodenheim, and Nierstein." His extraordinary attention to detail and love of facts for their own sake are illustrated by this further passage on wine:

"The *vin de paille* is made in the neighborhood of Colmar in Alsace. . . . It takes its name from the circumstance of spreading the grapes on straw, where they are preserved till spring, and then made into wine." It was also characteristic of Jefferson when he saw the tun of Heidelberg to measure it with care; he estimated it held 283,200 bottles.

His way out of Germany led him through Worms, Mannheim, Karlsruhe and Strasbourg, whence he crossed to Epernay and stopped to look at the champagne-producing country. Here he learned that sparkling wine, which was extra costly, was prepared almost wholly for foreign consumption, and was spring bottled. Still wines were made in September. By the time he reached Paris he had become so skilled a connoisseur that later when he was president of the

United States his table wines became famous. But at this epoch the nineteenth century had begun, and a puritanic Calvinism had come in which made this knowledge, particularly in the eyes of his critics, suspicious if not scandalous.

CHAPTER 29

A QUESTION OF BINDING

WHILE HE WAS arranging his affairs in Paris with the hope of an early visit to America, Jefferson sat down one day in September, 1789, and wrote to his closest political confidant, James Madison, one of his longest and most significant letters. It dealt with the question of whether one generation of men has a right to impose obligations on, or to "bind," another. The matter of "binding" recently had come much to the front in men's minds. Before the American colonies had revolted, there had been a long debate on the sovereign right and power of the British crown to "bind" its overseas subjects in all cases. Now the question had arisen again in the course of France's furious debate over what Jefferson called "the elementary principles of society." It will be a sufficient indication of his opinions to quote some of the passages from this carefully composed letter:

"I set out on this ground, which I suppose to be self-evident, that the *earth belongs in usufruct to the living;* that the dead have neither powers nor rights over it."

.   .   .   .   .

"The portion occupied by any individual ceases to be his when himself ceases to be, and reverts to the society."

.   .   .   .   .

"No generation can contract debts greater than may be paid during the course of its own existence."

.   .   .   .   .

"Neither the representatives of a nation, nor the whole nation itself assembled, can validly engage debts beyond what they may pay

160

in their own time, that is to say, within thirty-four years of the date of the engagement."

. . . . .

"No society can make a perpetual constitution, or even a perpetual law. The earth belongs always to the living generation."

. . . . .

"Persons and property make the sum of the objects of government. The constitution and the laws of their predecessors are extinguished then, in their natural course, with those whose will gave them being."

. . . . .

"A law of limited duration is much more manageable than one which needs a repeal."

. . . . .

Thus did Jefferson call for a revolt against another distinguishing principle of Europe's civilizations—a respect for the wishes of the dead as against those of the living. He urgently prayed that the new nation in America might always be on the side of living men rather than that of cemeteries.

It was characteristic of Jefferson to be able to turn directly from a discussion on the rights of living men to one on the merits of American salted beef. He was still hoping for an early departure for America when he wrote one of his last notes to Necker, the French finance minister, to suggest that Paris might relieve its shortage of food by importing salt meat from America, which now was being prepared "in the Irish manner." Jefferson also hinted that it might profit France to give its land to grain cultivation rather than to pasturage.

"Salt meat," he admitted, "is not as good as fresh for soups, but it gives a higher flavor to the vegetables boiled with it. The experience of a great part of America, which is fed almost entirely on it, proves it to be as wholesome as fresh meat. The sea scurvy, ascribed by some to the use of salt meat, is equally unknown in America as in Europe. It is the want of vegetables at sea which produces the scurvy." The truth of this last observation was not recognized by ship owners and masters for many years.

CHAPTER 30

JEFFERSON AND ABIGAIL ADAMS

"YOU INQUIRE OF ME how I like Paris," wrote Abigail Adams, wife of John Adams, to her niece Lucy Cranch, on arriving in France soon after Jefferson became minister there. "Why, they tell me I am no judge, for that I have not seen it yet. One thing I know, and that is that I have smelt it."

A portrait of Abigail as a young woman reveals the curled nostrils and skeptical eyebrows that accorded with her sometimes acidulous comments on men and countries. Yet this wife of the American minister to England had her amiable side, and no sooner had she moved into her temporary house at Auteuil, four miles from the center of Paris, than she and Jefferson, who was often a visitor there, became immediate friends. And as months passed a bond grew up between the sharp young married woman from Weymouth, Massachusetts, and the tall minister from the banks of the Rivanna in Virginia.

She could talk with Jefferson on matters he loved—the arts and sciences—with a "dish of politics," as her daughter noted; and when Jefferson, with his natural fondness for daughters, bestowed courteous attentions on little Abby, soon to become the wife of Colonel William Stephen Smith, Abigail eagerly responded by welcoming the frightened Polly Jefferson, fresh from the Eppes farm in Virginia, to her house in London. And when Jefferson wrote Abigail letters far more sprightly than he wrote to most correspondents, she replied in the same vein. Her letters were so good that recipients treasured them and they are preserved till today in bound volumes, meriting what her husband once said of them: "There are more good thoughts, fine strokes, and mother wit in them than I hear in the whole week." Jefferson shopped for the Adamses in Paris and they shopped for him

162

in London. He once wrote wittily to Abby:

"Mr. Jefferson has the honor to present his compliments to Mrs. Smith and to send her the two pair of corsets she desired. He wishes they may be suitable, as Mrs. Smith omitted to send her measure. . . . Should they be too small, however, she will be so good as to lay them by awhile. There are ebbs as well as flows in this world."

At another time he wrote gallantly to Abigail:

"I immediately ordered the shoes you desired which will be ready tomorrow. . . . I have also procured for you three plateaux de dessert with a silvered ballustrade around them, and four figures. . . . With respect to the figures I could only find three of those you named, matched in size. These were Minerva, Diana, and Apollo. I was obliged to add a fourth, unguided by your choice. They offered me a fine Venus; but I thought it out of taste to have two at table at the same time."

At this period Jefferson could not easily avoid a slap at the English, and in this letter to Mrs. Adams he added: "I fancy it must be the quantity of animal food eaten by the English which renders their character insusceptible of civilization. I suspect it is in their kitchens & not in their churches that their reformation must be worked."

This friendship between Mrs. Adams and Jefferson continued on an affectionate basis until the latter became president. Then one day Abigail's son, John Quincy Adams, was suddenly separated from his job as a customs officer in Massachusetts. Because Jefferson was head of the administration at Washington, Abigail never forgave him. She ceased to write to him or speak of him. She remained frozen until May, 1804, when she learned of Polly Jefferson's death. Then she wrote:

"The attachment which I formed for her when you committed her to my care upon her arrival in a foreign land . . . has remained with me to this hour; and the account of her death, which I read in a late paper, recalled to my recollection the tender scene of her separation from me, when, with the strongest sensibility, she clung around my neck and wet my bosom with her tears, saying, 'Oh, now I have learned to love you, why will they take me from you?' . . . That you may derive comfort and consolation, in this day of your sorrow and affliction, from that only source calculated to heal the broken heart, a firm belief in the being, perfections, and attributes of God, is the sincere and ardent wish of her who once took pleasure in subscribing herself your friend, Abigail Adams."

To this letter, with its chilling last line, Jefferson replied at length. He wrote: "I . . . am thankful for the occasion furnished me of expressing my regret that circumstances should have arisen which have seemed to draw a line of separation between us." He then brought up his own grievance against her husband for his "midnight appointments" when retiring from the presidency, but explained he had forgiven the matter "cordially." He added: "I have thus, my dear madam, opened myself to you without reserve, which I have long wished an opportunity of doing; without knowing how it will be received, I feel relief from being unbosomed."

Abigail, however, failed to respond. She remained resentful for years. Friendly relations were not resumed between Jefferson and the Adamses until 1811 when Dr. Benjamin Rush of Philadelphia brought John Adams and Jefferson together again, giving rise to a correspondence which surely was unlike any other ever carried on between two former presidents of the United States.

CHAPTER 31

HOMEWARD THOUGHTS

WHEN IN THE SPRING of 1789 permission for Jefferson to return to Virginia had not arrived, he wrote desperately to President Washington for his help: "I hope you found the request not an unreasonable one. I am excessively anxious to receive the permission without delay, that I may be able to get back before the winter sets in."

In the same letter he thus privately expressed himself: "There was nobody so well qualified as yourself to put our new machine into a regular course of action—nobody, the authority of whose name could have so effectually crushed opposition at home and produced respect abroad. . . . There are cases wherein it is a duty to risk all against nothing, and I believe this was exactly the case. We may presume . . . that, after doing a great deal of good, you will be found to have lost nothing but private repose." President Washington in a very short time had occasion to turn this letter against its own author.

To Mrs. Eppes in Virginia, who had been Polly's guardian, Jefferson wrote, "We look forward with impatience to the moment when we may be all reunited, though but for a little time. Kiss your dear children for us, the little and the big."

Among these children was Jack Eppes, who as a husband was fated to be the determiner of what remained of Polly Jefferson's life; hence this return home of the Jefferson family was fraught with importance in more than one sense.

But before Jefferson was able to foresee the date of his departure, he felt the hot breath of the nascent French Revolution upon his face in a way that frightened him; in fact, the revolution extended an arm into his very house. Late one afternoon in July, 1789, Lafayette brought a group of young men to visit Jefferson for a dinner and a talk. All were about thirty years old, Lafayette at thirty-two being the eldest. Jefferson, whose interest in the current tense situation between king and people was known, no doubt had become previously acquainted with all hands; certainly with Count Alexandre de Lameth, who had fought in the American Revolution in Virginia and was a deputy of the nobles in the States-General. He must have also known Antoine Barnave and Adrien Duport who formed with Lameth a triumvirate that controlled the most formidable bloc in the States-General, holding out for a reformed, or constitutional, system that would retain the monarchy but grant increased liberties.

Barnave was a lawyer belonging to a Protestant family in Grenoble. He was a spokesman for the French middle class which was trying to assert itself against the power of the nobles and upper clergy. Duport was also a lawyer and representative of the nobles, a Parisian aged only thirty. A third lawyer in the group was Jean Joseph Mounier, a right-wing Constitutionalist and at one time president of the Constituent Assembly. These men fled from France when the revolution rose to its extreme phase (except Barnave, who was guillotined), but at this moment they were in the advance guard of moderate liberals, or *Patriotes,* as they were called. Other and less important members of the group were Blaçon, Maubourg and Dagout.

It is necessary to place this group of men accurately in order to understand that Jefferson, whom they often consulted, was never a Jacobin sympathizer or a member of the extreme left-wing party, but consistently took a middle position. In fact, he repeatedly urged the *Patriotes* to be satisfied for the present with the king's grant of civil liberties and trust to the future for further gains; otherwise he thought despotism might return "with a tenfold fury."

When after dinner the discussion waxed warm at the host's table, Jefferson, who was much entertained by the brilliance exhibited, realized that this was no casual meeting, but an effort on Lafayette's part to reconcile two opposing factions. One headed by Mounier favored allowing the king an absolute veto over popular legislation; Barnave, Duport and Lameth would permit only a temporary and suspensive veto. Mounier refused to yield, dissociated himself from

the other three, and later took part in a split which led to his de-
nunciation by Marat as a traitor and reactionary: eventually he fled
to Switzerland. This left the triumvirate to head the left wing of
the rising revolutionary movement, and they grew rapidly in power
until Robespierre cut them down. Duport was regarded as having
the best organizing brains. He was a Free Mason, well-to-do and
educated. Having no gift of oratory and in person rather cold, he
worked behind the scenes.

Barnave was the speaker and writer, with an ardent temperament
and considerable personal charm despite an ugly face. Legend said
he had sworn to take vengeance on the class of nobles because one
evening at the opera his mother had been forced to give up her seat
to the Count de Clermont-Tonnerre. Of this group Lameth was the
man of action. He was a nephew of Marshal de Broglie. Gossip said
he had returned from America, where his two brothers had also
fought, with "his head turned by liberty." He was robust, handsome,
and as a cavalry colonel was supposed to be a lion among the ladies.
Courtiers whispered he had even raised his eyes to the queen, and
because she had ignored him, he had never forgiven her. A saying
ran through Paris:

"Duport thinks it, Barnave speaks it, Lameth does it."

The year after Jefferson sailed from France, these three men were
in virtual control of the early stages of the revolution.

Now at the end of this dinner-table debate, which lasted six
hours, Jefferson realized he had taken part in a possible subversive
gathering and was appalled. This was no time for foreigners to mix
in French politics. The next morning he hurried to report himself
to Montmorin, the foreign minister, and explained what had happened at his house. He was relieved when Montmorin received him
affably and, leaving Jefferson to guess that his secret service had been
at work, informed him that he knew all about the dinner and the
discussion that followed. Montmorin assured him that so far from
feeling offended, he wished the American would "habitually assist at
such conferences," believing he would have a moderating effect.

There was one other occasion when the revolution all but scorched
Jefferson. This was in the summer of 1789 when it became known
that the court party had procured foreign troops to protect them in

Paris. One June afternoon Jefferson in his carriage was approaching the Place Louis XV when he noticed that it was occupied by about one hundred German cavalry and two hundred Swiss soldiers. On one side were piles of stones collected for a bridge to be built. Around these stones the people had massed. They formed a lane through which Jefferson's carriage was allowed to move, but the moment it was past they attacked the Germans with the stones. The cavalry charged but could not withstand the hail of stones, and when the Swiss did not move to rescue them, they gave up and retreated. "This was the signal for universal insurrection," wrote Jefferson.

This was one of the last sights he witnessed in Paris.

CHAPTER 32

BACK HOME

PRESIDENT WASHINGTON HAVING CONSENTED to his leave of absence, Jefferson and his daughters left Paris in September, 1789, and started homeward by way of Havre to Cowes, England, where John Trumbull had engaged a ship to stop for them and where he had obtained Jefferson's exemption from all customs examinations. Probably it was here that Jefferson mused over the eloquent farewell to France which he wrote afterward:

"I cannot leave this great and good country, without expressing my sense of its preëminence of character among the nations of the earth. A more benevolent people I have never known, nor greater warmth and devotedness in their select friendships. Their kindness and accommodation to strangers is unparalleled, and the hospitality of Paris is beyond anything I had conceived to be practicable in a large city. Their eminence, too, in science, the communicative disposition of their scientific men, the politeness of the general manners, the ease and vivacity of their conversation, gave a charm to their society to be found nowhere else. . . . Ask the traveled inhabitants of any nation, in what country you would rather live? Certainly, in my own, where are all my friends, my relations, and the earliest and sweetest affections and recollections of my life. Which would be your second choice? France."

Arriving off the Virginia Capes, Jefferson's little ship, the *Clermont,* three thousand tons, at first was forced to beat about for three days before she dared to enter the bay and then when the ship was at last docked at Norfolk, she caught fire and the Jeffersons' baggage was barely saved. On shore the Jeffersons spent much time visiting friends, so that Monticello was reached only on December 23, almost

169

three months from their last glimpse of Paris.

"The negroes," wrote Martha afterward, "discovered the approach of the carriage as soon as it reached Shadwell, and such a scene I never witnessed in my life."

The slaves raised a shout and unhitching the horses, they pulled it all the way up the rugged road to the door of the house. When Jefferson stepped out, they crowded around him, laughing and crying, and tried to kiss his hands and feet. When the daughters appeared there was a gasp of wonder, for Martha, whom the slaves had last seen as a child, was now a smiling but dignified young woman, and Polly had become a young thing of beauty. But scarcely had Jefferson been able to give thanks that he was back home with his two children before he received a message from a very great man that altered all his plans.

On the journey from Norfolk to Monticello one of his stopping places had been at Eppington, Chesterfield county. This was the home of the Eppes family who had made Polly Jefferson one of themselves. Here Jefferson was able to rest and to enjoy that family affection in which he ever loved to steep himself. He was forty-six years old, he had had experience with public life in two hemispheres, but the world and his country were not yet willing to allow him to withdraw to the leisured life of the gentleman-farmer and slave owner. The summons back to action came from an unexpected source. A letter, dated October 13, 1789, from President George Washington declared his determination, "as well by motives of private regard as a conviction of public propriety," to nominate him to head the Department of State in succession to John Jay who so recently had been Jefferson's chief.

When Jefferson delayed his reply, James Madison came down, no doubt with Washington's encouragement, to counsel acceptance. Jefferson answered Washington in a long letter of December 15, 1789. He intimated he would not prefer a change from his Paris post; but he declared: "You are to marshal us as may be best for the public good. . . . If you think it better to transfer me to another post, my inclination must be no obstacle."

On the heels of this, Madison wrote to Washington: "All whom I have heard speak on the subject are remarkably solicitous for his acceptance, and I flatter myself that they will not in the event be disappointed."

So Jefferson again was to postpone rural quietude and step back into the brawling political life which to one facet of his character was detestable, but which to another was fascinating. At the moment, however, he had to think of other matters.

On February 23, 1790, Martha Jefferson, now eighteen years old, was married to the second cousin who had courted her in Paris, Thomas Mann Randolph, Jr., whose father once had been the ward at Tuckahoe of Peter Jefferson, father of Thomas. Young Randolph's mother was Ann Cary, daughter of Jefferson's friend the redoubtable Colonel Archibald Cary of Ampthill; and Ann Cary's mother had been Mary Randolph, daughter of Richard Randolph of Curles.

Martha's father must have given her up with a pang, for he had been almost mother as well as true father to her; and already she was exhibiting those traits that made John Randolph of Roanoke call her "the noblest woman in Virginia." Jefferson was pleased with the match and took obvious pride in his son-in-law, who was a gentleman-farmer like himself; was tall, dark and striking-looking; and was by temperament amiable but moody. Senator William Plumer of New Hampshire, who once visited him in Washington when he was a member of Congress, wrote: "Mr. Randolph is not a military man —yet he has a pair of pistols & sword laying on the mantle piece in his chamber in this house. . . . He is a bashful timid man— is a pleasant agreeable companion—a man of study—much devoted to books." At one time he was estranged from his family, but Jefferson's pleas brought him back.

The wedding over, Jefferson was free to go to New York, which was then the seat of government, and begin his duties as secretary of state. He left Monticello on March 1, 1790, and, after a stop at Richmond, was a fortnight on the muddy, snow-filled road from Richmond to New York. Occasionally he relieved the tedium of stage travel by riding a saddle horse he had bought in Alexandria for seventy-five pounds. At Philadelphia he stopped to pay his respects to the aging and feeble Benjamin Franklin, whom he was seeing now for the last time.

"My recent return," wrote Jefferson, "from a country in which he had left so many friends . . . revived all his anxieties to know what part they had taken, what had been their course, and what their fate. He went over all in succession with a rapidity and animation almost too much for his strength." A month later Franklin was dead.

Reaching New York, Jefferson stopped for a few days at the City Tavern, on Broadway next to Trinity Church. Then he found a house at 57 Maiden Lane and rented it from Robert and Peter Bruce at one hundred pounds a year. At the back he built a French alcove for his books, lamenting that New York yielded "fewer resources in the way of books than could have been imagined." Having made himself comfortable here, though sadly lonesome without his daughters, he wrote on April 2 three letters back to Paris. One was to Lafayette. It began with the words, "Behold me, my dear friend, elected Secretary of State." He closed with the hope that Lafayette would take care of himself, saying "we are not translated from despotism to liberty on a feather-bed."

A second letter was addressed to the Countess d'Houdetot saying he had found in America "a philosophic revolution, philosophically effected," and telling her of his visit to Franklin, whose face often flushed as he listened to Jefferson's account of the French Revolution. A third letter was to Madame de Corny. It thanked her for all civilities and kindnesses. "They have been greatly more," said Jefferson, "than I had a right to expect, and they have excited in me a warmth of esteem which it was imprudent in me to have given way to for a person whom I was one day to be separated from."

Other letters, lonely ones, were to his daughters back in Virginia, Martha in Richmond with her husband and Polly safely back in the home she loved best—her aunt's at Eppington. The latter was too immersed in her own affairs to write. "I wrote to you three weeks ago," said her father in reproach, "and have not yet received an answer. . . . I think it very long to have been absent from Virginia two months, and not to have received a line from yourself, your sister, or Mr. Randolph." To Martha he offered his resignation as the first person in her affections.

"The happiness of your life now depends on the continuing to please a single person," he wrote. "Cherish, then, for me my dear child, the affection of your husband, and continue to love me as you have done, and to render my life a blessing by the prospect it may hold up to me of seeing you happy."

His letters to Polly, who was now just short of twelve years old, asked a series of questions designed to emphasize the pragmatisms of life. "Tell me whether you see the sun rise every day? How many pages you read every day in Don Quixote? . . . Whether you repeat a grammar lesson every day . . . How many hours a day you sew? . . . Whether you know how to make a pudding yet, to cut out a beefsteak, to sow spinach? or to set a hen?" He also offered some moral advice: "Never be angry with any body, nor speak harm of them; try to let every body's faults be forgotten, as you would wish yours to be; take more pleasure in giving what is best to another than in having it yourself, and then all the world will love you, and I more than all the world."

CHAPTER 33

CANDLE HOLDER

WHEN JEFFERSON TOOK his seat at President Washington's council table at Cherry Street and Franklin Square, in New York, he found the three other members of the cabinet already present. They were Alexander Hamilton, secretary of the treasury; Henry Knox, secretary of war and Edmund Randolph, attorney general. Randolph was a Virginian and a cousin of Jefferson's. Knox was a Massachusetts general, while Hamilton was a New York lawyer who had been born in the West Indies. Of his reception from these and other prominent persons in New York Jefferson wrote:

"The President received me cordially, and my colleagues and the circle of principal citizens, apparently with welcome. The courtesies of dinner parties given me, as a stranger newly arrived among them, placed me at once in their familiar society. But I cannot describe the wonder and mortification with which the table conversations filled me. Politics were the chief topic, and a preference of kingly over republican government, was evidently the favorite sentiment. An apostate I could not be, nor yet a hypocrite; and I found myself, for the most part, the only advocate on the republican side of the question, unless among the guests there chanced to be some member of that party from the legislative houses."

It has been noted already that Jefferson when still in Paris had received from his correspondents in the United States reports of the reaction set up by Shays's Rebellion in Massachusetts. That reaction had now been strengthened by reports from the revolutionary front in France. Property, wealth and position were working up a propaganda not only against republicanism, but against democracy. Attempts had been made to surround President Washington with the

174

ritual and trappings of royalty. A crystallization of upper-class sentiment had occurred around the name of Alexander Hamilton, who
openly declared that the United States government would do well
to model itself after the British government, which, in his opinion,
was "the best in the world."

In fact, what was called "the leveling tendencies" set up by the
yeoman farmers who had fought in, and otherwise supported, the
Revolution were now giving way to the haughty manners of urban
dwellers who put their faith in stocks, banks and centralized power.
The tone of American society was being established by people who
favored creditors rather than debtors; and the planting states south
of the Potomac were losing influence to the mercantile states of
the North.

These muddied currents in public affairs saddened Jefferson and
made him uneasy. He was sometimes overcome by depressions accompanied by debilitating headaches that afflicted him almost
throughout the summer of 1790. For he believed that through
Hamilton's maneuvers, mercantilism was winning over his own
cherished agrarian notions; that the mercantile North was profiting
at the expense of the agricultural South; and that the post-war
republic would have to struggle hard to keep itself from being
identified with plutocracy rather than democracy.

The center of everything which Jefferson considered objection-
able in political life at this stage was Alexander Hamilton. Yet in
the midst of his dislike of Hamilton the politician, he remained a
friend of Hamilton the man. Twenty-eight years later he wrote of
this his chief opponent:

"Hamilton was, indeed, a singular character. Of acute understanding, disinterested, honest, and honorable in all private transactions,
amiable in society and duly valuing virtue in private life, yet so
bewitched and perverted by the British example, as to be under
thorough conviction that corruption was essential to the government of a nation."

As soon as Jefferson had settled down in New York he found the
young nation, which had just been embroiled by one of Hamilton's
"fiscal maneuvers," now in the grip of another. The first of two
measures proposed by Hamilton was known as the Funding Bill;

the second was called Assumption. In the first case were involved the paper certificates which had been issued to Revolutionary soldiers for services, or to farmers and merchants for supplies. Distressed holders long ago had sold this paper to speculators at heavy discounts. Hamilton drew up a bill to "fund," or pay off, this paper to the present owners, whether they were the original holders or speculative purchasers. Despite outcries, the measure passed, thus creating for the first time in America a class of moneyed men who felt no sense of responsibility toward their country and were indifferent toward the welfare of their countrymen.

It was Hamilton's second measure that drew Jefferson's heaviest indignation. This bill required that the federal treasury should "assume" the Revolutionary War debts incurred by the states; hence the name Assumption. Congress was deeply split by the question; and here for the first time was heard the dread word "secession" when furious representatives of various states threatened to quit the Union rather than yield their positions. Particularly were the Southern states bitter and suspicious. Hamilton recognized the strength of the opposition and resolved to break it down by making use of Jefferson's influence below the Potomac. To do this he employed one of the oldest devices in politics—a "deal."

President Washington was then occupying the McComb house on lower Broadway near Bowling Green. Jefferson was on his way to this house one day when he met Hamilton in the street. The latter buttonholed him about the split in Congress, pointing out that, because of the threats of secession and separation, the existence of the Union was in danger. During his arguments Hamilton walked Jefferson back and forth before the President's door until the latter agreed that to avert a dissolution of the Union "all partial and temporary evils should be yielded." He suggested that Hamilton, together with one or two other reasonable men, should dine with him next day and discuss a compromise. Since in order to carry the measure, it would be necessary for some members of Congress to change their votes and since it was recognized that "this pill would be peculiarly bitter to the Southern States," a little something to sweeten its passage was suggested. The rest is told in Jefferson's own words:

"There had before been propositions to fix the seat of government either at Philadelphia or at Georgetown on the Potomac; and it was thought that by giving it to Philadelphia for ten years, and to Georgetown permanently afterwards, this might, as an anodyne, calm in some degree the ferment which might be excited by the other measure alone." So that was the way Assumption was accomplished —as the result of a deal which enabled "twenty millions of stock" to be divided, as Jefferson put it, "among favored States, and thrown in as a pabulum to the stock-jobbing herd." Thus was Jefferson, in his own words, "made to hold the candle."

It was probably at this point, and as a consequence of this episode, that Jefferson's previously mild dislike of Hamilton became active suspicion. "A division, not very unequal, had already taken place in the honest part" of Congress, wrote Jefferson later; and these two parties now styled themselves Republican, or republic-men, and Federal, or strong-government men.

Between these parties there now opened a protracted struggle for the body of the infant United States. It was this war to the death that completely absorbed Jefferson's energies, so that even his dream of a return to rural life at Monticello lost its glow and was put aside. He felt that Hamilton's conception of, and propaganda for, upper-class rule must be countered and overthrown; yet even in his angriest moments Jefferson must have realized that the enemy carried strong weapons. Hamilton's actions were shaped by a single idea—that the infant government of the United States, to succeed, must receive the support of the wealthy and well-born classes; while Jefferson, though less grounded in economics, was equally convinced that all the people must share in government, the base of which must be men working and living on the land.

A third project of Hamilton's was designed, like the other two, to draw the wealthy investing class strongly to support the infant government. It took the form of a federal bank which was to have a capital subscribed one-fifth by the government and four-fifths by the public in shares costing four hundred dollars each. The bill was quickly passed and signed by President Washington. A fourth project, which drew less attention at the time, probably because the nation's industrial interests were as yet minor, was contained in Hamilton's

"Report on Manufactures," issued in December, 1791, in which he advocated government encouragement of manufacturers as a means of augmenting the nation's wealth. Implied was the necessity of tariffs not only for revenue but for protection of infant industries from foreign competition. In these measures Jefferson scented evil; but although critical of Hamilton's projects, he gave them no open battle. Possibly he had two good reasons: he was not combative by nature, and he was grounded less in economics than in political history. Hamilton, with his superior knowledge of what was then called political economy, in these early stages triumphed over Jefferson because he was able to make the government an economic as well as a political instrument adapted to the needs of the propertied classes. For example, the Bill of Rights attached to the United States Constitution came into effect without Jefferson's proposed clause in it aimed at monopolies. This omission caused Thomas Paine to write one of his harshest diatribes.

"Monopolies of every kind," he wrote, "marked your administration almost in the moment of its commencement. The lands obtained by the Revolution were lavished on partisans; the interest of the disbanded soldier was sold to the speculator; injustice was acted under the pretence of faith, and the chief of the army became the patron of fraud."

Paine, however, made the mistake of aiming these accusations at President Washington instead of at Hamilton. The bewildered Father of his Country indeed leaned toward Hamilton's opinions rather than Jefferson's, but he was never a shaper of fiscal policies and always did his best to keep at a polite level the arguments between those two most brilliant members of his cabinet.

In his calmer moments Jefferson could and did recognize the ability and personal honesty of Hamilton; but in the heat of argument his judgment sometimes erred. Hamilton admired monarchy, but in public office he never tried to grind his own political ax; while in his unvarying bias toward the wealthy and well-born, he was probably only revealing himself as the poor boy from the West Indies who had risen from zero by serving rich and powerful people, and who still considered them the only people of importance. That sometimes he suffered from self-doubts was possibly indicated by his giddy and over-talkative manner in public and by the forlorn confession he once made to Gouverneur Morris, to whom he was cousin in tastes and leanings:

"Every day proves to me more and more, that this American world was not made for me."

But Hamilton, in turn, was not always fair to Jefferson, as proved by remarks in a letter to James A. Bayard in 1801:

". . . his politics are tinctured with fanaticism."

". . . he is too much in earnest in his democracy."

". . . crafty and persevering in his objects."

". . . not scrupulous about the means of success, nor very mindful of truth."

". . . he is a contemptible hypocrite." [1]

---

[1] This epithet was possibly based on Jefferson's ability to admire and be genial to a man as a person though detesting his opinions.

CHAPTER 34

QUESTIONS OF COLOR
AND ARCHITECTURE

WHEN JEFFERSON WROTE in the Declaration of Independence of those self-evident truths, "that all men are created equal, and that they are endowed by their Creator with certain inalienable rights, that among these are life, liberty and the pursuit of happiness," he seems not to have been aware of the irony of pronouncing such sentiments when in eleven of the thirteen colonies there were some thousands of persons to whom neither equality nor liberty was allowed; and more than two hundred of them were living on his plantations. He was not publicly challenged by any of these people until this active year of 1791 when suddenly he received a letter from a free man of color living in Maryland, Benjamin Banneker, who although without formal schooling was both a mathematician and astronomer. Enclosed was an almanac for 1792 prepared from Banneker's own calculations. Banneker's letter to Jefferson was dated from "Maryland, Baltimore County, near Ellicott's Lower Mills, August 19, 1791." It expressed the hope that Jefferson would agree that "one universal father hath given being to us all," and recalled the time when he and others suffered under "the arms and tyranny of the British crown." He then proceeded to his main point:

"This, sir, was a time in which you clearly saw into the injustice of a state of slavery, and in which you had just apprehension of the horrors of its condition, it was now, sir, that your abhorrence thereof was so excited, that you publicly held forth this true and invaluable doctrine, which is worthy to be recorded and remembered in all succeeding ages. We hold these truths to be self-evident, that all men are created equal, and that they are endowed by their creator

180

with certain inalienable rights, that among these are life, liberty and the pursuit of happiness."

In his reply Jefferson was affable and sympathetic, but he failed altogether to refer to or answer Banneker's philosophical main point.

In his letter to Jefferson it is possible Banneker was aided by the surveyor Andrew Ellicott, who had prepared a United States Almanac, the earliest known, in 1782, and who when only fifteen years old had helped his father make a master clock of the grandfather type. The wars that afflicted the world in the late eighteenth century led Banneker to propose that the government cabinet have a secretary of peace. Here again we must suspect the hand of Ellicott, who was a Quaker.

The greatest honor that came to Banneker was his appointment as an assistant to the commission that laid out the ten square miles forming the District of Columbia. Employed by this body were Major Pierre Charles l'Enfant, designer of the Federal City which became Washington, and Banneker's friend, Andrew Ellicott, who had been an army engineer in the Revolutionary War. Banneker's biographer, Baker, says it was the latter who suggested Banneker's name, that Jefferson nominated him, and President Washington gave him the appointment. Banneker died at his farm home in 1806. A public school in Washington bears his name.

Although the federal territory on which Banneker was employed was surveyed and laid out by Ellicott, the Federal City was the creation of Major l'Enfant, who had preceded Lafayette to America as a volunteer in the Revolutionary War and who as an officer of engineers had been captured at Charleston. Jefferson employed L'Enfant in March, 1791, to work under Ellicott and to make drawings of the grounds most suitable for the federal site. Jefferson asked him to report on his progress twice a week. He lent L'Enfant maps and plans of numerous cities he had gathered in Europe, including Paris, Orleans, Marseilles, Turin, Milan, Amsterdam, Strasbourg and Frankfort on the Main, and showed eager interest in the work.

"I should propose," he wrote to L'Enfant, "that no street be narrower than one hundred feet, with footways of fifteen feet. Where a street is long and level, it might be one hundred twenty feet wide. I should prefer squares of at least two hundred yards every way, which will be about eight acres each. . . . I doubt much whether the obligation to build the houses at a given distance from the street contributes to its beauty. It produces a disgusting monotony; all persons make this complaint against Philadelphia. . . . In Paris it is forbidden to build a house beyond a given height; and it is admitted to be a good restriction." He also counseled L'Enfant:

"Whenever it is proposed to prepare plans for the Capitol I should prefer the adoption of some one of the models of antiquity which have the approbation of thousands of years, and for the President's house I should prefer the celebrated fronts of modern dwellings which have the approbation of all good judges. Such are the Galerie du Louvre, the Gardes Meubles and the two fronts of the Hotel de Salm."

Major l'Enfant accepted Jefferson's counsels as well as he could, so that Washington was later described as "Philadelphia griddled across Versailles," but that he was strongly influenced by the map of Paris was evident also. All went well until a sale of lots in the new Federal City was advertised. After that there was nothing but trouble between L'Enfant and the commissioners. That they must have been an exasperating group is evidenced by a letter from Ellicott, whose nature was much more tranquil than L'Enfant's, to his wife in which he said of them: "I have received treatment from them, that would justify me in any measure whatever. . . . Neither credit, nor reputation, will ever be the lot of a single person, who enters into their service. . . . I dislike the place, and every day adds to my disgust." [1]

Ellicott already had described the major to the same lady as "a most worthy French Gentleman and though not one of the most handsome of men he is from his good breeding and native politeness a first rate favourite among the ladies." Indeed, Major l'Enfant is described as a tall and courtly man who held himself very straight and wore an air of distinction. But when he went to the length of refusing to let the commissioners use his over-all design, President

---

[1] Catherine Van Cortlandt Mathews, *Andrew Ellicott: His Life & Letters,* New York, 1908.

Independence Hall National Museum
Dr. Benjamin Rush, pastel by James Sharpless

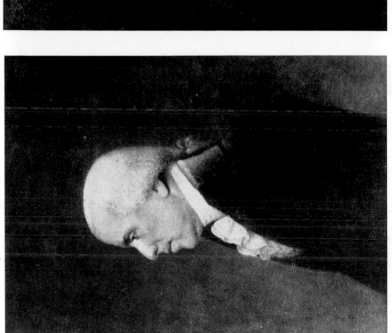

Oliver B. Jennings, owner. Courtesy,
Frick Art Reference Library
Aaron Burr, friend, rival and final enemy, by John
Vanderlyn

Mrs. John Adams by Gilbert Stuart. Jefferson pleased, then offended her

John Adams, who died on the same day as Jefferson, by Gilbert Stuart

Washington became annoyed with him for his "untoward disposition." Finally in 1792 Jefferson wrote the commissioners that it had
been found "impracticable" to employ Major l'Enfant any further,
and that Ellicott would finish "laying off the plan on the ground and
surveying and plotting the District." So Ellicott drew up a new plan
for the city, using parts of L'Enfant's design but incorporating material of his own.

It was not until many years later that the joint work of L'Enfant,
Ellicott and Jefferson, in making Washington one of the world's
most beautiful cities, was appreciated. L'Enfant died in a genteel
poverty. Ellicott went on in triumph to become coach to Lewis and
Clark, and finally to become professor of mathematics at West Point
as appointed by James Monroe, then secretary of war.

CHAPTER 35

ELEGANCE IN PHILADELPHIA

WHEN, IN ACCORDANCE with the deal made in New York, the seat of government was moved in 1790 to Philadelphia, Jefferson knew within his inner self that he must do further battle with Hamilton. And it did not help his spirits when he realized that Hamilton was regarded as the first or prime minister of the Washington administration. But Jefferson tried to save himself a crumb of comfort—"it is fortunate," he wrote, "that our first executive magistrate is purely and zealously republican." To favor a republic rather than a monarchy—that was Jefferson's chief test for any man in public life.

Before taking up residence in Philadelphia, Jefferson spent a few days at Monticello. On the trip south he was accompanied by James Madison, with whom his friendship was becoming ever tighter, and by young Thomas Lee Shippen, who was on his way to visit kinfolk in Virginia. Shippen had been provided by Jefferson with letters of introduction in Germany and Holland when in 1788 he had made a European tour with John Rutledge, Jr., of South Carolina; Shippen now wrote his father of his pleasure in traveling with "those charming men," Jefferson and Madison, saying:

"At Rock Hall, 12 miles from Chestertown [now Chester, Pa.], we waited all that day for want of a vessel to take us over [the Delaware river], and I never knew two men more agreeable than they. We talked and dined and strolled and rowed ourselves in boats, and feasted on delicious crabs." [1]

During his stay at Monticello Jefferson attended to farming matters and to repairs around the house. He employed five of his slaves to build a road twelve feet wide up to the "upper roundabout" in

---

[1] Dumbauld, *Thomas Jefferson, American Tourist.*

front of the house. He recorded in his *Garden Book* that they did 127 yards the first day and 165 yards the second. He appointed as his attorney Colonel Nicholas Lewis, whose nephew, Meriwether Lewis, one day was to become famous as an explorer under Jefferson's direction; and he shipped sixteen kinds of American trees and shrubs to the Countess de Tessé in France. One decision was significant. He reminded Colonel Lewis that on the Albemarle land he might "lay aside tobacco entirely" and in Bedford county as much as possible.

Jefferson's reaction against tobacco farming was growing; he was convinced it led to poverty. In its place he urged more attention to grains and fibers. He also hoped for a sugar crop by setting out maples. He was especially sanguine about a new variety of Maryland wheat, some seed of which had been given him by his fellow-farmer, President Washington. He also continued his lone experiments in planting upland rice. He had got the seed from a friend who had procured a supply from that found on the island of Timor, in the East Indies, by Captain William Bligh, who had been so unfortunate as to get caught by a mutiny on his famous ship, the *Bounty*.

On his return to Philadelphia in November, 1790, Jefferson again had to find a house and make it suitable for his meticulous needs. In High (later Market) Street, west of Eighth, he rented from Thomas Leiper for £ 250, or $666.66, a year a four-story house which he altered so as to have an alcove bedroom, a book room, a garden house and stables. "I shall want stables for five horses, and room for three carriages," he wrote the contractor, and added peremptorily: "No seats at the street door to collect lounging servants."

These, it must be said, are not the words or tone of a leveler. As president of the United States Jefferson was often accused of carelessness in dress and disregard of conventions. But certainly at this period he was no sloven either in person or house. Mrs. George Logan, at whose home in Stenton, near Philadelphia, he was often a visitor, wrote that after his return from France he "wore a suit of silk, ruffles, and an elegant topaz ring; but he soon adopted a more republican garb, and was reproached with going to the other extreme as a bait for popularity." [2] He once requested his grandson, Thomas Jefferson Randolph, to send him at Monticello "a half dozen pounds

[2] *Memoir of Dr. George Logan of Stenton.*

of scented hair powder," saying, "None is to be had here, and it is almost a necessity of life with me." And while living in Philadelphia, he wrote to Bache, a tailor there:

"If either now or at any time hence you can find a superfine French cloth of the very dark blue which you know I wear, I will be obliged to you to make and send me a coat of it. Furnish me also if you please a pair of black silk and a pair of black satin breeches."

While his High Street house was being altered, he complained to his daughter Polly of the slowness of the workmen. In December he foresaw himself occupying one chamber as "bedroom, study, dining-room, and parlor," but early in January he was at last able to dine at home and to hire a washwoman at twenty pounds a year. His garden house was to be a place for study and writing and was to have a skylight but no lateral windows. He gave orders to that effect; but when he returned from Virginia, he found the house had been "made with a window-door at each end, no sky light, and a set of joists which were in the way." From which we judge there are some things eternally recurring and unvarying down the centuries.

His house at length completed, Jefferson moved into it the contents of eighty-six packing cases he had brought over from France. They had been poked into by suspicious revolutionists at Havre but not damaged. Included were fifteen cases of books, also chairs, sofas, tables, beds, commodes, chiffoniers, mirrors, paintings, busts, statuary, curtains, draperies and other fabrics. His house and kitchen were presided over by Adrien Petit, who had been his steward in Paris. Jefferson's devotion to French cuisine aroused the deepest suspicions among compatriots who still clung to boiled bacon-and-greens as the summit of American colonial cooking; indeed, Patrick Henry once publicly attacked him for having "abjured his native victuals."

Jefferson never was one to accept the second-rate, and his writings show that he gave the same care to the compilation of a recipe as to that of a state paper. He amassed so many notes and directions on dishes and cooking that they have been gathered into *Thomas Jefferson's Cook Book*,[3] which indicates that macaroni and vanilla owe

---

[3] Marie Kimball, ed., Richmond, Va.

their introduction in America to Jefferson; and indeed there is evidence that he procured vanilla beans in Paris through the ever-obliging William Short, whom he left behind as the American chargé there. His passion for detail and statistics led him to make this curious entry in his account book:

"Tea out. The pound has lasted exactly 7 weeks, used 6 times a week. This is 8/21 or .4 of an oz. a time, for a single person. A pound of tea making 126 cups costs 2 D. 126 cups or ounces of coffee = 8 lb. cost 1.6. Campbell, 1 lb. Imperial tea 2."

But the comforts of his new Philadelphia house did not allay the loneliness that often beset him, and he besought James Madison, who was living in a boarding-house on Fifth Street, to rescue him from his solitude:

"Come and take a bed and plate with me. I have 4 rooms of which anyone is at your service. . . . To me it will be a relief from a solitude of which I have too much; and it will lessen your repugnance to be assured it will not increase my expenses an atom."

He also sought the company of James Monroe, saying: "I can accommodate you myself with a stable and coach house without any expense, as I happen to have two on hand; and indeed, in my new one I have had stalls enough prepared for 6 horses, which are 2 more than I keep."

Early in 1791 a new office was bestowed on Jefferson. His daughter Martha, now Mrs. Randolph, made him a grandfather in his forty-ninth year. He wrote to her: "Your last two letters gave me the greatest pleasure of any I ever received from you. The one announced that you were become a notable housewife; the other a mother. The last is undoubtedly the keystone of the arch of matrimonial happiness, as the first is its daily aliment." The baby was named Anne.

Jefferson regularly wrote to his two daughters in alternation, and though Martha answered with reasonable promptness, Polly continued either not to reply at all or to ignore the questions he was fond of asking her, especially those relating to gardens and birds. Such failures filled her father with despair; he could not reconcile himself to the recognition that in every child, however lovable, there dwells an element not to be reached by any parent, however devoted.

At length in April, 1791, he wrote in quiet desperation:

"I find I have counted too much on you as a Botanical and Zoological correspondent." And then he suddenly changed the subject to millinery as being something surer to provoke a response. He enclosed two veils, one for each sister. "Observe," he wrote with his usual love of detail, "that one of the strings is to be drawn tight round the root of the crown of the hat, and the veil then falling over the brim of the hat is drawn by the lower string as tight or loose as you please round the neck. When the veil is not chosen to be down, the lower string is also tied round the root of the crown, so as to give it the appearance of a puffed bandage for the hat. I send also the green lining for the calash. . . . Yours with tender love, Th. Jefferson." He added that on April 5, 9 and 11 the apricot, peach and cherry had blossomed.

In the spring of 1791 Jefferson prepared for a trip with Madison through New York State and New England to study the Hessian fly, which was becoming a pest to farmers, to botanize along the way, and also (his enemies charged) to enlarge and cement the growing opposition to the Federalist policies of Alexander Hamilton and John Adams. But before he departed, an explosion occurred in political circles that held him back momentarily. Edmund Burke in England had written his *Reflections on the Revolution in France,* containing his glamorous recollections of a holiday in France in 1773 and his lamentations over the twilight of royalty and nobility. Thomas Paine, then in England trying to sell his patent bridge, replied to it with his blistering *Rights of Man.* It was a sensation in two hemispheres, and Jefferson at once wrote Paine the pamphlet "has been much read here with avidity and pleasure." A copy of the English edition reached Philadelphia in advance of the American edition. It came into the hands of Madison, who lent it to Jefferson, and he returned it to the owner with a private note which said: "I am extremely pleased to find it will be reprinted here, and that something is at length to be publicly said against the political heresies which have sprung up among us." In a later letter to Paine he wrote: "I thank God that the people appear firm in their republicanism, notwithstanding the contrary hopes and aspirations of a sect here, high in name but small in number."

When similar sentiments were printed on the American pamphlet so as to appear to be an endorsement from Jefferson, a newspaper storm arose; and Jefferson felt obliged to write a letter of explanation to President Washington in which he said: "I certainly never made a secret of my being anti-monarchical, and anti-aristocratical; but I am sincerely mortified to be thus brought forward on the public stage, where to remain, to advance, or to retire, will be equally against my love of silence and quiet, and my abhorrence of dispute."

He wrote a similar letter of explanation to John Adams, who replied with chilly politeness. Meantime Adams's son, John Quincy Adams, aged twenty-four, had written a series of newspaper articles signed "Publicola" attacking Paine's pamphlet. The breach thus opened was not healed over till long after John Adams and Jefferson were old men.

Jefferson and Madison began their journey north almost at the moment that President Washington was making his tour of the Southern states. From Lakes George and Champlain in New York Jefferson wrote letters to his daughters on birch bark. His exhilaration was evident; his chronic headaches began to disappear. He and Madison fished successfully in Lake George, which he called "the most beautiful water I ever saw." They found their whole journey "prosperous and pleasant," but in a patriotic outburst he told his daughters to rejoice they had been born and were living in Virginia. He and Madison botanized happily, shot red squirrels, traveled through Vermont to the Connecticut river, then down to New York where they parted, Jefferson to return to Philadelphia and Madison to continue a personal errand.

On Long Island Jefferson bought from a nursery a stock of sugar maples, his latest enthusiasm. He had a dream of making his own sugar at Monticello, but, like his grape, rice and olive dreams, it came to small fruition. From Philadelphia he wrote to Martha telling her of his enjoyment of the tour. "I am in hopes the relaxation it gave me from business has freed me from the almost constant headache with which I had been persecuted during the whole winter and spring. Having been entirely free of it while travelling proves it to have been occasioned by the drudgery of business."

So busy was Jefferson with his multiple duties that in his writings we find few hints as to what Philadelphia, the capital and most important city in the United States, with a population of nearly seventy thousand, was then like. But from the French traveler J. P. Brissot de Warville, who first came to America in 1788, we find comments that illuminate as well as describe the Philadelphia scene.

The streets were fifty to sixty feet wide, except Market, which was one hundred feet wide, and were regularly laid out at right angles. All streets had public pumps. The sidewalks were of brick. Before each house were placed two benches on which the occupants might take the air. Few coaches were visible, but there were many handsome wagons. Luxury was creeping in, despite the Quaker influence. Carpets adorned rooms and halls even in the summer. The women wore hats and caps almost as varied as in Paris. "They bestow immense expenses on their toilet and head-dress." Gazettes and bookstores were numerous. Jefferson liked the town very well, except for the "disgusting monotony" of its streets.

CHAPTER 36

POET AS EDITOR

SOON AFTER THE government moved from New York to Philadelphia, Jefferson gave a place as translating clerk in the Department of State to Philip Freneau, sailor and former captain in the Revolutionary army, and once a captive on a British prison-ship. Freneau was a poet and journalist, and his salary as clerk was only $250 a year; nevertheless the appointment set off an outcry that must have astonished Jefferson and more so Madison, who had been Freneau's friend at Princeton and who had recommended him to Jefferson.

Freneau got out a newspaper, called the *National Gazette,* in which he attacked the Federalists and upheld republicanism with a wit and gaiety that soon earned him delighted subscribers and sour enemies, and brought upon Jefferson the charge that he had subsidized Freneau with a government salary. There were already two newspapers in Philadelphia: a neutral but friendly one edited by Benjamin Franklin Bache, grandson of Benjamin Franklin; and the other, an organ of the Federalists, edited by John Fenno, who had been sent down and backed by Massachusetts and New York followers of Hamilton. Called the *Gazette of the United States,* it attacked republican doctrines, scorned democratic practices, and denounced government by the people as anarchy.

Jefferson, Madison, Monroe and Henry Lee, then governor of Virginia, had long demanded a paper—a "free paper"—to offset Fenno's *Gazette.* Madison confessed his hope that "a free paper, meant for general circulation, and edited by a man of genius of republican principles and a friend of the Constitution, would be some antidote to the doctrines and discourses circulated in favor of Monarchy and Aristocracy." Jefferson paid for or solicited the first twenty-one subscriptions; but despite the charges against him of subsidization and subversion, it seems clear enough now that it was Madison and not Jefferson who was the chief agent in bringing Freneau to Philadelphia.

Freneau's paper, issued twice a week, never had two thousand cash subscribers; but because it was passed from hand to hand and often quoted in other papers, its influence was soon felt throughout the narrow little nation pinned between the Atlantic Ocean and the Mississippi river. Freneau was of Huguenot ancestry, and to a passionate devotion to the American Revolution, and a determination to preserve its fruits, he added a Gallic gift for witty satire and acid ridicule. At first his abstract essays on the sovereignty of the people, and such topics, aroused no opposition; but when he declaimed against exploiting "systems" and issued warnings against "saddles prepared for the back of the people," the economic and political royalists of the day began to watch his paper with hot eyes; and at last when he began to satirize official "levees" and careenings around in pretentious coaches, friends of George Washington and John Adams, as well as those of Alexander Hamilton, saw subversion being born; its father, they were sure, was Jefferson.

It now seems clear, however, that Jefferson was to a degree the follower rather than the mentor of Freneau. Jefferson, at this stage, was a republic-man only; his five horses, his five servants, the personal maid for his daughter Polly, the sumptuous furniture just arrived in Philadelphia from France, the slaves at Monticello, were insignia of the aristocratic planter. It was Freneau who, at a position well to the left of Jefferson, preached democracy as well as republicanism. It was Freneau, not Jefferson, who ridiculed the snobbish ceremonials surrounding President Washington—ceremonials that had been arranged by Hamilton, to whom Washington was prone to look for advice in social as well as political and economic matters; it was Freneau who insisted that the United States, freed of outworn British customs, must develop a social as well as a political democracy.

These doctrines, barbed by Freneau's humor and bolstered by articles from Madison, Henry Brackenridge and George Tucker, enraged the financial and mercantile groups led by Hamilton not only because these groups were human enough to dislike personal ridicule, but because they detested the very precepts which Freneau was preaching; their intention was to maintain in substance the British caste and class lines of pre-war colonial days and to gain and hold wealth. Independence having been won, they now wished to get down to business and avoid giving power to the common man.

In the small and yeoman farmers of the provinces, however, and in the artisans and mechanics of the towns, there had been born a hope that the Revolution was not to end merely with a political overturn; that the conditions of life in the new republic were to be more nearly equalized than before; and that the victory over monarchy was somehow to introduce a greater and freer civilization to be enjoyed and gloried in. Freneau, poet and sailor and former prisoner of war, was spokesman and defender of the smaller people; he was their man and his own; but his enemies believed he was the mouthpiece of Jefferson. They looked to Hamilton, who was far cleverer than they, to stop him. And Hamilton tried.

Unable to find a writer to match Freneau, Hamilton was driven to the expedient of writing himself for Fenno's *Gazette* anonymously. He replied to and attacked Freneau over the initials "T.L." and "Americus." His favorite target was Jefferson; he implied that Jefferson, already opposed to the Constitution, lacked dignity and honor. Washington, alarmed by this feud between the two stars of his cabinet, stepped in and wrote to both men requesting peace and harmony. Neither reply was comforting. Jefferson's letter contained these much-quoted lines:

"No government ought to be without censors; and where the press is free no one ever will. If virtuous, it need not fear the free operation of attack and defense."

Hamilton's answer had a tinge of that shortness, almost impudence, with which more than once he had addressed Washington; he said he could not "recede at the present." He declared Jefferson was trying "to render me and all the objects connected with my administration odious," and to "subvert the government." Were these among the anxieties that caused so many writers of the period to speak of Washington's depression and silence even on gay occasions, so that at dinners he drummed on the table with knife and fork as if moody or bored? One thing is sure, that Freneau's stinging pen finally annoyed Washington scarcely less than Hamilton, for one day the Country's Father lost his harassed temper at a cabinet meeting thus described by Jefferson:

"The President was much inflamed; got into one of those passions when he cannot command himself; ran on much on the personal abuse which had been bestowed on him; defied any man on earth to produce one single act of his since he had been in the government, which was not done on the purest motives; that he had never repented but once the having slipped the moment of resigning his office, and that was every moment since; that *by God* he had rather be in his grave than in his present situation; that he had rather be on his farm than to be made *Emperor of the world;* and yet that they were charging him with wanting to be a King. That that *rascal* Freneau sent him three of his papers every day, as if he thought he would become the distributor of his papers; that he could see in this, nothing but an impudent design to insult him."

It was the yellow fever epidemic in Philadelphia that ultimately put an end to the journal's weakened existence. Jefferson always insisted it was Freneau's writings that scotched "monocracy" in America and put an end to undemocratic pomp around public offices —which pomp was fostered largely by Colonel David Humphreys, who had apparently absorbed nothing from Jefferson during his residence with him in Paris. Freneau's return to rural life in New Jersey abated none of the Federalist hatred for his writings, as proved by the later Alien and Sedition Acts, which all but abolished free speech and a free press in a young and confused America. Everybody knew that those statutes were aimed at the Freneaus in the foreground but also at the Jeffersons in the back.

Jefferson showed much concern at this stage over the reopening of the chasm between the Northern and Southern states as a result of the financial maneuvers of Hamilton, especially with the national debt, which, said Jefferson, had placed "the owners of the debt . . . in the Southern, and the holders of it in the Northern division."

"North and South will hang together if they have you to hang on," he told Washington in a plea which plainly foreshadows the sectional war which was in open and active progress seventy years later. In-

deed, it is arresting to any reader of Jefferson's writings to discover
how often he pointed a finger directly at the evils, upheavals and
disasters that later came upon the American people in consequence
of violations of economic balance, political justice and social fair-
dealing.

The question of debt, and its sister, speculation, was at this period
much on Jefferson's mind. He insisted that no generation had a right
to bind another under public debt. In his opinion Hamilton was
trying to make the national debt into a permanent instrument for
regulating national policy.

"A national debt," Hamilton argued, "if it be not excessive, will
be to us a national blessing. . . . It will also create a necessity for
keeping up taxation to a degree which, without being oppressive,
will be a spur to industry."

Speculation continued to soar and at last, fostered by the financial
manipulations of William Duer, former employee of the Department
of the Treasury and friend of Hamilton, the tottering structure wob-
bled and fell. This was the first of the financial crashes, emanating
from the larger cities and eventuating in economic depression, that
have afflicted the American people at intervals since they founded
a nation. Duer went to jail and later so did Robert Morris, speculator
and financier, owner of the very house Washington lived in at Philadelphia.

CHAPTER 37

HAMILTON AND MRS. REYNOLDS

ABOUT THIS TIME began Alexander Hamilton's sordid intrigue with Mrs. Reynolds, an affair which his political enemies mistakenly thought had some connection with concealed financial skulduggery, particularly after they discovered Hamilton had been making secret payments to the husband in the case, a racketeer named James Reynolds. Eventually Hamilton had to make a full confession about his illicit amour, but in it was no evidence of dishonesty on his part, except toward his trusting wife, the former Eliza Schuyler.

The Reynolds woman apparently had studied Hamilton and selected him as a likely victim. Her first move was to call at his house in the role of a deserted wife in need of enough cash to return to her home in New York. He had not enough money with him (despite Hamilton's high financial position, he was often short of ready cash at this period), but later took the money in person to her home. There he found, in his own words, "that other than pecuniary consolation would be acceptable." Other meetings followed, and Hamilton had to confess most of them had been at his own house, his wife being absent with her children at the old Schuyler family home at Albany.

The intrigue had progressed to the point where Hamilton was well in the toils when Mrs. Reynolds' husband appeared and suggested his appointment to a place in the Treasury. Hamilton then began to suspect he was being victimized, and he had no defense when Reynolds threatened to inform Hamilton's wife about the whole business. To keep him quiet Hamilton paid him blackmail, one thousand dollars at first and then smaller sums in regular course.

This might have gone on indefinitely except that a clerk named Clingman got arrested for alleged subornation; he named James Reynolds as his partner in an attempted fraud. The upshot was that three members of Congress—Monroe, Muhlenberg and Venable—learned there was something suspicious between Reynolds and Hamilton. They went to Hamilton's office and requested an explanation. Hamilton was trapped. Unless he told the whole truth, he would be suspected of financial misdealings; while if he confessed, his amiable wife would learn what had occurred behind her back.

He chose to risk the latter course. Calling the three congressmen to his home and asking Oliver Wolcott, the Treasury comptroller, to be a witness, he opened and exposed the whole intrigue, showing also the clinching documents and letters. The three congressmen, no doubt, had entertained notions of hearing something that would damage Hamilton politically; when they learned it was a tale of amour and of later blackmail against a complaisant husband, they agreed to keep the whole matter in confidence.

Hamilton probably had put the affair out of his mind when five years later it suddenly broke out in the public prints. The author proved to be James T. Callender, the wandering newspaper writer who later printed an exposé of Jefferson's alleged attentions to a neighbor's wife. Hamilton, well aware how this might harm his career, demanded an explanation from the three congressmen who had heard his confession. Two of them denied all responsibility, but Monroe kept silence. At last Hamilton called on Monroe, taking with him his brother-in-law, John Barker Church, husband of Angelica—she who was a friend of Jefferson and a constant admirer of Hamilton. A hot interview took place in which Hamilton barely escaped a challenge to a duel, an institution which Hamilton's family had bitter cause to regret. All that Monroe would say was that he knew nothing of the publication; that he had sent the papers in Hamilton's case, sealed, "to his friend in Virginia," whom he did not name.

By now so much scandal had arisen that Hamilton felt impelled to publish a pamphlet refuting all accusations of speculation, but admitting his guilt in the Reynolds intrigue. His wife forgave him but, though she lived long after her husband, she never forgave Monroe. The affair simply piled more fuel on the burning hostility that mounted higher almost daily between the Jefferson followers who as yet called themselves Whigs and the Hamilton followers who became known as Federalists. In this battle, though the Jeffersonians lost the early skirmishes, in later stages they rallied strongly under skilled leadership and eventually crushed the Federalists just as the century ended.

While these things were going on in Philadelphia, Jefferson was getting news about the movements of some of his late associates in France that must have interested him no little. He learned that his friends of Lafayette's dinner party held at his own house—Barnave, Duport and Lameth—were now in virtual control of political life in Paris. In 1791 the French king and queen made the flight to Varennes which virtually ended the French monarchy but which began the friendship of Barnave for the queen, a friendship which later brought on Barnave's arrest and execution. The next year Lafayette, finding he could no longer induce the army to remain loyal to the monarchy, fled from France to the Netherlands. Here he was arrested by the Austrians and imprisoned by them at Antwerp and later at Olmütz. Around this latter prison both Washington and Jefferson pulled many diplomatic wires to obtain his release, but he remained there till 1797 when Napoleon freed him.

In the same year came the rise in France of the Jacobins and the formation of the royal and imperial allied armies which invaded France, intending to destroy the republic. In 1793 occurred the execution first of Louis XVI, then of Marie Antoinette, and next of Jefferson's dinner companion, Adrien Duport.

Throughout the world these events produced convulsive effects. In England a profound reaction occurred against everything French or liberal; and this reaction soon made itself felt in a filial America, where, although there had been a political separation, a social connection had been strongly maintained by upper-class elements. The Federalists now sought for means to quarantine France, to prevent the republican infection from spreading, and even to stir up a war against France. When in February, 1793, England and the new French republic declared war on each other, a deep split occurred in American sentiment. The propertied classes took the side of England; the masses came out with enthusiasm for France. Simultaneously there appeared a new and wider chasm between Hamilton's ideas and Jefferson's.

CHAPTER 38

THORNY CITIZEN FROM FRANCE

WHEN IN 1793 Edmond C. Genêt, young minister from revolutionary France, came ashore at Charleston, South Carolina, and bowed graciously before the exulting crowds that greeted him, a reaction and inflammation took place as violent as that which follows the injection of an alien substance into an unstable body. The Federalists were frightened by the riotous enthusiasm of American crowds for the new envoy from France; and they tried to find a way to halt Genêt's triumphant tour up the coast to Philadelphia. In this Jefferson saw the hope of Hamilton and of the British minister, Hammond, to use American neutrality for British purposes. "H. is panic-struck," he wrote, meaning Hamilton, "if we refuse our breach to every kick which Great Britain may choose to give it." He declared Hamilton's easy surrender to British views would "invite and merit habitual insults."

At Charleston Genêt showed no hurry to present himself to the government at Philadelphia; he had plenty of other business to attend to. There were privateers to outfit for raids on British shipping; brevet commissions to be issued to enthusiastic young Americans who wanted to fight for new France; and streams of admiring delegations to receive.

Genêt maintained that treaties between France and America obtained by Franklin were still in force; that the United States was the legal as well as natural ally of France; and that the United States was now receiving an opportunity to return her moral debt to France, particularly in allowing the use of American ports to French ships. Alexander Hamilton replied that the French treaties had been made with the French king, now deposed and dead; that it was a question

200

whether the treaties "ought not to be deemed temporarily and provisionally suspended"; and that American gratitude to France could be overdone. He even argued that men as individuals have one code of morality while men as governments have another. "The rule of morality in this respect," he argued, "is not precisely the same between nations as between individuals."

This reasoning made Jefferson impatient. He contended that the treaties in question had been made with the French nation, not the king, and hence remained fully binding even through changes in systems of government. Though Jefferson was inclined by every personal sentiment to be on France's side, Genêt's arrival and subsequent actions were more harassing to him than he was at first willing to admit. As secretary of state he had to pass upon case after case of alleged neutrality violations, with "Citizen" Genêt pushing him on one hand and the Federalists assailing him on the other. His correspondence with Genêt, at first warm and cordial, gradually cooled until spicules of ice lay between every two lines.

The trouble was that the Frenchman, no doubt carried away by the huzzas that greeted every personal appearance, lost all sense of tact and finesse; and instead of nursing his early advantage, pressed it and strained it until it cracked. Alexander Hamilton and his circle even put out a report that Genêt had threatened to appeal to the nation over the head of President Washington, who on Genêt's reaching Philadelphia, had received him coolly. This Genêt denied, but the report reduced his popularity.

Jefferson might have come to peaceful terms with Genêt, had he not discovered that the French government had given instructions under which the envoy was opening intrigues in the Mississippi valley and at the river's mouth. Indeed, Jefferson's friend, Colonel W. S. Smith, John Adams's son-in-law and secretary of the American legation at London, informed him that French officials had "told him they meant to begin the attack on Spain's possessions at the mouth of the Mississippi, and to sweep along the bay of Mexico, southwardly, and that they would have no objections to our incorporating into our government the two Floridas." [1]

To Jefferson the Mississippi valley was sacred ground, and in his

[1] *American Historical Review,* III, 655.

mind he had already dedicated it to the American union. He had long dreamed of adding to the United States all the territory west of the river as far as the Pacific Ocean. Judge of his feelings when he realized that revolutionary France might prove to be more of a menace in the West than even the British were. Hence Genêt, instead of being a welcomed friend, was a man to be watched. It can be surmised that Jefferson now carefully looked into Genêt's background and past.

Genêt had been one of Count de Vergennes's young assistants in the French foreign office, but there is no evidence he ever met Jefferson there. Brissot de Warville, Girondin leader and author in 1791 of *Nouveau Voyage dans les Etats-Unis,* had recommended him for the difficult post in America, for Genêt had showed superior ability in a dozen different fields. Vulgar history and prejudiced historians have managed to paint him in clownish colors, making it appear that he was an arrogant revolutionary with a raffish past and an impossible personality. On the contrary, he was a scholar, a linguist, a diplomat brought up in the old school and a man of scientific tastes. As a Girondin liberal, he believed that the American and French Revolutions had elevated mankind upon a new and glorious level. He came to America apparently with every good intention; his chief mistake was to read his instructions too thoroughly and to obey his superiors with an annoying and too enthusiastic fidelity.

One of his sisters was Madame Campan, companion of Marie Antoinette; the other sisters had made glamorous marriages; while Genêt was proving himself to be a boy prodigy, helping his father make official translations from English into French of papers on American liberty written by Benjamin Franklin and other members of the American mission. The young Edmond Charles was not yet twenty-one when he was attached to official missions in Germany, Vienna and England. At length he was sent to join the French embassy at Catherine II's court in Russia. There, when he endorsed the positions of the moderate *Patriotes* in France headed by Barnave, Duport and Lameth, who had attended Lafayette and Jefferson's dinner party, he was dismissed. He returned to Paris just in time to hear it proposed that "Capet," as Louis XVI was now called, be exiled to Louisiana with Genêt as his escort. Then came his appointment to the United States when he was just thirty years old. It was 1793, the year of the Terror.

From Charleston Genêt wrote home of the flattering welcome he had received from Governor Moultrie and the people of South Carolina while the aristocrats and partisans of England raged. In reply he received a warning of "the cold character" of the Americans which could be warmed up only by degrees. In other dispatches this "cold character" was emphasized, with hints that whisky might be a useful thawing agent.[2] From Philadelphia Genêt wrote: "My journey has been a succession of uninterrupted civic feasts and my entry into Philadelphia a triumph for liberty"; and in a following dispatch he added he was heeding his instructions thus: "I am stirring up the Canadians to free themselves from the yoke of England, I am arming the Kentuckians, and I am preparing by sea an expedition which will support their descent on New Orleans."

It was these activities, when they became known, that caused Jefferson's recoil; and it was the threat of these concealed "operations," as Genêt called them, that caused President Washington to warn Americans to give aid to neither France nor Britain.

"I told him," wrote Jefferson of Genêt, "that his enticing officers and soldiers from Kentucky to go against Spain, was really putting a halter about their necks, for they would assuredly be hung if they commenced hostilities against a nation at peace with the United States. That leaving out that article I did not care that insurrections might be excited in Louisiana."

However, to show his good will, Jefferson wrote for André Michaux, the French botanist then living at Charleston, who was one of Genêt's agents, a letter of introduction to Isaac Shelby, governor of Kentucky and one of the heroes of King's Mountain. These activities went on during the summer of 1793, the summer in which the Jacobins overthrew the Girondists in France. It was also the summer that brought an epidemic of yellow fever to Philadelphia, which slew hundreds of people and even laid low Alexander Hamilton and his wife. By the autumn of that year Jefferson had become exasperated with Genêt because of his defiant handling of French privateers

---

2 *Correspondence of the French Ministers to the United States, 1771-1777,* ed. F. J. Turner.

in American ports and finally burst out: "His conduct is indefensible by the most furious Jacobin. I only wish our countrymen may distinguish between him and his nation."

Jefferson's countrymen at first did not make these distinctions. They were convinced that France's declaration for liberty, equality and fraternity was simply an extension of the United States' declaration for life, liberty and the pursuit of happiness; and shouting these slogans impartially, they rioted up and down the streets of Philadelphia, frightening respectable citizens and causing John Adams to arm his servants; they even clamored before Washington's door. The official chill that affected Genêt's reception by Washington was at length felt in France and led to official warnings to Gênet to "treat with the government and not a portion of the people," and to be on his guard against alienating men useful to France. Genêt felt himself losing ground. He even criticized Jefferson in his home letters as "a man endowed with good qualities but weak enough to sign what he does not think and defend officially measures which he condemns in conversations and anonymous writings."

It was characteristic of Jefferson that in the middle of vexations concerning the behavior of Citizen Genêt and debates about international law, he could pause to write to James Madison on ploughs ("Have you ever," he wrote, "taken notice of Tull's horse-houghing plough?"), and to exchange letters with President Washington on the progress of agriculture in Virginia.

"Good husbandry," he wrote the President, "with us consists in abandoning Indian corn and tobacco, tending small grain, some red clover following, and endeavoring to have, while the lands are at rest, a spontaneous cover of white clover. . . . With moderate management of it, I can affirm that the James river lowgrounds, with the cultivation of small grain, will never be exhausted; because we know that under that cultivation we must now and then take them down with Indian corn, or they become, as they were originally, too rich to bring wheat."

A month later he followed this letter to Washington with a letter in which he announced he was leaving the administration. "At the close . . . of the ensuing month of September," he said, "I shall beg leave to retire to scenes of greater tranquillity." But when September came around, Philadelphia was in mortal combat with the yellow fever and Jefferson was unable to go home. He withdrew his residence to a country cottage on the banks of the Schuylkill river, near Gray's Ferry. To Martha Randolph he wrote concerning her sister Polly:

"She passes two or three days in the week with me under the trees, for I never go into the house but at the hour of bed. I never before knew the full value of trees. My house is entirely embosomed in high plane-trees, with good grass below; and under them I breakfast, write, read, and receive my company. What would I not give that the trees planted nearest round the house at Monticello were full-grown!" The sight of Bartram's and Gray's gardens across the river was also a comfort to him. At this spot President Washington came to see him, urging him to remain in office; but Jefferson would not consent beyond January 1.

Another shady spot beloved of Jefferson was Dr. George Logan's home at Stenton, then outside the city near Wayne Junction, but later a part of Philadelphia. Here Jefferson used to come to talk with the good doctor and his lively wife, the former Deborah Norris. Her memoir recalled that the secretary of state "used frequently to visit us in a social and intimate manner, sometimes with small parties whose company was agreeable to one another and sometimes alone. . . . He abounded in anecdotes of great interest."

Here, too, Jefferson sometimes had informal meetings with Citizen Genêt to argue with him concerning certain points.

Citizen Genêt became harder to deal with. He wrote home that the American people desired war alongside France despite "the base idolatry of the great capitalists and the fat merchants for the English constitution." He called the President a "Fayettetist" and "old Washington." Genêt convinced Jefferson that his appointment as minister for revolutionary France had been "calamitous." Indeed, the secretary of state wrote to Madison labeling Genêt as "hot headed, all imagination, no judgment, passionate, disrespectful and even indecent towards the P[resident]."

At last came the matter of the ship *Little Sarah,* a French prize converted into a privateer. Would she put to sea regardless of neutrality? Washington and Hamilton feared she might. Jefferson was sure she would not while Washington was absent at Mount Vernon. Washington returned to Philadelphia, and without warning the *Little Sarah* sailed. A cabinet meeting was called that lasted for two days. It was decided to demand Genêt's recall.

That ended the episode for the United States government. But not for Genêt. He was now in a dangerous position. He had no standing in America, and if he returned to France he would have no standing there. Indeed, if he went home his life might be in danger, for his friends among the Girondists were gone and the Terror was running under the iron hand of the Committee of Public Safety. That body took note of his recall, denounced him for "criminal conduct," and ordered his arrest. But Genêt submitted to no arrests. He sold his furniture and effects, moved to New York, and bought a farm near Jamaica, Long Island, intending, as he later wrote Jefferson, to bury himself "in retirement and silence; to meditate upon the great revolutions of the world; to try to penetrate the secrets of nature; and above all to isolate myself from the intrigues of courts and the discouraging cabals of people."

In time he became an American citizen and took an American girl of twenty as wife—Cornelia Clinton, daughter of Governor George Clinton, of New York State. Genêt long outlived Washington and Jefferson, whom he never quite forgave, and died respected and not a little honored for his interest in civic life and scientific research.

While Jefferson was busy with these battles and carrying on his duties as secretary of state, he found the time to enter anonymously a design for the President's house in the Federal City, later called the White House; for architectural drawing was one of his diversions in times of loneliness or stress. His design was rejected; fortunately, we think, for his building would have had a rather top-heavy dome and too numerous columns in the Palladian style. His drawing, 20¾" by 17½", still exists in the Fine Arts Division of the Library of Congress. The winner of the contest was young James Hoban of Charleston, South Carolina, an Irishman from county Kilkenny, whose design is supposed to have been based on the plan of the Duke of

Leinster's house in Dublin. Hoban went to Washington to work on other government buildings, including the Capitol, and was one of the few architects at the capital who did not harass Jefferson with protruding egotisms and gnawing jealousies.

CHAPTER 39

OUT OF OFFICE

GENÊT IN DEPARTING left behind two legacies, in the form of terms of speech, which had a determining influence on American political discussion. These two terms were "democratic" and "capitalist." Legend says Genêt introduced both words to common speech in Philadelphia; the first in naming the Democratic Societies that soon mushroomed all over the country and were denounced by Washington and the Federalists; and the second in assailing the influence which, allied with British diplomacy, constantly tried, he said, to block his efforts. In return the Federalists introduced the counter words "Jacobin" and "leveler" as terms of political loathing. From now on, the Jeffersonians had to meet those epithets plastered upon their every channel of activity. But at the moment Jefferson, fagged by his secretarial harassments, had but one thought—to get away. He wrote to Martha:

"Maria and I are scoring off the weeks which separate us from you. They wear off slowly. . . . My blessings to your little ones; love to you all, and friendly howd'ye's to my neighbors."

It was the fall of the year before he was able to leave Philadelphia with its fevers, both physical and spiritual, and hasten down for a Monticello holiday. He started back from there in November, 1793, overtaking President Washington at Baltimore and traveling with him to Germantown, to which village Congress had moved, because of the plague in Philadelphia. He complained to Martha of being "fleeced of seventy odd dollars" in getting over the road from Fredericksburg, Virginia. "The fever in Philadelphia," he added, "has so much abated as to have almost disappeared," but lodgings were scarce.

"As a great favor, I have got a bed in the corner of the public room of a tavern," he said, where he had to pay "four to six or eight dollars a week for cuddies without a bed."

This was the King of Prussia Tavern at what was later 5516-18-20 Germantown Avenue.[1] Later in the month he was able to leave this discomfort for a house at 5275-7 Germantown Avenue, whence he wrote joyfully to James Madison who, together with James Monroe, was his constant care: "I have got good lodgings for Monroe and yourself—that is to say, a good room with a fire-place and two beds, in a pleasant and convenient position, with a quiet family. They will breakfast you, but you must mess in a tavern."

Now came some long-delayed personal messages from France through Angelica Church in England. First came a note from her delivered by the Viscount de Noailles, a cousin of Lafayette. Noailles was despised by Genêt as a hanger-on of royalty. Jefferson answered Angelica eagerly. "You recall to my mind remembrances which are very dear to it," he said. "What is become of Madame de Corny? . . . Where is Mrs. Cosway? I have heard she was become a mother; but is the new object to absorb all her affections?"

Again came a letter from Angelica containing a message from Lafayette, now imprisoned by the Austrians. "Your letter," Jefferson answered, "gives me the first information that our dear friend Madame de Corny has been, as to her fortune, among the victims of the times. . . . And Madam Cosway in a convent! I knew that to much goodness of heart she joined enthusiasm and religion; but I thought that very enthusiasm would have prevented her from shutting up her adoration of the God of the universe within the walls of a cloister; that she would rather have sought the *mountain-top*. How happy should I be that it were mine that you, she, and Madame Corny would seek."

It cannot escape notice that, under attack as he was from the "monocrats" led by Hamilton, Jefferson kept up the correspondence in the old, familiar vein with Hamilton's sister-in-law, Mrs. Church, who was Hamilton's adorer; and that he clung to his friendships with other women of the fortunate classes. He was still a republic-man, and hated only kings, priests and nobles; he still thought the agricultural

---

[1] Dumbauld.

class was the only productive class, and still had no confidence in the mechanics and artisans of the towns. The instincts of democracy were developing up from the American people, and daily he was learning something from them and from such teachers as Paine and Freneau.

When cleansing rains and cold weather put an end to the epidemic in Philadelphia, he moved back into town, lodging first at 7th and Market Streets and then with John Francis, a Frenchman who kept a hotel near the Indian Queen on South 4th Street. On December 21, 1793, President Washington made what Jefferson described to Martha as "the last set at me to continue"; Jefferson added this belligerent note: "Our affairs with England and Spain have a turbid appearance. The letting loose the Algerines on us, which has been contrived by England, has produced peculiar irritation. I think Congress will indemnify themselves by high duties on all articles of British importation. If this should produce war, though not wished for, it seems not to be feared."

This note illustrates one of the gaps in his comprehension. At this stage he seems to have had little grasp of the fact that economics was taking charge of politics; and small understanding that, between nations as well as between individuals, to retaliate for an evil by another is to introduce two evils for one; and that high duties lead to more high duties, and hence multiply economic iniquity. Likewise he failed to see that the interference of politics in economics produces abortions or worse. Here is a clear foreshadowing of one of Jefferson's worst political mistakes—the embargo in the war with England which his own nationalism helped to bring on.

In December, 1793, he sent to Washington his formal letter of resignation. "I carry into my retirement," he said, "a lively sense of your goodness." In reply Washington praised his "integrity and talents . . . confirmed by the fullest experience." Just after the new year, 1794, Jefferson returned to Monticello and to the eight other farms comprising his landed estate. He felicitated himself that after ten years of battle he was forever done with public life. After a look around, he wrote a depressed letter to Washington saying the "ravages of overseers" had brought on his lands "a degree of degradation far beyond what I had expected."

It was fortunate for his peace of mind that Jefferson failed to realize that his cultivated land would never completely recover. It had
been all but ruined by two factors: careless slave labor misdirected
by ignorant overseers, and a system of cash-cropping that often produced neither sufficient cash nor crops. Fortunate, too, it was for
Jefferson that he could not foresee how this depleted soil would
affect the being whom he loved better than all other things in the
world—Martha Randolph, his oldest child and most faithful helper.
This year was to see Martha as the mother of three children, and
Polly as a singularly lovely girl of seventeen, nubile and dreaming
of marriage.

With his daughters near him, Jefferson was almost completely
happy; and his cup ran over when he could put on a farmer's coat
and begin work on the garden and orchard and on the house, which
he decided to remodel. To a prospective new overseer at $120 a year
he wrote this heretical letter, attacking the very foundations of Southern farming:

"The farm is of about 5 or 600 acres of cleared land, very hilly,
originally as rich as any highlands in the world, but much worried
by Indian corn & tobacco. It is still however very strong, & remarkably friendly to wheat & rye. These will be my first object. Next will
be grasses, cattle, sheep, & the introduction of potatoes for the use of
the farm, instead of Indian corn, in as great a degree as possible. . . .
I have long banished tobacco, & wish to do the same by Indian corn
in a great degree. . . . It is usual with us to give a fixed allowance
of pork; I shall much rather substitute beef and mutton, as I consider pork to be as destructive an article in a farm as Indian corn." [2]

Thus did Jefferson plan to do battle with that dry rot of the land
of which his friend the Duke de la Rochefoucauld later left this
picture of the country lying between Richmond and Petersburg:
"These fields are never manured, hardly ever are they ploughed;
and it seldom happens that their owners for two successive years
exact from them these scanty crops. . . . The country . . . everywhere exhibits the features of laziness, of ignorance, and consequently of poverty."

Though in 1794 Jefferson was sometimes bedridden by illness,

---

[2] Massachusetts Historical Collection, quoted by Betts, *Jefferson's Garden Book.*

chiefly from rheumatism, he was cheerful in his outdoor work, and when Washington sounded him as to his rejoining the cabinet, he told Edmund Randolph: "No circumstances, my dear sir, will ever tempt me to engage in anything public."

He thought he meant it; indeed, his ailments made him think he was becoming an old man about to relinquish "the tedium of life." Actually, he was only fifty-one, with the great days of his life yet to come.

Jefferson's remedy for worn-out land was rotation of crops, and he had some correspondence on the subject with John Taylor of Caroline, who was a much more experienced farmer. "You keep half your lands in culture, the other half at nurse; so I propose to do," he wrote. "Your scheme indeed requires only four years & mine six; but the proportion of labor and rest is the same." In a long letter to Taylor written near the close of 1794 he foreshadowed the mold-board plough that became one of his most famous inventions. He said:

"I have imagined and executed a mold-board which may be mathematically demonstrated to be perfect, as far as perfection depends on mathematical principles. . . . It is on the principle of two wedges combined at right angles, the first in the direct line of the furrow to raise the turf gradually, the other across the furrow to turn it over gradually. For both these purposes the wedge is the instrument of least resistance." [3] He also wrote happily to his old mentor, George Wythe: "I ever wish to have opportunity of enjoying your society, knowing your fondness for figs, I have daily wished you could have partaken of ours this year. . . . We are now living in a brick-kiln, for my house, in it's present state, is nothing better. I shall recommence my operations on it the next summer."

Although Jefferson was unlucky in most of his plantation overseers, he was fortunate enough to find a good gardener named Bailey who served him many years "for £15 a year & 500 lb pork, with bread for his family."

Even with the best fortune, however, Jefferson realized that three or four years would be required to bring his farms back to profitable

---

[3] *Garden Book.*

production. Hence, in order to earn some ready money, he set up, in disregard of his own warnings against industry, a plantation factory of nails. "My new trade of nail-making," he wrote, "is to me in this country what an additional title of nobility or the ensigns of a new order are in Europe." He was for a time an employer of child labor. His first workers were a dozen Negro boys aged from ten to sixteen. He was his own superintendent and almost from the first he began to make a profit on which he could get along while he was alone, for Martha and her husband spent the winter at the Randolph farm, Edgehill, while Polly went to the Eppes place. Jefferson's enjoyment of his labors continued throughout 1795, and he was still in a pleased mood when on June 1, he wrote General Henry Knox:

"I live on my horse from morning to night almost. Intervals are filled up with attentions to a nailery I carry on. I rarely look into a book, and more rarely take up a pen. I have proscribed newspapers, not taking a single one, nor scarcely ever looking into one. My next reformation will be to allow neither pen, ink, nor paper to be kept on the farm."

CHAPTER 40

VICE-PRESIDENT

To THE STUDENT of Jefferson's career and papers, it is odd to note how in one moment he is protesting his hatred of public life and his devotion to his farm, his family and his books; and how in the next moment he is accepting an office that will take him back into the very center of politics. Jefferson had been returned to the rural peace of Monticello scarcely more than three years when he was offered the vice-presidency of the United States, and he at once accepted.

For this acceptance he probably had more than one reason. In the first place, there was absent at Monticello the one element which could have anchored him there—the society of his two daughters. Without their presence, Monticello was only a camp (it was in process of being remodeled), not a home. In the second place, Washington was leaving the presidency, and without his hold on the respect of the people, the infant republic might be expected to reel and rock. Third was the fact that Alexander Hamilton was also quitting the government, leaving a vacuum into which interests even more hostile to Jefferson's ideas might rush in. Fourth was John Jay's treaty with England which had sent the "Anglo-men" into ecstasies and convinced them they would soon control United States policy. Fifth was Jefferson's opinion that never since 1783 had affairs at the capital (still in Philadelphia) worn "so gloomy an aspect"; and he probably could not fight off the temptation to get back into a position whence he could occasionally give the national helm a turn. And finally there is the possibility that he needed the money.

To friends who doubted whether he would regard the vice-presidency as in accord with his dignity, he wrote that he had been for years junior to John Adams and would not mind being so again;

President Thomas Jefferson by Gilbert Stuart. This is the portrait preferred by his daughters

William Clark, the genial "Billy," who accompanied Lewis, by C. W. Peale

Meriwether Lewis, Jefferson's secretary who led the expedition to the Pacific, by C. W. Peale

while to his friend and fellow-scientist, Dr. Benjamin Rush, he said: "It will give me philosophical evenings in the winter and rural days in summer." He even asked his friends to support Adams for the presidency, although he knew that Adams despised common men and feared democracy. In this he may have been governed by the knowledge that Hamilton had been secretly knifing Adam's candidacy; and by the belief that Adams's barks against rule by the people would be worse than his actual bites. At any rate, March, 1796, saw Jefferson riding back into Philadelphia in his carriage, thus renewing a tie with political life that was to last for thirteen years. With him was a box full of mastodon bones which he was taking to the American Philosophical Society, of which he had lately been elected president. Old bones and politics—these were two things that Jefferson could not resist.

Hardly was Jefferson installed again in Francis's hotel than he found himself the target of a new hurricane of abuse. In April, 1796, he had written from Monticello to Philip Mazzei in Tuscany a long and rambling letter of news, comment and gossip in which, after asking his old Tuscan friend to "put a few seeds in every letter you may write to me," he had included this view of contemporary politics:

"In place of that noble love of liberty & republican government which carried us triumphantly thro the war, an Anglican monarchial, & aristocratical party has sprung up, whose avowed object is to draw over us the substance, as they have already done the forms, of the British government. The main body of our citizens, however, remain true to their republican principles; the whole landed interest is republican, and so is a great mass of talents. Against us are the Executive, the Judiciary, two out of three branches of the legislature, all the officers of the government, all who want to be officers, all timid men who prefer the calm of despotism to the boisterous sea of liberty, British merchants & Americans trading on British capitals, speculators and holders in the banks & public funds, a contrivance invented for the purposes of corruption, & for assimilating us in all things to the rotten as well as the sound parts of the British model. It would give you a fever were I to name to you the apostates who have gone over to these heresies, men who were Samsons in the field and Solomons in the council, but who have had their heads shorn by the harlot England."

Mazzei allowed these comments to appear in translation in a Florence, Italy, newspaper, whence they were copied in French by the Paris *Moniteur,* and from there they were reproduced over all the American states. The result was violent criticism from the Federalists, particularly because of the reference to Samsons and Solomons, which they proclaimed was a barb aimed at George Washington.

A coolness had already opened between the two men. To Madison, Jefferson declared sardonically that "the bank and paper-mania," by which he no doubt meant the currency inflation which was swelling all prices, was producing ruin, and that "the President is fortunate to get off just as the bubble is bursting, leaving others to hold the bag." To Archibald Stuart he wrote early in 1797 that Washington's "mind has been so long used to unlimited applause that it could not brook contradiction, or even advice offered unasked. To advice, when asked, he is very open. I have long thought therefore it was best for the republican interest to soothe him by flattering where they could approve his measures, & to be silent where they disapprove."

This letter to Mazzei contained certain overstatements; possibly they were due to Jefferson's long-suppressed resentment against President Washington for having so often sided with Hamilton and taken counsel from him; but in Europe it was accepted as an accurate summary of affairs in the United States. Particularly did Europe take note of Jefferson's assertion that "the whole landed interest" in the United States was republican, but that other interests, including the governmental interests, were aristocratic and pro-British. In the United States echoes of the Mazzei letter returned to plague Jefferson for many years. He tried to explain it away, but never disavowed its chief observations.

The central figure he had in mind, however, was probably not Washington but Hamilton. It was Hamilton who corresponded with Gouverneur Morris and Rufus King about setting up a government on "foundations much firmer than have yet been devised," and Hamilton who "trusted that in the changes and chances of time we should be involved in some war" that might change constitutional provisions and practices. Jefferson's suspicions of the pro-British parties of this period may appear at this distance to be strained and overstated; yet when we see what conceptions later influenced Aaron Burr, we cannot say he was wide of the target.

In the middle of 1797 Jefferson wrote his daughter Maria (this name by now had displaced her earlier names of Mary and Polly):

"I feel the desire of never separating from you grow daily stronger, for nothing can compensate with me the want of your society."

On the very heels of this, he got a letter from Martha Randolph announcing Maria's engagement to John (Jack) Wayles Eppes, her cousin and long her playmate at Eppington plantation in Maria's happy days before her father summoned her to Paris. This news, though it deprived Jefferson of a beloved child, brought him great relief, for he could now see the family fireside "formed into a group, no one member of which has a fibre in their composition which can ever produce any jarring or jealousies." He wrote to Martha and Maria long and fatherly letters. To the former he said:

"I receive with inexpressible pleasure the information your letter contained," and declared Maria could not have chosen a partner more in accord with his wishes. "I become more and more disgusted with the jealousies, the hatred, and the rancorous and malignant passions of this scene," he added. "I have seen enough of political honors to know that they are but splendid torments."

To Maria he wrote an essay of advice on matrimony in which appeared a vein of his Stoic philosophy. These are extracts:

"Harmony in the married state is the very first object to be aimed at. Nothing can preserve affections uninterrupted but a firm resolution never to differ in will."

.   .   .   .   .   .

"How light . . . is the sacrifice of any other wish when weighed against the affections of one with whom we are to pass our whole life!"

.   .   .   .   .

"When we see ourselves in a situation which must be endured and gone through, it is best to make up our minds to it." [This concerned the misfortune of a sister who had married a ne'er-do-well drunk-ard.]

.   .   .   .   .

"Other sources of discontent . . . are the little cross-purposes of husband and wife, in common conversation, a disposition in either to criticise and question whatever the other says, a desire always to demonstrate and make him feel himself in the wrong, and especially in company. Nothing is so goading."

.   .   .   .   .

"What is the use of rectifying him if the thing be unimportant; and if important, let it pass for the present, and wait a softer moment."

.   .   .   .   .

"The article of dress is perhaps that in which economy is least to be recommended."

.   .   .   .   .

"If a debt is once contracted by a farmer, it is never paid but by a sale."

.   .   .   .   .

This last observation was in connection with what Jefferson called "the unprofitable condition of Virginia estates in general," which made it "next to impossible for the holder to avoid ruin." Here was a clear foreshadowing of a state of affairs that gave Jefferson, not only then but years later, days of anxiety. The tide was running against the great landed estates; and their owners, many of them friends of Jefferson, died in debt and bequeathed debt to their children. The Page family with its great house, Rosewell, was one of the victims of this changed economy which siphoned off the wealth from the countryside and channeled it into the towns; and Jefferson's boyhood friend, John Page, once governor of Virginia, was glad to accept a small paying office from Jefferson when president.

Repeatedly Jefferson wrote in his letters to his daughters of the "envy, hatred, malice, revenge" and the like that characterized the political storms in which he was living; to Edward Rutledge of South

Carolina he declared that "men who have been intimate all their lives, cross the street to avoid meeting, and turn their heads another way, lest they should be obliged to touch their hats"; and to Thomas Pinckney, also of South Carolina, he said: "The good are rare enough at best. There is no reason to subdivide them by artificial dikes."

These quarrels and Jefferson's pessimism were due to a general fear that the United States would soon be pushed into a profitless war with England or France or perhaps both. "We shall now either be forced into a war, or have our commerce and navigation at least totally annihilated, and the produce of our farms for some years left to rot on our hands." Finally, Jefferson's feelings burst out in a letter to his old friend, Elbridge Gerry:

"I can scarcely withhold myself from joining in the wish of Silas Deane [once agent of the American colonies in France] that there were an ocean of fire between us and the old world." When in June, 1797, Gerry was appointed one of the trio of envoys extraordinary to France, Jefferson begged him to accept. The other two were General C. C. Pinckney of South Carolina and John Marshall of Virginia, Jefferson's kinsman. These three were soon to become the famous American participants in the XYZ case.

At this period Jefferson wrote letters to his friends with great caution, for he had reason to believe his mail was being opened and copied. In this same year, 1797, there was the beginning of a great economic depression, the nation's first taste of the reactions of mercantilism.

"The bankruptcies here continue," wrote Jefferson to Madison. "The prison is full of the most reputable merchants. . . . Prices have fallen greatly."

By the middle of 1797 Napoleon Bonaparte's victories in Europe drew this comment from Jefferson to Madison: "Nothing less than the miraculous string of events which have taken place, to wit, the victories of the Rhine and Italy, peace with Austria, bankruptcy of England, mutiny in her fleet . . . could have cooled the British faction." He added in a letter to Aaron Burr that "the executive temper was for war" on France. "I consider the future character of our republic as in the air; indeed its future fortune will be in the air, if war is made on us by France, & if Louisiana becomes a Gallo-American colony."

With other correspondents Jefferson repeatedly discussed the possibility of an invasion of England by Napoleon. "I do not indeed wish," wrote Jefferson, "to see any nation have a form of government forced on them; but if it is to be done, I should rejoice at its being a free one."

CHAPTER 41

DRAMATIC YEAR

WHEN 1798, a year of fierce drama, came, Jefferson began to shape a policy and draw together an organization that would enable the scattered Republicans to meet the aggressive onslaughts of the Federalists.

The latter had fostered an attempt to put down the Democratic Societies; had applauded Washington's dispatch of an army of fifteen thousand men to crush the Pennsylvania farmers who rose in the Whisky Rebellion in a campaign which Alexander Hamilton, who had always nursed a secret hankering after military fame, wanted to lead; had supported John Jay's execrated treaty with Great Britain; and finally had demanded that the cold war with France be converted into a shooting one. When in the spring of this year President John Adams disclosed that his trio of envoys to France had been asked for bribes and tributes by so-called agents of the French Directory known only as X, Y and Z, thus causing General C. C. Pinckney to declare dramatically, "Millions for defense, not a cent for tribute," the nation burst into flame, especially, Jefferson noted, in "the trading towns." A navy was created; the army was enlarged; the newspapers screeched; political arguments became obscene and raucous. Jefferson, under constant abuse for his peaceful sentiments, tried to be calm, but had spells of depression when he saw the nation so easily pushed toward war.

"I never was more homesick or heart-sick," he wrote his son-in-law, Jack Eppes.

When the American commissioners got back home, John Marshall, their chief spokesman, became the hero of the day as a repeller of XYZ; and won a popularity that eventually carried him into the head seat in the United States Supreme Court. Jefferson, however, was skeptical of the politics being played. "You know what a wicked use has been made of the French negotiation," he wrote Edmund Pendleton, "and particularly the X.Y.Z. dish cooked up by Marshall, where the swindlers are made to appear as the French government." Almost from this moment Marshall and Jefferson became enemies, and this enmity had not abated when the one had become chief justice and the other president of the United States.

The national propaganda machine now constantly portrayed revolutionary France as evil incarnate; while England was never aught but sturdy virtue. The mercantile or war party believed it had a conflict with France due when an unofficial envoy suddenly intervened. This was Jefferson's friend, Dr. George Logan of Stenton, outside Philadelphia, where Jefferson had often been a guest. Logan took it on himself to go to Europe and singlehandedly try to avert what seemed to him to be an impending but useless war. Jefferson at the moment was exerting every effort to circumvent the Federalists in their support of the war hawks; was Logan's voyage one of his devices? Logan always denied he was any man's agent; but that Jefferson was privy to his visit to France is indicated by the fact that he supplied Logan with letters of introduction in Europe. Logan landed at Hamburg where he got in touch with Lafayette, who procured his admission to France.

In Paris, Logan easily obtained interviews with high officials in cluding Merlin of the French Directory and the cynical Talleyrand, Napoleon's finance minister, who was suspected of having inspired the French agents in the XYZ affair. Everywhere Logan found evidence that France, aware of its previous haste and truculence, was anxious to avoid war with America and was willing to make concessions to American wishes. Armed with conciliating messages, he returned to America; but if he dreamed the road to peace and understanding would now be short, the good doctor was violently awakened.

He made the mistake, in the first place, of making his first report to Timothy Pickering, the sour successor to and pupil of Alexander Hamilton as secretary of state. Pickering showed Logan no sympathy, but George Washington, to whom Logan then reported at Trenton, showed him even less. Both Pickering and Washington were no doubt influenced by the outcry which filled the Federalist papers, saying that Logan had "meddled," that he had pretended to have an authority which had never been given him, and that he must be punished as an impostor. It was even charged in Congress that he had memorialized the French Directory with a bogus official address. Logan was able to disprove all these assertions and to show that he had gone abroad to give his own views at his own expense. But Logan's friends were not able to prevent the passage in an atmosphere of hysteria of the Logan Act, which forbade any citizen to engage in "correspondence or intercourse" with any agent of a foreign government in relation to disputes with the United States.

At this point it might be well to search for an explanation of the enmity, replacing the mutual admiration of Franklin's time, that had suddenly arisen between those two young and powerful republics, France and the United States. First, we can trace it to a natural reaction from the excessive fondness of the two nations during revolutionary days. Second, there was the influence of the fright felt by England when it appeared that the upheaval in France might affect thrones and royal governments elsewhere—a fright that was soon communicated to the conservative and propertied classes of America. For other explanations we may look to Bernard Faÿ's *L'Esprit Révolutionnaire en France et aux Etats-Unis à la fin du XVIII° Siècle* published in Paris in 1925.

He thinks French judgment of the United States was based on the three great American personalities known in Europe—Franklin, Washington and Jefferson. France forgot that many Americans were merchants, and she could not understand it when the United States laid a tax on French ships entering American ports. France's reply was to shut down on the American fish oils and tobacco for which Jefferson had so long toiled in Paris. Added was the influence of those Americans, hostile to revolutionary France, who dreamed of forging an alliance between Great Britain and the United States; among these were Gouverneur Morris and Alexander Hamilton, both scorners of democracy. A final factor was the vari-colored and gross exaggerations of the British press, and of the American press which frequently copied it, in regard to the more violent phases of the French Revolution. Concerning the violence in Paris and some of the provinces, Jefferson almost alone among highly placed Americans was able to see it in perspective, thus:

"In the struggle which was necessary, many guilty persons fell without the form of trial, and with them some innocent. These I deplore as much as anybody, and shall deplore some of them to the day of my death. But . . . was ever such a prize won with so little innocent blood?"

Jefferson's opinions, however, were not able to heal the breach between the two republics. The influence of trade and finance in the Eastern cities was strong; merchants and bankers constantly strove for closer ties with Great Britain, despite British raids on American commerce and British encouragement of Indian depredations on frontier settlements. In the course of years, American support became a British asset which enabled the British Empire to expand in safety and put down formidable enemies; meanwhile France's influence in the Atlantic Ocean and the Caribbean Sea, deprived of American sympathy, declined until it fell almost to zero. These facts had a determining influence on both American and European history during and after the closing years of the eighteenth century.

CHAPTER 42

NO WAR

"GENERAL WASHINGTON HAS RESUMED his station at the head of our armies, I am second in command."

So ran an exultant letter by Alexander Hamilton to Rufus King, the United States minister to England, while the war fever mounted. King at that time was in constant contact in London with Sebastian Francisco de Miranda, Venezuela soldier of fortune; and, in association with the British government, was encouraging Miranda in the hope that both the United States and Britain would help him realize his dream of overturning Spain's power in South America. Miranda's scheme included an army to be furnished by the United States while Britain would supply ships and prestige.

Hamilton was in correspondence with him through King; for, dazzled by his own dreams of military glory, Hamilton had virtually given up his New York law practice to place himself at the head of the war party. He had obtained appointment as inspector general of the army which was being readied to fight France—and, he hoped, Spain—and was now not only virtually the active commander, since Washington had retired, but the virtual secretary of war in place of the inept McHenry. Hamilton was in charge of the northern department; General C. C. Pinckney held the southern command; while the western recruiting was looked after by General James Wilkinson, who later became a figure in the Burr conspiracy.

Wilkinson was a brigadier, but although once he had been a party to the Revolutionary War cabal aimed at General Washington, Hamilton, although admitting "doubts" had been entertained about him, urged Washington to make him a major general. Meantime he wrote: "Besides eventual security against invasion, we ought certainly to look to the possession of the Floridas and Louisiana, and we ought to squint at South America."

Here, then, were not only the ingredients of a war, but the germs of an aggressive imperialism. Lucky was the United States to escape this crisis with its integrity intact; for the war party might have taken the nation down the road upon which Europe, chained to its militarisms, had met disaster upon disaster.

"With regard to the enterprise in question," Hamilton wrote King, "I wish it much to be undertaken, but I should be glad that the principal agency be in the United States,—they to furnish the whole land force if necessary. The command in this case would very naturally fall upon me, and I hope I shall disappoint no favorable expectation." [1]

Jefferson looked on this military activity with considerable fear, but also considerable skepticism. "Can such an army under Hamilton be disbanded?" he wrote. "I doubt it, and therefore rest my principal hope on their inability to raise anything but officers."

Jefferson guessed rightly. The war party raised plenty of officers, chiefly from Federalist families (Hamilton had to warn McHenry, the war secretary, against a too exclusive policy of appointing only "friends of the Govern't"); but the people as a whole failed to respond to the war alarms, and were not dazzled by dreams of military glory and conquest.

To go to war with Spain as a partner of Miranda was not Hamilton's only military dream. Edward Everett Hale in *Memories of a Hundred Years* wrote that Hamilton once had nursed a plan of working with Wilkinson to raise an army and float down the Mississippi to seize New Orleans, from which base forays might be made into the Caribbean Sea and into Latin America. How often did this dream linger in the imagination of American leadership, finally to culminate and burst in the case of Aaron Burr? But destiny had no military adventures for Hamilton beyond those already bestowed on him in the Revolutionary War when he was a spruce young captain in the Third Virginia Regiment in which his fellow-officers were Lieutenant James Monroe, Captain John Marshall and Colonel Aaron Burr.

---

[1] Schachner, *Hamilton*, p. 384.

At the end of 1799 came the death of Washington. Losing Washington, Hamilton knew he could no longer soar above his contemporaries. In fact, at that moment, his fortunes sloped downward while those of his rival, Jefferson, grew daily stronger. As for Miranda, England, after encouraging his gaudiest dreams, dropped him; President Adams showed no interest in his schemes. Jefferson was much more impressed with them, for Jefferson knew that Spain's hold on her colonies was daily weakening.

As for the all-out war on France, which so many interests, financial and military, were now working for, President Adams seemed to be pushed closer to it minute by minute, until suddenly he balked. It had dawned upon him that his cabinet members were not his own liege men but Hamilton's; and that decisions were being made in which he was not being consulted. Besides, he had received assurance from France that an American envoy would be well received there. Saying nothing to his treacherous cabinet, Adams sent to the Senate the name of William Vans Murray as the envoy to France. Thus it was determined there should be peace instead of war. The war party was enraged but helpless. The Federalist leaders never forgave Adams for thus eluding their control, and though they rallied strongly, they never quite recovered from their chagrin; from this moment, indeed, their party began to go downhill, slowly at first, but finally with a slide and an ultimate crash.

"The body of the American people is substantially republican," wrote Jefferson. "But their virtuous feelings have been played on by some fact with more fiction; they have been the dupes of artful manoeuvres, and made for a moment to be willing instruments in forging chains for themselves. The Anglomen and monocrats had so artfully confounded the cause of France with that of Freedom, that both went down in the same scale."

From Philadelphia the French minister, P. A. Adet, wrote to his superiors in Paris: "Jefferson, I say, is American, and by that title cannot be sincerely our friend. An American is the born enemy of all the European peoples."

CHAPTER 43

REPRESSION AND RANCOR

THE AGITATION for more freedom and less war brought out into the open elements of the republican population whose crudeness and passion frightened the Adams government. The consequence was the enactment of the Alien and Sedition Laws which formed the major mistake and chief curse of John Adams's administration. What the infantile American democracy needed was growth, but these laws introduced repression. In some degree they were accurate reflections of the worse sides of John Adams's mind and temperament, with his hasty choler, sensitiveness to opposition and criticism, obstinate adherence to the wealthy and well-born as the only desirable elements of the population, and his sour doubts of democracy. "Remember," he once exclaimed to John Taylor of Caroline, "democracy never lasts long."

The Alien and Sedition Laws were evidence that mercantilism, which the administrations of Washington and Adams honestly sought to foster, was not interested in preserving freedom but only in advancing its own welfare. The country at large thought that such repressive laws "could not happen here"; but they did happen, and they were enforced with a rancor which amazed those persons who believed that the American traditions of tolerance and liberty were firmly established and could not be overturned.

It was assumed that the Alien Bill was aimed at the French who had come to the United States either as visitors or refugees; Jefferson believed so, for he wrote Madison: "A ship, chartered by themselves . . . will sail within about a fortnight for France, with as many as she can carry. Among these I believe will be Volney [Count de Volney, author of *The Ruins* and a libertarian known to two

228

hemispheres], who has in truth been the principal object aimed at by the law." But no sooner was the bill passed than it was seen it would threaten not only honored men like Volney and Kosciusko; Dr. Joseph Priestley, the scientist and theologian who had fled to America after being mobbed in England; and Albert Gallatin, the Swiss emigrant who later became Jefferson's efficient secretary of the treasury; but would also strike at "subversion" in the form of Irish refugees: they had been partisans of Wolfe Tone and had lately fled from the English army led by Lord Cornwallis, who had been assigned to subdue a rebelling Ireland after failing to subdue a rebelling America.

In fact, wild tales were circulated that the United Irish refugees would combine with the French emigrants to overturn the United States government; showing that when repression is once set in motion, there is no limit to the silliness it engenders. Meantime no obstacle was put in the way of dispossessed French royalists, one of whom ran away with a daughter of Jefferson's former friend, Mrs. William Bingham, who now never included Jefferson when she sent out invitations to her crowded "evenings."

But it was the Sedition Law that most aroused Jefferson's ire. It provided punishment for anyone who maligned any branch of the government; stamped the French people as enemies of the American people; and menaced with a jail term anyone who criticized or ques tioned the constitutionality—even the justice—of a government measure.

"For the present," Jefferson wrote John Taylor, "I should be for resolving the alien & sedition laws to be against the constitution & merely void, and for addressing the other States to obtain similar declarations. . . . It is a singular phenomenon, that while our State governments are the very *best in the world,* without exception or comparison, our general government has, in the rapid course of 9 or 10 years, become more arbitrary, and has swallowed more of the public liberty than even that of England."

Jefferson, like other students of government, had been under the belief that a republic was innately liberal; but years of struggle ensued before the infant American republic became a politically liberal democracy, and even then it was subject to savage reactions.

He who reads the history of this period, including the stirring year of 1798, cannot fail to be impressed by the constant recurrence of the notion of the separation, or secession, from the Union of disaffected states. No wonder that when in the next century the dreadful sixties came, the minds of the American people were already prepared to see secession arise.

In the Adams cabinet the agitation for the formation among the New England states, particularly Massachusetts and Connecticut, of a Northern Confederacy, was kept up by Timothy Pickering, the sour secretary of state; this movement was countered in Jefferson's home state by John Taylor of Caroline with a proposal that Virginia and North Carolina withdraw into a "separate mass." In a letter to Taylor, Jefferson deplored this notion.

"If," he wrote, "to rid ourselves of the present rule of Massachusetts and Connecticut, we break the Union, will the evil stop there? . . . Are we not men still to the south of that, and with all the passions of men? . . . If we reduce our Union to Virginia and North Carolina . . . they will end by breaking into their simple units. . . . Seeing that we must have somebody to quarrel with, I had rather keep our New England associates for that purpose, than to see our bickerings transferred to others."

Though Jefferson did not mention it, there was a reason for these bickerings. New England, with its ships, ports and merchants, was the capital of mercantilism and nascent nationalism; but Virginia and North Carolina were still agrarian communities. And Jefferson was their prophet. New England's prophet at the moment was John Adams, while New York and Philadelphia abided by Alexander Hamilton.

It is a testimony of the times that Jefferson felt impelled to caution Taylor, after writing him the above quoted letter, "to let nothing of mine get before the public; a single sentence got hold of by the Porcupines [the Cobbetts, Fennoes and other Federalist editors], will suffice to abuse and persecute me in their papers for months." Indeed, under the Sedition Law, Jefferson, as a critic of government, might have been not only persecuted but prosecuted.

He added something else of significance: the high price of tobacco, he confessed, had tempted him, though he realized the risk, "to go entirely into that culture." Meantime all his revised farming plans were "in abeyance."

Did the Federalists lay the foundation for their own defeat and disappearance as a national party in encouraging or conniving at the punishments and repressions that followed the passage of the Alien and Sedition Laws? At the moment the Federalists sat safely atop the American political world; yet in another two years they were hardly visible. Seldom has any party plunged so completely from zenith to nadir, and it must be assumed that the resentment of the American voters was in part, at least, responsible. The punishment of Matthew Lyon, a Vermont editor, by a jail sentence and fine led to Lyon's election to Congress by 4,576 votes to 2,444 for his nearest competitor. Anthony Haswell, another Vermont editor, received a jail sentence for sympathizing with Lyon. David Brown, a ragged Revolutionary soldier, helped to put up a liberty pole at Dedham, Massachusetts, bearing the incoherent words "No Stamp Tax, No Sedition" and went to jail for two years. Thomas Adams, a Massachusetts editor, was prosecuted not under an American statute but under the common law of England. William Duane, Irish editor, was indicted several times. Dr. Thomas Cooper, a fiery professor and judge, was the author of an article that brought upon him a heavy fine and jail sentence. James Callender, a Scotch immigrant writer, was tried and convicted for writing a pamphlet. There were other prosecutions for opinions, some of which, it is true, were reckless and violently expressed, until Jefferson suddenly declared a state's right to proclaim certain laws null and void. Here was a new and heretical doctrine.

Jefferson regarded the Alien and Sedition Laws as a test to determine what Americans would bear. If such laws endured, he expected to see presidents in office for life or a monarchy established. This gloomy idea of restored monarchy became obsessive. But neither Alexander Hamilton nor Gouverneur Morris, the leading pro-monarchists, believed that royalty could be re-established in the United States; and if any of their followers expected to see royal courts result from the formal "levees" permitted by Presidents Washington and Adams, the illusion was soon burst.

"The spirit of 1776 is not dead," wrote Jefferson in March, 1799.

"It has only been slumbering. The body of the American people is substantially republican."

Republican, yes; but not yet democratic.

Recognizing that the war fever had cooled and that thus one of the most dangerous periods in the nation's life had been safely passed, Jefferson now turned to the discussion of two salient evils in American political life. To Edmund Randolph he wrote: "Of all the doctrines which have ever been broached by the federal government, the novel one, of the common law being in force and cognizable as an existing law in their courts, is to me the most formidable." Here lay a foreshadowing of Jefferson's later attacks on usurpation by the judiciary.

The other reform, which evidently he had had in mind for some time, he now laid before John Taylor of Caroline, whose knowledge of certain economic principles he had learned to respect.

"I wish it were possible," he wrote Taylor in November, 1798, "to obtain a single amendment to our Constitution. . . . I mean an additional article taking from the federal government the power of borrowing. I now deny their power of making paper money or anything else a legal tender. I know that to pay all proper expenses within the year, would, in case of war, be hard on us. But not so hard as ten wars instead of one. For wars would be reduced in that proportion."

In this statement can be seen Jefferson's ever-present fear of the tendencies of government to encroach not only on the liberties of peoples but on their earnings. Hence his devotion to systems of checks, balances and "general equilibrium."

CHAPTER 44

VOIDS AND NULLITIES

WHEN IN 1798 it appeared that the Federalists were in too domi-
nating a position in the government easily to be overthrown, the
Republicans began to withdraw their representatives from Congress
and to concentrate them in the state legislatures; and soon it became
evident that a battle was developing between the advocates of states'
rights and those cherishing the federal power. Plans for resistance
to encroaching governments were decided upon at a meeting in
Jefferson's Monticello home where just three men were present:
Jefferson himself and the two formidable Nicholas brothers—George
and Wilson Cary.

These were the sons of Robert Carter Nicholas, the conservative
patriot, whose widow had moved her family from Tidewater to
Albemarle county. George Nicholas was the man who once had introduced in the Virginia legislature a resolution asking for an investigation of Jefferson's measures as war governor. When the proposal
was dropped, he and Jefferson became reconciled. Nicholas, who
had moved to Kentucky, became one of Jefferson's stoutest supporters. As for Wilson Cary Nicholas, he became governor of Virginia and an important factor in Jefferson's life near its end.

At this conference Jefferson agreed to "sketch" resolutions aimed
at the Federalists' "enterprises on the Constitution," which George
Nicholas would offer to the Kentucky legislature. The result was one
of the most debated documents in American political history. The
first resolution as prepared by Jefferson laid down certain conten-
tions which formed the very foundation of the Jeffersonian political
doctrine:

   1. That the United States Constitution is a compact.

2. That the several states could not admit "unlimited submission" to the central government.

3. That they had delegated to the government certain definite powers.

4. That the government as created by the compact could not be "the exclusive or final judge" of its own powers.

5. That when the government assumed undelegated powers, "its acts are unauthoritative, void, and of no force."

These fighting words were the fruit of several actions, including the spying on Jefferson's private mail and acts ("I know not," he wrote, "which mortifies me most, that I should fear to write what I think, or my country bear such a state of things"); the Alien and Sedition Laws under which civil rights were all but dead; the raising of an army ostensibly for defense against France and for the rescue of South American peoples from Spain, but an army which Jefferson suspected might eventually be used, as in Shays's Rebellion and the Whisky Rebellion, by the federal government against the states and dissenting groups. Alexander Hamilton was preaching that the people were only "a great beast," while President John Adams was proclaiming, in his blunt way, that only the wealthy and well-born were fit to rule.

These resolutions, a trifle modified, were adopted by the Kentucky legislature in November, 1798, and, again modified as drafted by Madison, by the Virginia assembly a month later. They became the subject of discussion for many years; and at length evolved into the nullification controversy which had John C. Calhoun on one side and Andrew Jackson on the other in the darkening years before the Civil War.

Alexander Hamilton, who although out of office, remained, through his influence on the War and Treasury Departments, one of two key men of the United States, did not fail to call the attention of men "of information and property" to the Kentucky and Virginia resolutions as encouraging "direct resistance to certain laws of the Union." In a letter to Speaker Dayton he recommended these countermeasures: extension of the judiciary system by the cutting up of each state into small districts, assigning to each a judge; improvement and extension of roads and canals; consolidating the

strength of the government by developing army and navy establishments, particularly authorizing "calling out of the militia to suppress
unlawful combinations and insurrections"; declaring all writings
"which at common law are libels, if levelled against any officer
whatsoever of the United States," to be "cognizable by the courts."
In this same year, 1798, Hamilton also recommended to the Senate
military committee the enlargement of military supplies.

"If we engage in war," he wrote, "our game will be to attack where
we can. France is not to be considered as separated from her ally
[Spain]. Tempting objects will be within our grasp!"

If Jefferson dreamed at odd moments of the delights of architecture
or science, Hamilton's constantly recurring dream was that of military glory, with himself leading an American army in co-operation
with and assisting the British navy. He thought this combination
might well rule the world.

The Federalists' reply to the Virginia and Kentucky resolutions
was a strong effort to beat the Republicans in the Virginia elections
in the spring of 1799. General Washington prevailed on Patrick
Henry to run for the Virginia legislature to defeat "the endeavors
of a certain party among us to disquiet the public mind." Henry's
last speech, defending the Alien and Sedition Laws and conjuring up
a picture of Washington "inflicting military execution" on Virginia
people, was answered by a figure new to Virginia politics—a thin
young man with luminous eyes and light hair combed back into
a queue, dressed in a blue frock and buff small-clothes, the bony
leanness of his legs concealed by top boots. This was one of those
numerous Randolphs akin to Jefferson—John Randolph of Roanoke.
He had won a seat in Congress that year over Powhatan Bolling,
the Federalist candidate. Bolling wore a scarlet coat to show he had
no sympathy for Randolph's revolutionary blue and buff.

The Federalists made great gains, not enough to carry the assembly
but encouraging to Washington, who now hoped "the tide was
turned." It was the last year of any tide for both Patrick Henry
and George Washington. Before this year was ended, the grave had
claimed them both.

Jefferson's summary of Washington's attributes was generous. He
thought the Father of His Country had not a mind of the first order,

but "his character was, in its mass, perfect, in nothing bad, in few points indifferent; and it may be truly said, that never did nature and fortune combine more perfectly to make a man great, and to place him in the same constellation with whatever worthies have merited from man an everlasting remembrance."

To offset what he regarded as the Federalist and administration propaganda for war, Jefferson now made huge exertions to foster an immense campaign for peace.

"This summer," he wrote Madison in the middle of 1798, "is the season for systematic energies and sacrifices. . . . Let me pray and beseech you to set apart a certain portion of every post day to write what may be proper for the public."

But the news of uprisings in Pennsylvania against a window tax disquieted him. No force must be used by the rebels, he warned, lest the government win undeserved sympathy. In case war was declared, he favored sinking political differences; "but," he wrote Kosciusko, "whether at the close of such a war, we shall be as free as we are now, God knows." Jefferson regarded all the liberties that had been won by the Revolutionary War as now under threat; in fact, he deemed the whole year of 1798 critical for the American people; for while President Adams was denouncing France, Hamilton, newly appointed executive head of the American army under Washington, was confidently writing Rufus King in London regarding the proposed Miranda adventure in South America: "Are we ready for this undertaking? Not quite. But we ripen fast." And again in 1799 he wrote: " 'Tis to be regretted that the preparation of an adequate military force does not advance more rapidly."

Almost at the same time Jefferson was writing his daughter, Maria Eppes, from Philadelphia: "Without an object here which is not alien to me, and barren of every delight, I turn to your situation with pleasure, in the midst of a good family which loves you, and merits all your love"; again he wrote of being "environed here in scores of constant torment, malice and obliquy." In a later letter to Martha Randolph we hear among the affectionate expressions the masterful tones of Jefferson, the plantation owner: "Jupiter, with my horses, must be at Fredericksburg on Tuesday evening, the 5th of March. . . . I am already light-hearted at the approach of my departure."

This was in the last year of the eighteenth century. Before the year was gone, Jefferson welcomed a new arrival from France, P. S. du Pont de Nemours. This was the founder of physiocracy [1] and friend of Turgot and Franklin. He was one of the many foreigners who recognized in Jefferson the figure of a world-man. Du Pont's support of Louis XVI had forced him out of his native land. His was destined to be a great name in Franco-American history.

To Jefferson the closing year of the century was important for another reason: Maria Eppes, his younger daughter, was with child, and his letters to her became extra tender and anxious. "Continue me," he wrote, "your most tender affections so necessary to my happiness, and be assured of mine for ever."

As the century came to an end, Jefferson received from Louisiana a gift that probably pleased him more than any gift received during the year. It was a barrel filled with "paccan" [pecan] nuts, which could be planted all around Monticello. The gift was from Daniel Clark, Jr., a leading citizen of New Orleans. Jefferson loved to give away pecans to his friends, foreign and home, and he sent many to France.

And so comes the end of the eighteenth century and the birth of the nineteenth. Already certain changes in the fabric of society are signalized as science overtakes the social graces, and commercial practicality overcomes romance. There comes a significant change in men's costumes: breeches and silk stockings are laid aside for prosaic pantaloons; Jefferson himself sometimes dons them. The suavities of the drawing room are invaded by rude men like Napoleon and Andrew Jackson. Individual enterprise is succeeded by great associations and companies which override provincial and national boundaries and compel statesmen to act as their commercial agents. Even a staunch defender of agriculture as a way of life like Jefferson is compelled to yield ground to manufactures. It is evident that new structures are rising, and with them, come new concepts and new stresses.

---

[1] The physiocrats emphasized the land and its products as the true source of national wealth.

CHAPTER 45

THE FEDERAL CITY

IN 1800 THE CAPITAL of the United States was moved to the new Federal City in the territory, later the District, of Columbia, consisting of ten miles square. This was in accordance with the deal in which Jefferson had been made to "hold the candle" for Hamilton in the matter of the government's assumption of the states' war debts. Despite his chagrin at this recollection, Jefferson could not help being pleased by the government's removal from Philadelphia to Washington; he would be much nearer to home and farm and family.

The men who had had most hope for the new city and most to do with its construction on sound lines were Washington and Jefferson. As the former's sympathy for Federalism and the latter's for Republicanism developed, politics drew them apart; but in creating an imposing city where once had been only the muddy cornfields of Maryland and Virginia, their collaboration was close and amiable. Washington foresaw "a city, though not as large as London, yet with a magnitude inferior to few others in Europe"; Jefferson forecast a population of one hundred thousand in a hundred years and perhaps two hundred thousand ultimately.

On March 31, 1791, Jefferson had written Washington: "The acquisition of ground is really noble." Major l'Enfant, who had noble conceptions but who had to be held closely in check by Jefferson as secretary of state under Washington, placed the Congress House, later the Capitol, on Jenkins' Heights. The President's House, still unfinished in 1800—much to Mrs. John Adams's annoyance—stood on a ridge a mile and a half to the west. Connecting it with the Congress House was a causeway 160 feet wide. This developed into Pennsylvania Avenue, bordered by Jefferson's poplars. Near this

238

avenue at the foot of the hill was a spring concealed by bushes where in summer bobwhites sounded their call.

The Federal City was a red clay tract of fields, woods and bushes interspersed with a few scattered clumps of buildings, brick kilns and the windowless shacks of laborers. Mrs. Adams found the President's House (not called the White House until it had been repainted after being burned by the British in 1812) "upon a grand and superb scale," but without heat, bells, fences, yards, "or other convenience without."

Jefferson's lodging in the Federal City was in a suite of rooms in Conrad and McMunn's boarding-house. He shared this at one time with Samuel Smith of Maryland. He made no complaint about his lodgings. In this respect, his disposition was to accept things philosophically and serenely.

Another occupant of Conrad and McMunn's boarding-house was Albert Gallatin of Pennsylvania, young leader of the republic-men in the House of Representatives. With Varnum of Massachusetts he shared a room for which, "including attendance, wood, candles, and liquor," as he wrote his wife, he paid fifteen dollars a week. Including Jefferson, from twenty-four to thirty persons daily gathered around the boarding-house table. Gallatin found the assembly "somewhat monkish." Besides the two congressmen mentioned, there were Senators John Langdon, Abraham Baldwin and Wilson Cary Nicholas; also Representatives George Nicholas, John Brown of Kentucky and Theodorus Bailey of New York. The wives of the latter two men kept the company from being too monotonously male. Finding that Jefferson sat at the foot of the common table, they tried to induce him to move to the head, but without success. He remained there until he moved into the President's House.

Gallatin complained there were few vegetables served, beef "not very good," mutton and poultry better. Referring to his fellow-boarders, he told his wife: "A few indeed drink, and some gamble, but the majority think naught but politics." He gave these further details: "Around the capitol are seven or eight boarding-houses, one tailor, one shoe-maker, one printer, a washing-woman, a grocery shop, a pamphlets and stationery shop, a small dry-goods shop, and an oyster house. This makes the whole of the Federal City as connected with the Capitol." [1]

The Reverend Manasseh Cutler, of the fourth middle district of Massachusetts, wrote home that on Sundays the occupants of these boarding-houses sang psalm-tunes on the "Forte-Piano"—such as "Old Hundred," "Canterbury," "Denmark" and "St. Martin." About the chief structures of the Federal City he was more cheerful: "The buildings are brick, and erected in what are called large blocks. . . . The block in which I live contains six houses, four stories high, and very handsomely furnished. . . . I am not much pleased with the Capitol. It is a huge pile, built, indeed, with handsome stone, very heavy in its appearance without, and not very pleasant within. The President's house is superb, well proportioned and pleasingly situated."

A new idea was born to Jefferson this year. He wrote Dr. Joseph Priestley in Pennsylvania about it. It concerned a design for a "central university" in Virginia, its plan to be "broad and liberal and modern." It was to be suited to American, not European, conditions. It was to lay heavy emphasis on the sciences and practical arts. We get a glimpse of what Jefferson's university would avoid in his remarks on Napoleon Bonaparte: "Wherever he has meddled, we have seen nothing but fragments of the old Roman governments stuck into materials with which they can form no cohesion." This reference to Bonaparte brought up a parallel thought:

"The enemies of our Constitution are preparing a fearful operation," he wrote. "Our Bonaparte, surrounded by his comrades in arms, may step in to give us political salvation in his way." It was evident that by "our Bonaparte" he meant Alexander Hamilton, who, Washington being dead, was now head of the United States military forces and was well-nigh in virtual control of the civil government.

Early in this new year of 1800 the political pot began to simmer. The republic-men, having had their confidence strengthened by several small political successes, now suddenly decided to bid for national power by nominating Jefferson for the presidency and Aaron Burr of New York for the vice-presidency. The Federalists countered with the nomination of President John Adams to succeed himself.

---

[1] Adams, *Life of Gallatin*, Philadelphia, 1880.

For the vice-presidency they nominated Charles Cotesworth Pinckney of South Carolina, a major general in the augmented American army and a former minister to, and a known critic of, France.

To the political and military forces led by Hamilton the prospect of Adams's succeeding himself was horrifying. Hamilton had fallen out with Adams. In addition, he was now without the powerful support and prestige of Washington's friendship—that cover which had carried him triumphantly past so many dangers. Moreover, Adams had become deeply suspicious of Hamilton's influence over the three key men of Adams's cabinet—Pickering of the State Department, McHenry of War, and Wolcott, comptroller of the Treasury.

Suddenly the Republicans won the election in New York State. With equal suddenness Adams used the ax on Pickering and McHenry, placing John Marshall of Virginia in the State Department and Samuel Dexter of Massachusetts in War. Oliver Wolcott was kept in the Treasury, possibly out of a desire not to offend supporting Federalists too deeply. To Hamilton the New York result was alarming; he at once proposed to John Jay, governor of New York, a measure designed to keep Jefferson out of the "chief magistracy" on the ground that the anti-Federalists were aiming at overthrow of the government. This measure would be the calling together of the New York legislature to choose electors by districts instead of direct popular vote. "In times like these," wrote Hamilton, "it will not do to be over scrupulous."

Jay rejected the measure as unbecoming. Hamilton then went to work gathering material against President Adams which subsequently he printed under the title of *The Public Conduct and Character of John Adams, Esq., President of the United States.* It was one of the major mistakes of Hamilton's career; for the public not only was shocked by the tone of his attack on President Adams but by that of his defense of his own actions, particularly his declaration that as regards Great Britain, "my opinions while in the Administration, to the best of my recollection, coincided with those of Mr. Jefferson"; for everyone knew that he never coincided with Jefferson in anything.

Aaron Burr got hold of an early copy of Hamilton's document

and circulated it where it would do its author most harm, thereby fostering an already burgeoning enmity which brought upon Hamilton his last and most tragic quarrel.

Jefferson's memoranda at this time in 1800 show that he was paying federal taxes on 5,786 acres of land in Albemarle county and on sixty-five Negroes, though he gave the number of his slaves there as ninety-three. In this year he gathered the heaviest crop of wheat in the plantation's history, but times were hard for farmers and Jefferson's tobacco crop went unsold. He tried to economize, but could not resist buying a "forte-piano" from Philadelphia. It was an upright, with perpendicular instead of horizontal strings, "as easily turned as a spinette," and Jefferson was delighted with it.

As the summer's presidential campaign came on, Jefferson was the target of unholy mud from his enemies, including the clergy of New England. For this clerical vituperation Jefferson's hard-won "freedom of religion" statute in Virginia was probably most to blame; for through that statute the clergy of the Established Church had lost both income and position. For the rest, they had translated Jefferson's unitarianism into "French atheism"; besides, like their pewholders in most of the larger towns, they were Federalists through sympathy with property, birth and education; and all had the Federalists' disbelief in common man.

The Reverend Cotton Mather Smith of Shena, Connecticut, declared from the pulpit that Jefferson had obtained his property by fraud and robbery, particularly of widows and fatherless children; the Reverend Dr. John M. Mason of New York published a pamphlet accusing Jefferson of atheism and French infidelity; while the Reverend Dr. Timothy Dwight, president of Yale College, foresaw in an emotional nightmare "the consummation of Democratic blessedness" when "the ties of marriage, with all its felicities, are severed and destroyed" and "our wives and daughters are thrown into the stews."

Jefferson wrote concerning these agitated clergymen: "I have sworn upon the altar of God eternal hostility against every form of tyranny over the mind of man. But this is all they have to fear from me."

Near the end of this year President Adams announced that the three American commissioners to France had been received with respect in Paris. Thus did the XYZ episode, which had embarked the United States on an enlarged military and naval program and called forth much belligerent patriotism, come to an end without an open war with France. This escape from war was a disappointment to certain interests; but it was pleasing to Jefferson, who had consistently preached that his young country could not afford to risk its strength in war. When the envoys, headed by General W. R. Davie of North Carolina, brought back from France a treaty or convention, to be laid before Congress, Jefferson wrote to Madison:

"Davie is here with the convention, as it is called; but it is a real treaty, and without limitation of time. It has some disagreeable features, and will endanger the compromising us with Great Britain."

At this stage Jefferson looked across the ocean with mounting anxiety, for he could see France only as a "den of robbers" and England only as a "nation of pirates."

CHAPTER 46

BURR AND BALLOTS

IN THE CAMPAIGN of 1800 Hamilton fared badly. He had no sooner torpedoed President Adams than he discovered a movement among certain Federalists to shift support to Aaron Burr for the presidency. Burr! "Little Burr!"

In every political corridor Hamilton was now running into the influences set in motion by this now suave, now saturnine, New Yorker who had built up a threatening machine in New York City largely by his conversion of the Tammany Society, originally a social club, into a political organization. By comparison Jefferson began to appear saint-like; Jefferson (Hamilton wrote) at least had "pretensions to character," while Burr was "a dangerous man" and "bankrupt beyond redemption except by the plunder of his country." Hamilton, possibly recalling the old political adage, *"If you can't beat 'em, join 'em,"* now brought his ship up on another tack and proposed to his followers an understanding with Jefferson:

"Let our situation be improved to obtain from Jefferson assurances on certain points—the maintenance of the present system, especially on the cardinal articles of public credit—a navy, neutrality."

Thus, Hamilton, dropping old differences, was ready to do business with Jefferson if the latter would bind himself to preserve the fiscal structure that Hamilton had set up, and if Jefferson would accept the program of a big navy and non-hostility to Britain. From Jefferson came only silence; so Hamilton had to give up his hope of a deal. One day at a banquet given in New York he pronounced this toast: "May our government never fall a prey to the dreams of a Condorcet nor the vices of a Catiline." Everyone knew these were double stabs; the first aimed at Jefferson, the latter at Burr.

But he did not escape criticism himself. In South Carolina Charles Pinckney attacked Hamilton's proposed tax system as favoring the mercantile as against the planting class.

"Our government," he wrote, "by this invidious distinction has placed the landholders and the planter in an oppressive and degrading predicament. . . . Clearly to exempt all the monied interest, which is by far the largest in the Northern States and the greatest favorite of the federal party from bearing any share of the public burdens and throwing all direct taxes entirely upon the landed and planting interests." [1]

In the same state John Rutledge echoed the Federalist viewpoint by writing to Hamilton his fears that Jefferson would try to change the Constitution so as to give the government to the people and "end by throwing everything into their hands."

In the heat and clamor of the 1800 campaign, it was not always clear to the few hundred thousand American voters what the orators were saying; but they did understand to some degree that the difference between Hamilton's ideas and Jefferson's was basic and reached down to the very inner fabric of human societies. Hamilton was for stability; Jefferson for liberty. Hamilton was for power at the center; Jefferson for power distributed over the parts, giving it to the center only when the parts might be ineffective (as in foreign relations). Hamilton would have given absolute sovereignty to a centralized government; Jefferson to the people. Hamilton believed in a firm, efficient control from above; Jefferson held that good government is not a substitute for self-government. Hamilton's concepts were those derived from Old World societies; Jefferson had been convinced by his observations in Europe that the New World offered a superior life, political, economic and social, to the masses of men. Hamilton's philosophy was static and conserving where Jefferson's was dynamic and expansionist.

"It is impossible not to look forward," Jefferson wrote Monroe, "to distant times, when our rapid multiplication will expand itself . . . and cover the whole northern, if not the southern continent, with a people speaking the same language, governed in similar forms and by similar laws."

[1] Wolfe, *Jeffersonian Democracy in South Carolina*, Chapel Hill, N.C., 1940.

When the votes of the presidential electors had been canvassed, it was found that Jefferson and Burr each had received 73 votes, while President Adams had received only 65, C. C. Pinckney 64, and John Jay 1. The Federalist party was thus all but knocked out. But the high vote received by Burr was amazing to Republicans and Federalists alike. The American union then comprised sixteen states. Eight were Republican, six Federal, two divided. A Jefferson-Burr tie would throw the election into the House of Representatives. If the Federalists would support Burr, Jefferson could be kept out of the presidency.

But at the name of Burr, Hamilton revolted. Anything but this "Catiline of America." Nevertheless, his old lieutenants proposed a deal to Burr, who, busy with the marriage of his adored daughter Theodosia, rejected their offer. The approach to Burr signified that Hamilton as a political manager was finished; without the prestige of Washington's support he had never done well. Now he was ignored by his own party. As for Jefferson, he kept up his writing of voluminous letters in his room in Conrad and McMunn's boarding-house. He corresponded with R. R. Livingston of New York about steam engines, water tanks and mammoth bones; with Colonel Benjamin Hawkins, later North Carolina senator and Indian agent, about Indian vocabularies; with Dr. Hugh Williamson, also of North Carolina, about turkeys; and with William Dunbar of Mississippi about temperatures.

"I have no doubt," Jefferson wrote feelingly as to the last from his chilly Washington boarding-house in January, "but that cold is the source of more sufferance to all animal nature than hunger, thirst, sickness, and all the other pains of life and death itself put together."

On February 11, 1801, the representatives that met in the domeless Capitol began their balloting for the presidency. So close was it that a bed-ridden sick man, Joseph H. Nicholson of Maryland, was brought in to cast his vote each time, and so far from injuring him, the exercise improved him. Day after day the balloting brought no decision. Members slept in committee rooms and came out sleepily, with nightcaps on, to cast their votes. The Southern states, except South Carolina, steadily supported Jefferson; New England uniformly backed Burr. The business was kept up for six days. Then a

Mrs. James Madison (Dolly Payne), who helped Jefferson as White House
hostess, portrait attributed to Ezra Ames

John Quincy Adams, dinner guest and critic of
Jefferson, by J. W. Jarvis

Albert Gallatin, Jefferson's brilliant treasurer, by
William H. Powell

Vermont Federalist withdrew. Maryland Federalists and one from Delaware, James A. Bayard, cast blank ballots. So did South Carolina.

That ended the contest and elected Jefferson. Burr became vice-president. Inauguration was set for March 4. But a dying Federalism made one more effort. John Adams employed his last hours as president in making as many federal appointments as possible, including those of a number of "midnight judges." John Marshall was one of these judges; he was made chief justice of the United States Supreme Court. Adams forsook the President's House at 4 A.M., March 4, without so much as a farewell to Jefferson.

"You have no idea," wrote Albert Gallatin, whom Jefferson had already marked for the Treasury, "of the meanness, indecency, almost insanity of his [Adams's] conduct." Yet Jefferson, knowing Adams's temperament, refused to give up his friendship for him.

CHAPTER 47

PRESIDENT JEFFERSON BEGINS
HIS FIRST TERM

FROM CONRAD and McMunn's boarding-house on the south side of Capitol Hill, Jefferson in March, 1801, walked to the two-winged and ugly uncompleted Capitol (the dome was not in place then) to be inaugurated as president of the United States.[1]

Jefferson was now fifty-seven years old. He was the leader of a movement and party which had just won a tidal victory; sweeping back (though not destroying) in America the Old World conception that power ought to belong exclusively to the wealthy and well-born. He accepted his triumph quietly; neither in his bearing nor in his letters appeared any evidence of exultation. In the Senate chamber, where he was sworn in, the inauguration was carried out with a simple dignity. On Jefferson's right hand stood Aaron Burr, the vice-president; on his left, John Marshall, the new chief justice.

On this stage containing these three actors an onlooker gifted with a knowledge of the past and future might have beheld much drama. John Marshall was Jefferson's blood kinsman, but also his political enemy—one destined to do Jefferson's ideas much harm. Burr had just missed the culmination of an avid ambition: "By deceiving one man (a great blockhead), and tempting two (not incorruptible)," wrote James A. Bayard to Alexander Hamilton four days after the inauguration, "he might have secured a majority of the States." And all three men were soon to be involved in a drama far surpassing this

---

[1] The tradition that he rode a horse to the Capitol and hitched it "to the palisades" was founded on a story told by a lone Englishman, John David, who published a travel book in London in 1803. There is no other authority for this story. Sir Augustus J. Foster, of the British legation, mentioned having seen Jefferson hitch his horse to shop fronts. That may be the basis for the legend.

inauguration scene in significance.

With Jefferson a favorite adage was: "Take hold of things by their smooth handle." Now, reading in a low voice, he showed in his formal address how balanced and conciliatory his policy was to be. Certain of the calm but pungent passages of his address from that moment became a basic part of American political thinking:

1. *"Though the will of the majority is to prevail, that will, to be rightful, must be reasonable . . . the minority possess their equal rights, which equal laws must protect, and to violate which would be oppression."*

2. *"Let us reflect that having banished from our land that religious intolerance under which mankind so long bled and suffered, we have yet gained little if we countenance a political intolerance as despotic, as wicked, and capable of as bitter and bloody persecutions."*

3. *"We are all Republicans—we are all Federalists. If there be any among us who would wish to dissolve this Union, or to change its republican form, let them stand undisturbed as monuments of the safety with which error of opinion may be tolerated where reason is left free to combat it."*

4. *"Sometimes it is said that man cannot be trusted with the government of himself. Can he then be trusted with the government of others?"*

5. *"A wise and frugal government, which shall restrain men from injuring one another, which shall leave them otherwise free to regulate their own pursuits of industry and improvement, and shall not take from the mouth of labor the bread it has earned."*

6. *"Peace, commerce, and honest friendship with all nations— entangling alliances with none."*

There was one witness, a woman, who did not look on this scene unmoved. "I cannot describe the agitation I felt," wrote Margaret Bayard Smith, daughter of a Federalist, to her sister Susan on March 4, 1801, "while I looked around on the various multitude. . . . If doubt of the integrity and talents of Mr. Jefferson ever existed in the minds of any one, methinks this address must forever eradicate them." [2]

---

[2] Margaret Bayard Smith, *The First Forty Years of Washington Society.*

Margaret Bayard Smith came to the capital as the wife of Samuel Harrison Smith, editor of the *National Intelligencer*. Smith was the son of a former member of the Continental Congress. Margaret was his cousin. Her father was Colonel John Bayard, a Federalist. His nephew and adopted son was Senator James A. Bayard of Delaware, long a Jefferson opponent. Virtually all of Margaret's upbringing had led her to regard Jefferson as having horns and a forked tail; and even after she came to Washington at the age of twenty-two, she thought of Jefferson as an inhuman monster who bore the brand of revolutionary France.

"I did believe," she wrote, "that he was an ambitious and violent demagogue, coarse and vulgar in his manners, awkward and rude in his appearance, for such had the public journals and private conversations of the federal party represented him to be."

Yet the very first time she met Jefferson she melted and became his adorer and reverent admirer. "His face owes all its charm to its expression and intelligence," she wrote. "But his manners—how gentle, how humble, how kind."

The most complete statement of the new administration's intentions came from Jefferson himself in a letter written in April, 1802, to Count de Volney. Referring to the ferment in France, Jefferson said:

"Believing that forms of government have been attempted to which the national character is not adapted, I expect something will finally be settled as free as their habits of thinking and acting will permit." This was a new statement of an opinion which Jefferson stressed more and more as he grew older: that a government, to succeed, must mold itself to the character and habits of its people.

Then coming down to a scornful discussion of the opposition to Republican teachings, he wrote concerning the recent campaign: "Principles and pursuits were then brought forward the most adverse to those of the nation in its sound state of mind and maintained for a short period by delusion, terror, corruption, and every artifice which those who [held] the power and resources of the nation could put into exercise. . . . We are returning our government to the original simplicity of its form, suppressing offices useless to the public and created only to increase the patronage and strength of the executive beyond the control of the legislative branch of the government."

Referring to the calumnies against him, for which he regarded "the empire of the priesthood" in New England as largely to blame, he wrote sarcastically: "Happily those vehicles, like the flues of our chimnies, give an innocent conveyance and discharge to smoke vapours which might be dangerous if put up in their bowels."

The Republican aim, he said, was to prove that "a people easy in their circumstances as ours are, are capable of conducting themselves under a government founded not on the fear and follies of man, but in his reason, on the predominance of his social over his dissocial passions, so free as to restrict him in no moral right, and . . . [illegible] as to protect him from every moral wrong; which shall leave him, in short, in possession of all his natural rights; nothing being more demonstrable than that he has no natural right in opposition to his social duties."

Thus did Jefferson summarize his tenets at the beginning of his presidency. Never did he make plainer his beliefs as a social moralist and philosopher of human societies. To the beaten Federalists, muttering even as they retreated, Jefferson gave this parting blow: "Though the people in mass have joined us, their leaders had committed themselves too far to retract. Pride keeps them hostile; they brood over their angry passions, and give them vent in the newspapers which they maintain. They still make as much noise as if they were the whole nation. Unfortunately, those being the mercantile papers, published chiefly in the seaports, are the only ones which find their way to Europe, and make very false impressions there."

Jefferson's inaugural sentiments were received with due respect by most of his countrymen. Only among the die-hard clergy and indurate Federalists was there skepticism and snorting. The Reverend Manasseh Cutler wrote home to Massachusetts: "Jefferson's speech, though a mixed medly of Jacobinism, Republicanism, and Federalism, of religion and atheism, of sentiments consistent and inconsistent with the constitution of an energetic government, yet it is extremely smooth, and must be highly popular with the people at large." A little later Cutler again wrote to a friend in Ipswich, Massachusetts: "There appears no doubt that the Democrats intend to destroy the present Judiciary system."

These curdled remarks from a Massachusetts representative in Congress partly offset the sensation created in the Capitol by another Massachusetts man of an opposite belief, Elder John Leland of Grafton, Massachusetts, who for some years had been a Baptist preacher in Virginia. Soon after Jefferson's inauguration Leland conceived the impressive idea of sending to the President, as a tribute from the New England dairy industry, the largest cheese in the world. Every dairyman who admired Jefferson was invited to contribute one day's milk; only federal cows were excluded. There resulted a mammoth cheese of sixteen hundred pounds. It was placed on a sleigh and was three weeks reaching the capital while citizens gathered en route to smell and cheer. At the President's House the cheese was installed in what Jefferson called the "mammoth room" where members of Congress were invited for a view. Among others Cutler came, and though he admitted "we were received with politeness and entertained with cake and wine," the cheese, savoring both of Baptism and Democracy, was to him only a "monument of weakness and folly."

Indeed, Cutler was never able to reconcile himself either to Jefferson or Elder Leland. During Jefferson's term religious services were conducted every Sunday in the Capitol. There, the first Sunday in 1802, Cutler recorded that "the two Houses of Congress were insulted by the introduction of Leland, the cheese monger, as a preacher," whom he classified as "poor, ignorant, illiterate" and "clownish." But in Cutler's eyes Leland capped offense with insult when on the arrival of Jefferson as a member of the congregation, Leland arose and gave out the text: *Behold, a greater than Solomon is here.*

"Such a farrago," wrote Cutler, "bawled with stunning voice, horrid tone, frightful grimaces, and extravagant gestures, I believe, was never heard by any decent auditory before." [3] A month later Cutler

---

[3] This view of Elder John Leland does not accord with that indicated by L. H. Butterfield in *Proceedings American Antiquarian Society, LXII, Part II,* which depicts Leland as an intelligent and humorous preacher who preferred to be an independent evangelist rather than a formal pastor. Though born in Massachusetts, he preached some years in Virginia, moving to the dairy region around Cheshire, Massachusetts, in 1792, where regularly he led his flock to the polls to vote for Jefferson though all

ODE
TO THE
MAMMOTH CHEESE,
Prefented to Thomas Jefferson,

PRESIDENT OF THE UNITED STATES,

BY THE INHABITANTS OF CHESHIRE, MASSACHUSETTS,

JANUARY 1, 1802.

MOST Excellent--far fam'd and far fetch'd Cheese!
Superior far in fmell, tafte, weight and fize,
To any ever form'd 'neath foreign fkies,
And highly honour'd—thou wert made to pleafe,
The man belov'd by all—but ftop a trice,
Before he's praifed—I too muft have a flice.

II.

Rich too thou art, and pleafant tho' fo large
As any Millftone—or a North-weft Moon ;
To meafure thee 'twould take an afternoon—
Few tables can fupport the pond'rous charge,
Into what cupboard Mammoth canft thou enter,
And where's the knife can cut clean thro' thy centre.

III.

'Twould take a Gallatin to afcertain
How many meals for Congrefs--clerks and all·
The fupernumeraries about their Hall,
Thy fpacious limits actually contain :
What number of WELSH RABBITS, thou wouldft make
How many thoufand loaves there's caufe to bake.

IV.

For cent'ries paft--in Europe--fometimes here,
Placemen were faid to fhare the *loaves* and *fifhes*,
(And where's the man that for a fhare ne'er wifhes)
But now Americans have better cheer,
And to their worthy fervants 'ftead of thefe,
They've wifely fubftituted—LOAVES and CHEESE.

V.

Cheefe is the attendant of a New-Year's day,
Cheefe is the Blithe-meat * when a bairn is born,

* In Scotland.

Cheefe, may thofe tafte thee ne'er, who tafting fcor·
Cheefe--ftill proceeding from the milky way,
Is nature', pureft, plain and fimple food ;
Cheefe is a lux'ry, when like this 'tis good.

VI.

God blefs the Cheefe--and kindly blefs the makers,
The givers--generous--good and fweet and fair,
And the receiver--great beyond compare,
All thofe who fhall be happy as partakers ;·
O ! may no traitor to his country's caufe
E'er have a bit of thee between his jaws.

VII.

Some folks may fneer, with envy in their fmiles,
And with low wit at ridicule endeavour,
Their fenfe and breeding's fhewn by their behaviour,
Well--let them ufe Ariftocratic wiles,
Do what they can--and fay juft what they pleafe,
RATS love to nibble at good Chefhire Cheefe.

VIII.

'Tis a good New-Year's Gift I think indeed,
But the Cheefe-Mafter muft be on his guard,
And againft *longing women* be prepar'd,
Once they begin to eat--do pray take heed ;
Once they begin--when they may ftop's unknown,
Perhaps they will not till the whole is gone.

IX.

To others leaving wealth, and place and pow'r,
I'll to my home and to my HARRIS hie,
Our wants are few--thofe induftry fupply ;
All that we want or wifh for in life's hour,
Heaven ftill will grant us--they are only thefe,
Poetry--Health--Peace--Virtue--Bread and *Cheefe*.·

was still not rid of his anti-cheese prejudices, for he recorded in a note which gives us an appetizing view of the way in which Jefferson entertained his guests, even his political enemies:

"Dined at the President's. . . . Rice soup, round of beef, turkey, mutton, ham, loin of veal, cutlets of mutton or veal, fried eggs, fried beef, a pie called macaroni, which appeared to be a rich crust filled with the strillions of onions, or shallots, which I took it to be, tasted very strong, and not agreeable. . . . Ice cream very good, crust wholly dried, crumbled into thin flakes; a dish somewhat like a pudding—inside white as milk or curd, very porous and light, covered with cream-sauce,—very fine. Many other gimcracks, a great variety of fruit, plenty of wines, and good. President social. We drank tea and viewed again the great cheese." Later Cutler wrote another dining note: "The President's two daughters, Mrs. Randolph and Mrs. Eppes, were at the table. They appeared well-accomplished women—very delicate and tolerably handsome. . . . The President was very social." But this did not mean Cutler was yet reconciled to Jefferson, for on March 14, 1802, he made this comment:

"When the time comes, depend upon it, there is a *Bonaparte* ready to hurl Jefferson from his chair, and to take the reins of government into his own hands."

This note must be regarded as of more than passing significance. While the late campaign was in progress, there were repeated rumors that the Federalists would take up arms rather than accept Republican rule; on the other hand, the reported fostering by James Monroe, who was now governor of Virginia, of armories in his state was reported as a countermove. As for Jefferson, he often warned his followers against any show of forcible methods. There is one more observation by Cutler which must be recorded. His journal for January 2, 1802, mentions a trip by himself and associates to Mount Vernon where they were hospitably received by Mrs. George Washington.

---

the neighboring counties were Federalist. The cheese he had made for Jefferson consisted of the milk drawn from nine hundred cows and weighed 1,230 pounds. Leland was often quoted as saying: "The new world was found by Columbus, delivered by Washington, and taught by Jefferson." In 1940 a concrete replica of the Jefferson cheese and its press was erected in Cheshire in honor both of Jefferson and Leland. The latter died in North Adams, Massachusetts, at the age of eighty-seven.

"We were all Federalists," wrote Cutler, "which evidently gave her particular pleasure. Her remarks were frequently pointed, and sometimes very sarcastic, on the new order of things and the present administration. She spoke of the election of Mr. Jefferson, whom she considered as one of the most detestable of mankind, as the greatest misfortune our country has ever experienced."

At this time it was often the theme of gossip that Martha Washington was even more Federalist than her great husband had been, and that Jefferson was not a *persona grata* in her home. Jefferson apparently did not sense this hostility, for in a letter of January 4, 1801, to his daughter Maria at Bermuda Hundred, he wrote: "I went yesterday to Mount Vernon, where Mrs. Washington and Mrs. Lewis inquired very kindly after you."

One thing is certain: those anti-democratic Americans for whom Cutler was a spokesman never gave up their belief that Jefferson and democracy were plunging the country into ruin, darkness and damnation, and not for a moment did they relax their suspicious watch on the President.

CHAPTER 48

QUEST FOR AN EXPLORER

ONE DAY IN 1783 Jefferson, then the American minister in France, read in a gazette just arrived from London an item that caused the hackles on the back of his neck to rise. It set forth that a semi-official British exploring party, wishing to enlarge the boundaries of knowledge, purposed to enter the unknown American country lying between the Mississippi river and the Pacific coast.

This announcement alarmed Jefferson for three reasons: one was that as a patriot he wanted to keep the land-hungry British out of Western territory; a second was that as an amateur scientist he had long wanted to know what lay in this unknown region, and particularly whether the Missouri river provided a natural channel of communication between the Mississippi valley and the Pacific coast; a third reason was that he disliked the whole monarchical British government, and wanted no part of it operating on American soil.

He had long foreseen that pushful American pioneers and settlers, who already had broken over the old barrier of the Alleghenies, soon would be crowding up to the Mississippi. What then? This menacing item in an English gazette hardened a resolve that had been gradually forming in his mind: *the United States must beat the British to the West.*

At once he sat down and wrote a letter to that old battler of the British, George Rogers Clark. Here was a man to whom he could tell his fears. Clark had once been a near neighbor in Albemarle county, Virginia. He had beaten the British at Vincennes and Kaskaskia in 1778, and had rescued the Illinois and Kentucky country from their colonizing hands. He was used to hardships in rough country.

"I find they have subscribed a very large sum of money in England," Jefferson wrote, "for exploring the country from the Mississippi to California. . . . They pretend it is only to promote knowledge. I am afraid they have thoughts of colonizing into that quarter. . . . Some of us have been talking here in a feeble way of making the attempt to search that country. . . . How would you like to lead such a party?"

But General Clark declined. He thought his health and present circumstances would not allow him to undertake the mission. Jefferson, disappointed, laid the scheme aside. But not for keeps. It lay and simmered in the back of his mind. West of the Mississippi stretched the vast Louisiana territory. It had been explored in parts and at times by the French, governed by the Spanish and eyed by the British. But none of them must have it; it must be saved for the American union. But who would get there first?

Three years later, in 1786, Jefferson, then in Paris as the United States minister, met a young man who he believed would be even better than General Clark as an explorer to the Far West. This discovery was a lithe and roving young Connecticut Yankee named John Ledyard.

Ledyard was one of the first American marines to stamp his name on history. He had served as a volunteer with Captain Cook on his third voyage around the world and had been made a corporal of marines. Jefferson learned that Ledyard was nursing a project whereby he might reach the Pacific coast where the fur trade promised money and adventure. He listened to the young fellow closely, and liked him. Ledyard seemed to have spirit and enterprise; might even prove to be a genius, so Jefferson told a friend, adding: "If he escapes safely, he will give us new, curious, and useful information." He made Ledyard an offer, and the young man snapped at it.

"It will be one of the remaining pleasures of my life to thank you for the many instances of your friendship," he wrote Jefferson later, "and wherever I am, to pursue you with the tale of my gratitude."

He and Jefferson worked out a plan which was to be carried out at once. Ledyard was to cross Europe into Russsia, and from there make his way to Kamchatka. Thence he would procure passage on some Russian vessel to Nootka Sound. Then he would try to reach the mouth of the Missouri river, or of the Oregon, on the Pacific coast, whence he would follow the bed of the Missouri until the Mississippi and civilization would again be reached. His notes he would bring at once to Jefferson, wherever he might be.

Alas, this mission so eagerly begun was not destined to be carried out by Ledyard. At Tobolsk the Empress Catherine II had him stopped, and suspecting he might be a spy, she sent him back through Poland. Thence Ledyard, bitterly disappointed, wandered to Cairo where in 1789 he died.

But Jefferson did not give up. In 1789 he ended his stay in France and went home. When in 1792 the Boston skipper, Robert Gray, discovered the mouth of the Columbia river, Jefferson's yearning to know more about the spaces that filled the Northwest between the Mississippi and the Pacific Ocean came back upon him.

André Michaux, the French botanist, was in the United States that year, collecting plants; and Jefferson, who was himself a life-long student of plant life and vice-president of the American Philosophical Society, on learning that Michaux was anxious to carry his scientific explorations beyond the Appalachian Mountains, took it on himself to raise subscriptions to a fund of four hundred dollars which should enable the Frenchman to explore the country along the Missouri river "by the shortest way and the lowest latitudes to the Pacific Ocean." The largest subscribers were George Washington twenty-five dollars, Robert Morris twenty dollars, Alexander Hamilton and Jefferson twelve dollars and fifty cents each.

In January, 1793, Jefferson himself wrote down the society's detailed instructions to Michaux. He also gave him a letter of introduction to Governor Isaac Shelby of Kentucky. Michaux was to stick to the Missouri river as a channel of communication; and Jefferson mentioned that as far as the town of Kaskaskia the society would procure the botanist a conveyance "in company with the Indians of that town now in Philadelphia." Thence Michaux was to cross the Mississippi and pass by land to the nearest part of the Missouri above the Spanish settlements.

"It would seem by the latest maps," wrote Jefferson, "as if a river called Oregon interlocked with the Missouri for a considerable distance and entered the Pacific Ocean not far southward of Nootka

Sound."

He hinted that Michaux might verify this. In any case, he was to note the "soil, rivers, mountains, its productions—animal, vegetable, and mineral—so far as they may be new to us . . . the names, members and dwellings of the inhabitants"; and particularly the history of the mammoth, and learn whether the llama or paca of Peru was to be found in those parts. Jefferson even directed Michaux how to preserve his notes—"on the skin might be best for such as may be the most important," though certain details might be committed to paper-birch bark, "a substance which may not excite suspicions among the Indians and is little liable to injury from wet or other common accidents."

While Michaux waited for some part of the exploring fund to be paid him, there arrived in the United States as minister from the French republic, Edmond C. Genêt. When he became aggressive in behalf of his country, Jefferson became colder and colder, and his notes to Genêt became blunter and blunter. The suspicions against Genêt were summed up in the evidence that part of his mission was to raise and finance a core of American frontiersmen who were to attack the Spanish and British possessions on and beyond the Mississippi.

To further these ends Genêt engaged Michaux as one of his agents. Another agent was General George Rogers Clark, who had declined to lead Jefferson's exploring party but who was willing to lead Genêt's. Clark outlined a fantastic scheme to raise a force of riflemen to attack New Orleans and other Spanish posts. He wellnigh ruined himself in the venture. Clark by now had moved from Virginia to Kentucky, where he had become a leader of those farmers and traders who were constantly pressing the Spanish to open the Mississippi permanently to the growing traffic of the region.

Citizen Genêt was to finance these agents out of the debts to France which were to be collected from the young American republic. But this scheme was aborted by the opposition of Alexander Hamilton, financial secretary in Washington's cabinet. Michaux, who had got as far as Kentucky, where he was supposed to be botanizing exclusively, but where he was also forwarding the French government's messages to Clark, was forced to turn back because of lack of funds. He returned to Charleston, South Carolina, near which he had a large botanic garden.

Hence for a second time Jefferson's dream of sending an exploring party up the Missouri to the Pacific Northwest came to nothing. But again this dream was only laid aside, not abandoned. Jefferson was rarely aggressive; but in persistence, in sheer hanging on to a purpose, he had a long and sinewy tenacity.

When in 1801 Jefferson took office as president of the United States, he engaged as his secretary the son of a couple who for years had been his neighbors in Albemarle county, Virginia. His name was Meriwether Lewis. He was twenty-seven years old, in the prime of health and vigor. Jefferson watched him closely; how would he do as an explorer? Here was a young man who could be extremely useful; he was as fearless as John Ledyard, and he was steadier in dealing with men; while as a woodsman he was widely experienced.

Lewis had been a hunter since he was able to shoulder a rifle. His guardian, his uncle Nicholas Lewis, had been an Indian fighter. Meriwether himself had been a soldier in the federal force that had put down the Whisky Rebellion in Pennsylvania. Enlisting as a private under General Anthony Wayne, in a few years he had become captain and paymaster in a line regiment. He had made trips as far west as Detroit and in the course of his duties he had developed a hobby for making notes on nature's doings. Jefferson studied him as he went about the business of managing his widowed mother's farm, and then offered him a permanent post as his private secretary. The letter he sent to Lewis was carefully designed to pull strongly on the strings of Lewis's heart and imagination. The salary would be modest, only five hundred dollars a year, but the work would be light, there would be plenty of opportunity to meet distinguished men, and meantime he would live in the President's House as a member of his family.

In the two years that Lewis served Jefferson as secretary, he met every expectation, becoming one of the able young men whom Jefferson delighted to have in his circle. Afterward he wrote of Lewis in eloquent terms—"courage undaunted"; "honest, disinterested, liberal, of sound understanding, and a fidelity to truth so scrupulous that whatever he should report would be as certain as if seen by ourselves." Only one fault Meriwether Lewis had: he was sometimes moody and given to spells of melancholy. But as these moments of depression passed off, leaving no trace behind, Jefferson dismissed all thought of them and had no hesitation in fixing upon his secretary as the man who was qualified to lead the long-dreamed-of expedition into the Northwestern region to mark it down in the name of the United States, and to keep ahead of the British with their unquenchable hunger for land, trade and territory.

The President's opening gambit was made early in 1803 in the form of a secret message to Congress. Secrecy was the medium in which Jefferson always preferred to move, carefully veiling the doings of his right hand from his left, even though neither hand might be up to deeds of high importance. This was a trait that often raised the ire of his enemies and caused them to see in every harmless diversion some sinister machination. The President's message of January 18, 1803, took the form of a discussion of the growth of American trading posts established on the Mississippi and its tributaries. It pointed out particularly that the Mississippi river offered, "according to the best accounts, a continued navigation from its source, and possibly with a single portage from the Western Ocean," and that "other civilized nations have encountered great expense to enlarge the boundaries of knowledge by undertaking voyages of discovery, and for other literary purposes." Finally the message proposed that an appropriation of twenty-five thousand dollars be made "for the purpose of extending the external commerce of the United States" so as to "cover the undertaking from notice" and prevent obstructions.

Jefferson's next move was to send Lewis to Philadelphia, center of science and learning, to prepare himself for the journey by study and to purchase the power equipment. He particularly enjoined Lewis to seek advice from four of the Quaker city's leading scientists: Doctors Benjamin Rush, Caspar Wistar, Robert Patterson and Benjamin Smith Barton. To Dr. Rush, physician and civic leader, and to Dr. Wistar, medical professor at the University of Pennsylvania (for whom the flowering vine wistaria is named), he wrote personal letters asking them to receive Lewis when he should call and to make written suggestions for his guidance.

"I wish to mention to you in confidence," he wrote Dr. Rush, "that I have obtained authority from Congress to undertake the long desired object of exploring the Missouri and whatever river, heading with that, leads into the western ocean. About 10 chosen woodsmen headed by Capt. Lewis my secretary, will set out on it immediately and probably accomplish it in two seasons." To Dr. Wistar he wrote: "What follows is to be perfectly confidential. I have at length succeeded in procuring an essay to be made of exploring the Missouri and whatever river heading with that runs into the western ocean. Congress by a secret authority enables me to do it."

Jefferson also sent Lewis to Lancaster, Pennsylvania, where lived numbers of armorers and gunsmiths, including Jacob Deckard, maker of the thin-barreled Deckard rifle of a pattern which later because of its great use there, became known as the Kentucky rifle. In Lancaster also lived Andrew Ellicott, the surveyor, who later laid out the city of Washington and who readily consented to give Lewis instruction in the use of surveying and mathematical instruments. All during the spring and early summer of 1803 eager letters flew back and forth between Lewis and the President; and to look on those letters now is to recognize that in the preparations for the great journey Jefferson, nearing sixty, was as happy as his young secretary. There was in Jefferson at all times a considerable element of Tom Sawyer and boy scout, and no schoolboy could be more eager than the graying President of the United States about collecting the jaw-bones of a mammoth or the shank of a mastodon. He even believed the legend that somewhere in the Western country there was a solid mountain of salt. In fact, Jefferson had a deep and insatiable curiosity about things, common to schoolboys and scientists. It was a passion shared with his Virginia neighbor and successor, James Madison, and was one of the bases of their long friendship. (Madison wrote Jefferson in Paris in 1785: "Received the two pamphlets on animal magnetism and the last aeronautic expedition together with the phosphoritic matches. These articles were a great treat to my curiosity.")

"I have not been able to hear anything of you," wrote Jefferson reproachfully to Lewis at Philadelphia in April, 1803, "since Mar. 7, till two or three days ago . . . I will . . . thank you to purchase for

me a Leopard or tyger's skin, such as the covers of our saddles were
cut out of. in [1] North 3d street & North 4th street a few doors only
from Market street there used to be a considerable furrier's store in
each. at one of these it was that I saw a robe of what they called the
Peruvian sheep, and I took to be of the Lama or Vigogna. it was made
up of several skins and was of the price of 12 D. If there be such a
thing there now, you can either observe & report it to me, or if you
think it good (for I have almost forgot it) I would take it at once."
Four days later Jefferson wrote again, saying: "The idea that you are
going to explore the Missisipi [sic] has been generally given out;
it satisfies public curiosity and masks sufficiently the real destination." Three days later he wrote once more to remind Lewis to take
along "some cast iron corn mills to give to the Indians or to trade
with them, as well as for your own use."

In May, Lewis wrote from Philadelphia that Dr. Patterson and
Surveyor Ellicott both disapproved of his taking along a theodolite;
instead they recommended two sextants, an artificial horizon or two,
a good Arnold's watch or chronometer, a surveyor's compass and a
set of plotting instruments. Jefferson replied that their advice should
rule. At the end of May Lewis wrote from Philadelphia that he had
been studying under Drs. Rush, Wistar and Barton as well as Patterson, that he had bought for Jefferson a Vigogna (vicuña?) blanket—
"a very pretty thing"—but had been unable to find a tiger's skin.
Such was the way the captain and the President wrote each other
about the minutiae of preparation, although—or was it because?—
Jefferson during this very spring of 1803 was busy with the preliminary negotiations leading to the Louisiana Purchase; in fact, the
treaty of transfer was signed on May 2, 1803, and Jefferson informed
Lewis of it in a letter dated July 15, 1803.

News that this vast deal was about to culminate prompted Jefferson to request Lewis to invite his friend and fellow-Virginian, William ("Billy") Clark, younger brother of General George Rogers
Clark, to join the expedition as coadjutor and second in command.
William Clark was four years older than Lewis. He, like Lewis, had
won his commission fighting the Indians on the Western frontier

---

[1] It was a habit of Jefferson, in the free and easy eighteenth-century way, to begin a
sentence without capitals.

under Anthony Wayne. Lewis, no doubt at Jefferson's suggestion, promised Clark all the honors and rewards that he himself was to get. Clark accepted and became Lewis's loyal and able co-commander; but for some unexplained reason he was never awarded the captaincy promised him. Instead, he was retained as a second lieutenant of artillery until he resigned from the army in 1807. The men of the expedition, however, insisted on calling him "Cap'n Billy" and accorded him the same respect given to Captain Lewis.

In judging men, Jefferson of course made occasional mistakes, but on the whole his selecting ability was very high. In choosing these two young men, he showed something like genius. They made a perfect team, and they carried out a nearly perfect expedition.

Armed with detailed instructions and a letter of credit written by Jefferson's own hand, they left Pittsburgh on what Jefferson insisted on calling "a literary journey" at the end of August, 1803. Clark carried with him a questionnaire about the habits of Western Indians which could have been framed by no one but Jefferson. These are sample questions as taken down by Clark, whose spelling was somewhat weak:

"At what age do both Sexes usially [sic] marry?

"How long do the Woman usually succle their Children?

"What are the Vices most common among the Indians?

"What species of grain or pulse do they cultivate?

"At what season of the year do they usially [sic] go to war?

"What is the cerimony of reciving a Stranger at their Village?"

In January, 1804, Jefferson wrote Lewis that the public was showing a rising interest in the exploration. "The Fed. [eralists] alone still treat it as philosophism and would rejoice in its failure." He added that New Orleans had been delivered to the United States government on December 20. In March Lewis sent his first specimens of plant life to Jefferson—slips of the Osage plum and orange, which he called an apple. On May 14 Lewis led his party out from St. Louis. Five months later they were at Fort Mandan (above Bismarck, North Dakota) where they spent the winter. In April, 1805, Lewis shipped by bateau to Jefferson a quantity of skins, horns, Indian weapons and other articles, seed and a few live squirrels and birds. For many years some of these articles were kept on display at Monticello, Jefferson proudly showing them to distinguished visitors. In November, 1805, the party of thirty-three men and the Indian "bird-woman," Sacagawea, reached the mouth of the Columbia river. In January, 1806, Jefferson wrote to Reuben Lewis, brother of Meriwether, to say a message had been received from the United States Indian agent at St. Louis reporting that some Osage chiefs had brought word that Captain Lewis and party had reached that part of the Missouri river near the mountains where the Indian trace "leads across (in 8 days' march) to the Columbia river."

"Knowing the anxiety of a mother in such a case," wrote Jefferson, "I mention this information praying you to present her my respects and to accept my friendly salutations."

On September 23, 1806, Meriwether Lewis wrote to Jefferson that he had returned safely to St. Louis. The expedition had done its work in two and one-third years. "In obedience to your orders," Lewis wrote, "we have penetrated the Continent of North America to the Pacific Ocean. . . . I am very anxious to learn the state of my friends in Albemarle—particularly whether my mother is yet living." In reply Jefferson wrote:

"I recieved [sic], my dear Sir, with unspeakable joy your letter of Sep. 23 announcing the return of yourself, Capt. Clarke and your party in good health to St. Louis. . . . I salute you with sincere affection." From the wilds beyond the Mississippi the explorers returned to civilization to be lionized, especially by the ladies. From Washington, March 5, 1807, Clark wrote his brother, Major Edmund Clark, in Kentucky: "I have become quite a galant, and [am] somewhat taken with the fair creatures."

One of Lewis's rewards was to be appointed governor of the new Louisiana Territory in that year, while Clark was made governor of Missouri. Lewis did not live long to enjoy his elevation. Jefferson wrote of him in a *Memoir:* "Governor Lewis had, from early life, been subject to hypochondriac affections. It was a constitutional disposition in all the nearer branches of the family of his name, and was more immediately inherited by him from his father.[2] They had not, however, been so strong as to give uneasiness to his family.

---

2 Jefferson had been a deskmate of Thomas Lewis, Meriwether Lewis's father, at Parson Douglas's school for boys.

While he lived with me in Washington, I observed at times sensible depressions of mind; but, knowing their constitutional source, I estimated their course by what I had seen in the family. During his Western expedition the constant exertion which that required of all the faculties of body and mind suspended these distressing affections; but, after his establishment at St. Louis in sedentary occupations, they returned upon him with redoubled vigour, and began seriously to alarm his friends."

Continuing this memoir, Jefferson then described a journey to Washington that Lewis started in September, 1807. Going through the Chickasaw country in Tennessee Lewis stopped for the night at the "stand" of a white man named Grinder on the old Natchez Trace. His body, pierced with a bullet, was found in his room next day. Jefferson always believed Lewis had killed himself. But other persons believed he had been assassinated and robbed. He was only thirty-five years old. The mystery has never been cleared up. On one face of his monument in Lewis county, Tennessee, are these sentences by Jefferson:

"His courage was undaunted. His firmness and perseverance yielded to nothing but impossibilities. A rigid disciplinarian, yet tender as a father to those committed to his charge; honest, disinterested, liberal, with a sound understanding, and a scrupulous fidelity to truth."

Time has a way of defacing reputations and corroding memories. But Meriwether Lewis's name has survived all tests. He fully justified Jefferson's choice of him as a pathfinder. Even the handwriting of his reports to Jefferson remains firm, fine and clear like his character. A fit companion for him was the genial Billy Clark, who was still governor of Missouri when in 1820 it became a state.

Lewis and Clark's success was overshadowed by other events of the period, but their expedition remains one of American history's great achievements. Jefferson fathered the conception, planned its details, and clung resolutely to it until it was fully carried out. By means of this expedition as linked to the Louisiana Purchase, he gave the United States, once cooped up in a narrow ribbon on the Atlantic coast, an empire that leaped the great Mississippi, ascended the Missouri, and reached the Pacific coast. Because of it the American nation suffered only a minimum of the commercial imperialism that kept the world embroiled throughout the nineteenth century; and through it the American nation was able to keep many generations busy, peaceful and comparatively harmless to their neighbors.

The whole enterprise was engraved with characteristic Jefferson markings. It was typical of Jefferson's way of doing good by stealth and indirection. He would never lead an enterprise himself if he could find competent agents to do it. That Jefferson could thus mingle politics, secret diplomacy and natural history was testimony to the veiled methods that so many times convinced his enemies that he was up to the most sinister deviltry when actually he was laboring in some cause much larger than himself. Jefferson's disinterestedness formed an enclosing armor hardly penetrable by the sharpest critical spear, while his lack of any visible ax to be ground was often exasperating and baffling to his opponents. He never claimed credit for the Lewis and Clark expedition and never mentioned it among the enterprises in which he took pride; and strange to say, he omitted it altogether from the list of achievements which he wished inscribed upon his tomb.

Did a Negro risen from slavery in a foreign island enable the United States to make the Louisiana Purchase?

To give an answer to this question we must go back to 1789 when the French masses rose in revolution against monarchy. The emotions thus raised spread to the island of Haiti at the western end of which lay the rich colony of San Domingo, where a few thousand French planters grew rich from the labor of half a million black slaves. In 1791 these slaves revolted. To escape massacre many families of the planting class fled to the United States and established themselves in the chief cities of the Atlantic coast all the way from Charleston to Philadelphia.

The risen Negroes in San Domingo found a leader in Toussaint Breda, who took the surname of L'Ouverture. He organized an army and administration that frightened the colonial governments of Europe, and even those old rivals, England and France, put their heads together. They asked each other:

"How far is this flame of revolt to spread? For our mutual benefit, hadn't we better unite to put down this threat in the West Indies?"

Napoleon Bonaparte answered for France. He wrote to his foreign minister a note intended for the private eye of the British government:

"In the course which I have taken of annihilating the black government at St. Domingo, I have been less guided by considerations of commerce and finance than by the necessity of stifling in every part of the world every kind of germ of disquiet and trouble." [3]

A few months after Jefferson became president of the United States, Napoleon dispatched from Brest a powerful army destined for Hispaniola, the older name of the island, under the command of General Leclerc, husband of Pauline Bonaparte, Napoleon's sister. Almost in the same week R. R. Livingston, Jefferson's envoy, landed in France and in a few days learned enough about this expedition to cause him to write: "I know that the armament destined in the first instance for Hispaniola, is to proceed to Louisiana provided Toussaint makes no opposition." San Domingo for years had been dependent on American supplies. Toussaint wished these supplies to continue. Napoleon wanted them stopped and believed the island could be fully supplied from Louisiana.

Louisiana and San Domingo: with these two colonies closely linked under French control, he believed France could extend her empire in the New World, overawe the young United States, and keep England at bay.

In 1793 when Jefferson was secretary of state, he had written to Governor Monroe of Virginia: "The situation of San Domingo fugitives (aristocrats as they are) calls aloud for pity and charity. Never was so deep a tragedy presented to the feelings of man." In 1799 he wrote to James Madison concerning a bill to continue furnishing supplies to San Domingo: "Even South Carolinians in the House of Representatives voted for it. We may expect, therefore, black crews, and super cargoes, and missionaries thence into the Southern States; and when that leaven begins to work, I would gladly compound with

_____
[3] Adams, *History of the United States,* 1889, I, 391.

a great part of our northern country, if they would honestly stand neuter. If this combustion can be introduced among us under any veil whatever, we have to fear it."

These extracts make it appear that Jefferson, himself a great planter, was uneasy lest the San Domingo revolt affect the slaves in America; but elsewhere the rebellion was identified with what seemed to be a world-wide and spreading infection of Jacobinism; for at the time the Leclerc expedition to crush Toussaint was organized, Otto, the French envoy in London, told his government that the British ministry had said to him:

"The interest of the two governments is absolutely the same, namely, the destruction of Jacobinism [in general] and that of the blacks in particular"; and Napoleon in his order to Leclerc said: "Jefferson has promised that the instant the French army arrives all measures will be taken to reduce Toussaint to starvation and aid the army." [4]

This is not to be accepted as fact, since, when it suited his purposes, Napoleon was an unprincipled fabricator, but enough survives of this diplomatic correspondence to indicate that the United States was in two minds about the Negro revolt: on one hand, it wished the rebellion not to succeed; on the other, it valued the trade with San Domingo, whether it came from Toussaint or the French government. At any rate, General Leclerc obtained Toussaint's arrest by a stratagem and sent him in exile to a mountain dungeon in France. But at the very moment when it appeared that the French army had triumphed, it began to melt away with fever and other tropical diseases; Leclerc then demanded a fresh army of ten thousand men and many tons of new supplies. In a few months Leclerc himself was dead of yellow fever, and nothing remained of the French invaders but a few bones and faded uniforms.

At this crisis, Napoleon realized his dream of a French empire in the New World was gone; for to begin again where Leclerc had left off would require a navy, which he did not have, and much money, which he could not spare. Ever one to cut his losses, Napoleon decided that with San Domingo prostrate, he could not hold Louisiana

4 Quoted by Carl L. Lokke, *American Historical Review*, XXXIII, 327-8.

any longer, and he gave the order for the negotiation of sale to the United States.

It would seem, then, that Louisiana was saved to the United States by the uprising led by the San Domingo Negro, Toussaint L'Ouverture. At least, historians are beginning to see it that way now.

CHAPTER 49

AN EMPIRE—CHEAP

WHEN UPPER LOUISIANA was transferred to France by Spain on March 9, 1804, and turned over to the United States by France the next day, Meriwether Lewis was present at the ceremonies of St. Louis; and so, no doubt, were William Clark and other members of the exploring party. They were bound to be interested, for their journey had caused them to touch at least seven of the states later formed out of the lands lying within the Louisiana Purchase. In fact, the Lewis and Clark expedition cut right across the face of the new territory.

For his part in the Louisiana Purchase, Jefferson was attacked by enemy politicians and since has been criticized by historians, the burden of their condemnation being its unconstitutionality. But the whole business of the purchase might have been called non-constitutional rather than unconstitutional; and as regards the transaction as a whole, it ought to be said that so far from Jefferson having been a plotter for or seeker of the purchase, he seems to have been caught in a stream that carried him irresistibly toward the goal. He was like a man who goes to a stream to catch a minnow and comes back with a ten-pound bass.

The buying by the United States of the territory known as Louisiana was the result of financial fencing between Napoleon Bonaparte and Jefferson. In the deal, each believed he had got the better of the other; but history declares Jefferson was the winner by an incalculable margin. At the beginning of the nineteenth century the struggle over the control of the Mississippi was two decades old, but the immediate question was: who should own the New Orleans gateway to the great river valley? Jefferson dramatized its position thus:

271

"There is on the globe one single spot the possessor of which is our natural and habitual enemy. It is New Orleans, through which the produce of three-eighths of our territory must pass to market. France, placing herself in that door, assumes to us the attitude of defiance. Spain might have retained it quietly for years. . . . The day France takes possession of New Orleans fixes the sentence which is to restrain her forever within her low-water mark. It seals the union of two nations which in conjunction can maintain exclusive possession of the ocean. From that moment we must marry ourselves to the British fleet and nation." He wrote this to R. R. Livingston, minister to France, on April 18, 1802.

Up to 1762 France had owned Louisiana by virtue of the explorations of Robert Cavelier de la Salle begun in 1681. It took France eighty-one years to learn that owning and managing the colony was a costly and troublous business, and she was relieved to be able secretly to convey the province to Spain. Thirty-nine years later Spain, the government of which had been alarmed by the rapid growth of the American states, retroceded *la Louisianne* and the Floridas to France through the secret treaties of San Ildefonso framed by Napoleon Bonaparte with the promise that the territory should not be ceded or alienated to any other nation without Spain's consent.

Although the Spanish government did not sign the treaties until 1802, their contents were pretty well known in the United States in 1801, the year Jefferson took office as president. Better than any other man at Washington, Jefferson knew the import of this reconveyance of Louisiana to France. His knowledge of George Rogers Clark's military ambitions; his study of the Western regions while he was encouraging the explorations of John Ledyard, of André Michaux, and of Lewis and Clark; had made him well aware of the trouble that might ensue if these territories were to be used by the European powers as centers of political and economic intrigue. To Rufus King at London he wrote calling the Louisiana transaction "an inauspicious circumstance for us." To James Monroe he wrote of it as "very ominous." But he could only watch while Napoleon set about building a colonial empire in this hemisphere, which was momentarily halted by the Negro leader, Toussaint L'Ouverture, and by yellow fever in San Domingo.

In October, 1802, the Spanish authorities at New Orleans, who had not yet formally turned over the port to Napoleon, closed the mouth of the Mississippi to American vessels. The result was a convulsion that threw the whole situation into Jefferson's lap. Shippers of tobacco, flour, pork, lead, cordage and apples protested loudly to Washington. Settlers demanded defense by United States troops. Americans living or trading in the Mississippi valley petitioned Congress angrily. It was one of the most harassing dilemmas of Jefferson's life. Either to move or not move might precipitate a war. To keep the young republic out of wars was one of his steadiest principles. Wars would cripple the immature nation, hamper its growth, divert its energies, and twist its development. *No war*—that was a guiding Jeffersonian principle.

His solution was to write a tranquil message to Congress. "Tactful," his friends called it. "Cunning," said his enemies. He was careful not to excite nationalistic feelings; to Congress he merely remarked that the Louisiana cession "if carried into effect" would cause a change in our foreign relations. The key to this message lay in the phrase *"if carried into effect."* Here was a warning to France that the United States might ally herself with Britain; to Spain that its government had gone too far; to the American states that they should keep cool while he acted.

To his confidential friends his tone was in another key. To Du Pont de Nemours, the French physiocrat, he remarked that it was "a crisis the most important the United States have met since their independence and which is to decide their future character and career." For a long time it was supposed the suggestion that the United States buy Louisiana and the Floridas from France came from Napoleon or his foreign minister, Talleyrand; but the Jefferson papers preserved in the Library of Congress make it pretty clear that at least one such suggestion came early in 1802 from Du Pont de Nemours, who had been visiting in America and who was on friendly terms with Jefferson. Du Pont even named the sum of six million dollars, pointing out a fact that he knew would impress Jefferson: that purchase would be much more economical than war.

Having made up his mind that he was ready to go to any extreme to prevent France or any other European power from getting a new foothold on the American continent, Jefferson made several rapid and decisive moves. Having sent R. R. Livingston, lawyer and business man, to Paris as minister, with instructions to ask for the transfer of the Floridas, or at least West Florida, including Mobile Bay, he followed this by asking the Senate to appoint his confidential friend, Colonel James Monroe, special envoy to France "for the purpose of enlarging and more effectually securing our rights and interests in the river Mississippi and in the territories westward thereof."

He then procured a congressional appropriation of two million dollars to defray the expenses of negotiation. His instructions to Monroe and Livingston declared that should a greater sum than that be demanded by France, "the President has made up his mind to go as far as fifty millions of *livres tournois* rather than lose the main object." Seemingly he had forgotten he had told Du Pont the country was in no position to pay six million dollars for the desired territories. (The *livre tournois* at the time it was replaced in 1795 by the franc was worth slightly over nineteen cents.)

Much backing and filling ensued. Livingston, ignorant that Du Pont de Nemours was corresponding with Jefferson from Paris, despaired of coming to terms with France. "I think nothing will be effected here," he wrote; and even Jefferson confessed on April 30, 1803, that he was "not sanguine in obtaining a cession of New Orleans for money."

And then came a sudden change in the face of things. Napoleon, foreseeing a war to the death with England, lacking a navy, and disappointed by the loss of a French army in the West Indies, decided he could not hold Louisiana, that he had better sell it, and use the money to the best military advantage. He ordered his finance minister, Barbé-Marbois, to offer the whole of Louisiana to Livingston (Monroe not having arrived) for fifty million francs. Marbois eventually put the price at sixty million francs, or fifteen million dollars, provided the United States would meet the claims of its citizens for damages done their shipping by France. On May 2, 1803, Livingston and Monroe signed the treaty transferring Louisiana to the United States. Livingston exclaimed to his fellow-ministers: "This is the noblest work of our whole lives."

But Jefferson was curiously backward both in praising his envoys and in rejoicing over the winning of Louisiana. Was his silence due to an uneasy conscience? He had to acknowledge that "the Executive . . . have done an act beyond the Constitution." He had to warn his friends to lie low about "constitutional difficulties," and in asking for ratification he had to beg Congress to cast behind it "metaphysical subleties." The Federalists and other political enemies raged; but Jefferson's fellow-citizens, eager for land and trade, shouted their approval. So far from admitting any pleasure in the deal, Jefferson even confessed he was a bit disappointed at not obtaining the Floridas from the Spanish, but he added with a quiet cunning: "If we push them strongly with one hand, holding out a price with the other, we shall certainly obtain the Floridas, and all in good time."

The tale of the completion of the Louisiana Purchase has often been told, but the wonder of its still remains. The area of the province was greater than that of Great Britain, France, Spain, Germany, Italy and Portugal combined. By this one inexpensive deal Jefferson virtually doubled the United States territory lying within the original thirteen states. Thirteen other states have been formed from the area—Louisiana, Arkansas, Missouri, Iowa, Minnesota, North Dakota, South Dakota, Nebraska, Kansas, Oklahoma, and the main part of Colorado, Wyoming and Montana—all bought for fifteen million dollars.

Jefferson the idealist might have been expected to admit the new territory to the same terms of self-government enjoyed by the existing states; but Jefferson the practical politician thought its inhabitants were not ready for self-determination. As to the form of government being prepared for the Louisianians, he told Du Pont de Nemours:

"We shall make it mild and free, as they are able to bear, all persons residing there concurring in the information that they were neither gratified, nor willing to exercise the rights of an elective government. The immense swarm flocking thither of Americans used to that exercise, will soon prepare them to receive the necessary change."

Thus did the author of the Declaration of Independence forget that governments "derive their just powers from the consent of the governed," and allowed himself to become a Caesar over the thirty thousand Louisiana inhabitants. Congress in March, 1804, gave him complete control of the administrative machinery by authorizing him to appoint the territory's governor, its law-making council and its superior court judges.

The irony of this situation impressed itself on a young man who was peculiarly qualified to be a critic. He was Edward Livingston, of the up-the-Hudson, New York, family of clever Scotch-descended landholders. He was a brother of R. R. Livingston, the American minister to France. Edward Livingston had been mayor of New York. Upon the opening of the new territory he moved there and became the spokesman of the vassal Louisianians. He helped them draw up a memorial that said: "Taxation without representation, an obligation to obey laws without any voice in their foundation, the undue influence of the executive upon legislative proceedings, and a dependent judiciary, formed, we believe, very prominent articles in the list of grievances complained of by the United States at the commencement of their glorious contest for freedom. Were the patriots who composed your councils mistaken in their political principles?"

But Jefferson was not yet done with the extension of American control over new lands. The vagueness of the treaty with France on the subject of the Floridas, eastern and western, irked him; and after studying old maps and claims, an exercise he loved, he convinced himself that the United States had a claim on West Florida up to and including the Perdido river. In February, 1804, while Meriwether Lewis stood poised at St. Louis before starting his westward journey, Jefferson induced Congress to empower him as president to establish "the shores, waters, and inlets of the bay and river of Mobile" into a United States customs district. Feebly Spain protested. Yet she dared not go to war. Her weakness was so evident that her colonies, long held for purposes of exploitation only, began to dream of independence. And indeed Francisco Miranda almost at once made the effort to break Venezuela away. He failed; but Simon Bolivar, Miranda's lieutenant, succeeded, launching a movement which did not exhaust itself until all the Spanish colonies in South America were free.

Bolivar died four years after Jefferson. And in a sense it might be said that if George Washington was the father of his country's freedom, Jefferson was the uncle of South American liberation. As for the Floridas, their conquest remained to be completed in 1819 under President Madison, Jefferson's political heir and adviser. So that at the very opening of the nineteenth century, it was evident that Jefferson was shaping the embryo of that political declaration which, although it was suggested by England, became known as the doctrine of James Monroe, the second of Jefferson's political heirs and pupils.

CHAPTER 50

TANGLE IN A PETTICOAT

WHILE THESE EVENTS were developing, Jefferson was being harassed by a scandal that might have affected his nerves or frightened him into silence, if he had been a weak man. He met it, dealt with it, put it in its place; but since it charged him with coveting his neighbor's wife, it must have cost him some of the most wretched moments of his life, knowing as he did that the Anglo-Saxon peoples throughout their history have reacted strongly against any accusation of sexual irregularity involving an eminent man.

It was ironic that Jefferson should have been touched with this scandal owing to one of his most amiable traits, his quick help to men he deemed unfortunate or persecuted. In this instance the man he befriended was James Thompson Callender, a Scotch journalist from Philadelphia who had been fined and jailed under President John Adams's Alien and Sedition Acts. Jefferson as Adams's successor caused Callender's fine to be remitted. But when Callender, on being relieved of the charges against him, asked for the postmaster's place at Richmond, Jefferson, who had become disillusioned about Callender's character, refused. Callender was enraged. Gaining control of a newspaper, the *Recorder,* in Richmond, he poured on his benefactor the scrapings of taproom gutters. Among other accusations Callender declared that Jefferson, when appointed minister to France, had taken to Paris with him in 1784 a black woman named Sarah or Sally,[1] and that her son, Tom, bore "a striking though sable resemblance" to the President; and that Jefferson had "made up" to the wife of his neighbor and friend, John ("Jack")

---

[1] This was a bright mulatto girl whose father, according to Monticello gossip, was an unknown white man. She escorted Maria Jefferson to Paris.

John Marshall, Jefferson's cousin and enemy, by
Rembrandt Peale

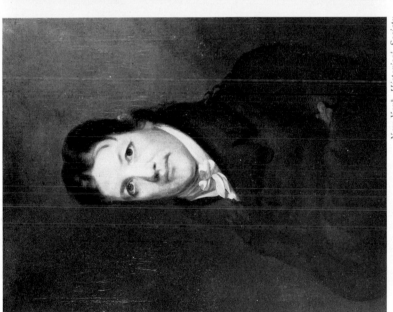
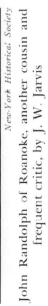

John Randolph of Roanoke, another cousin and
frequent critic, by J. W. Jarvis

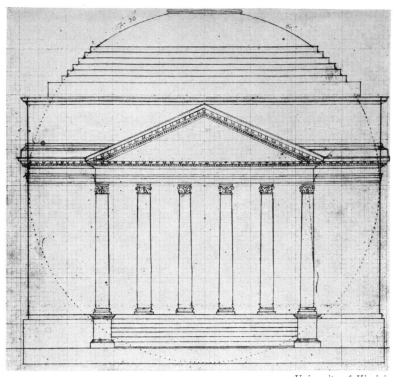

Jefferson's design for the Rotunda at the University of Virginia

The Rotunda, central building of the University of Virginia, adapted by Jefferson from the Pantheon of Rome

Walker, who was the son of Dr. Thomas Walker, close friend of Jefferson's father.

Early in 1805 these charges were taken up, added to, and embellished by the printers of a Massachusetts paper, the *New England Palladium*, which accused Jefferson of having played the coward when the British army, under Cornwallis, invaded Virginia. The paper declared he had said a belief in the existence of a god was of no social importance; that he had helped the atheist Thomas Paine to return to the United States from France; that he had dismantled the navy; that he had secretly given money to Callender for political purposes; and lastly, that he had "assaulted the domestic happiness of Mr. Walker."

All his life Jefferson was an acutely sensitive man. He loathed the obscenity of political combat and despised brawls and dirt. Yet here he was in the depths of a septic pit, the worst and deepest of his existence. The whole scandal must have been painful beyond words —all the more so because it was in part true. Yet he had to take the cup of gall and swallow it, even though Lewis and Clark, Napoleon, Spain and Louisiana might have to be put aside.

The scandal was doubtless the more disagreeable because it brought in the name of Jack Walker, friend of his boyhood and a student chum at William and Mary College, and that of Walker's wife, who was Elizabeth Moore, the granddaughter of Governor Spottswood. Walker's mother was the daughter of Nicholas Meriwether, uncle of Meriwether Lewis. All these were names well known to both the upland yeomanry and Tidewater aristocracy of Virginia. Such names made the smoke of the scandal spread far beyond official circles. One of Jefferson's most savage enemies at this period was his kinsman, Henry Lee. The young American republic had no proper employment for the erratic Harry Lee, and in his endeavors to make money out of land and speculation, he encountered many troubles. Having failed in real estate promotion, Lee went into politics, becoming one of the vocal Federalists who believed Jefferson had brought home from France doctrines which would subvert the nation. Lee brooded on and nursed his feelings about Jefferson until his suspicions had festered into a hatred which could be appeased only by his doing some visible hurt. When the scandal involving

Jefferson and his neighbor's wife first began to burgeon, Lee went to Walker as the injured husband and persuaded him to make and sign a statement.

In outlining this statement Walker, who had waited forty years to make it, forgot he had been Jefferson's chum in childhood and his intimate at college, and that Jefferson once had written him playful letters in a kind of burlesque Latin. Walker declared that Jefferson in 1769 or 1770 began a series of attempts on Mrs. Walker's virtue that lasted for some years, even after Jefferson was married. His statement said that Jefferson's attentions to Mrs. Walker began when her husband in 1768 (Jefferson was then twenty-five years old and unmarried) was absent four months as clerk to the Virginia commissioners.

The statement continued: "At Shadwell, his own house, in '69 or '70, on a visit common to us being neighbors he renewed his caresses, placed in Mrs. Walker's sleeve cuff, a paper tending to convince her of the innocence of promiscuous love. This Mrs. Walker, on the first glance, tore to pieces"; yet not so emphatically as to discourage Jefferson, said Walker, from stealing later into a room at the house of Colonel Coles where Mrs. Walker was undressing or in bed. "He was repulsed," said the statement, "with indignation and menaces of alarm, and stole off."

Nevertheless, Walker continued, Jefferson, although in '71 he was married, renewed his molestations, which went on until 1779. The statement mentions a particular incident in which Jefferson, "found in his shirt," tried to molest Mrs. Walker when he and Mrs. Jefferson were guests at the Walker home. Walker declared his wife had said nothing of these incidents until Jefferson had sailed for France, for fear of consequences to her husband's health.

By July, 1805, the noise made over these charges obliged Jefferson to make an explanation to his cabinet members and particular friends. To Robert Smith, his secretary of the navy, he wrote: "You will perceive that I plead guilty to one of the charges, that when young and single I offered love to a handsome lady. I acknoledge [sic] its correctness. It is the only one founded in truth in all their allegations against me."

What reception the President's associates gave to this explanation is not known beyond the brief note written by Madison to Monroe on April 20, 1805: "The affair between the President and J. Walker has had a happy *éclairecissement*. Even this general communication is for your own bosom as already privy to the affair."

This reference to a happy clearing up of the affair accorded with Lee's note on his interview with Jefferson regarding the scandal in which he recorded the hope "that social intercourse may be restored between two friends from earliest years. I was truly satisfied in finding kindred feelings in his [Walker's] breast." [2]

One supporter who took up the cudgels for Jefferson was Thomas Paine. In answer to one Thomas Turner of Virginia, who had attacked Jefferson for various offenses including the alleged affair with Mrs. Walker, Paine, using a pen name because, he said, "I do not wish Mr. Jefferson to be *obliged* to know it is from me," wrote in 1805 the following comment for publication in the *American Citizen:*

"Turner's fourth calumny is a tale about Mrs. Walker, who, if now living, must be upwards of 60 years of age; a tale, of which the public knows no fact, and is possessed by no evidence. . . . We have heard of a ten years' siege of Troy; but who ever heard of a ten years' siege to seduce? and what is equally as wonderful, that a woman should keep it a secret ten years. Ten years, [says Turner and then repeats it in capitals] TEN YEARS, was Mr. Jefferson repeatedly and assiduously making attempts which were as repeatedly and with horror repelled. There could not be much horror in the case or it would have killed any woman in less than a tenth part of that time." [3]

---

[2] Jefferson papers, Library of Congress.
[3] *Complete Writings of Thomas Paine*, ed. Foner, New York, 1945.

CHAPTER 51

"TOO BIG FOR HER"

"So you are at the head of your wise country," wrote Du Pont de Nemours from France to Jefferson on hearing of his election as president. "She has unreservedly placed her greatest man in her greatest position. . . . For God has given you *judgment*." Du Pont added later: "I fear that you are too big for her."

The United States was indeed a small country, having only about five and a quarter million inhabitants. About seven thousand people lived in its unfinished capital, which was streaked with mud in winter and seared with heat in summer. The town was so crude that when the French minister, Turreau, appeared there in a uniform hung with much gold lace, Jefferson was afraid the small boys would follow him in the streets and "chunk" him with stones.

As for the British minister Anthony Merry, he and his wife, after living luxuriously in Paris and Spain, were obliged on moving to Washington to take a house that had neither pump nor well; and Thomas Moore, the Irish poet, after being a guest of the Merrys in Washington, went away and wrote these lines:

> "Take Christians, Mohawks, democrats and all,
> From the wide wigwam to the Congress hall,—
> From man the savage, whether slaved or free,
> To man the civilized, less tame than he:
> 'Tis one dull chaos, one unfertile strife,
> Betwixt half-polished and half-barbarous life;
> Where every ill the ancient world can brew
> Is mixed with every grossness of the new;
> Where all corrupts, though little can entice,
> And nothing's known of luxury but vice."

282

To say that "all corrupts" was of course a rhetorical statement; but that all was not beautiful on the Potomac was admitted by Jefferson himself when in writing to Du Pont on the eve of the latter's departure from France for America he said:

"The present agonizing state of commerce, and the swarms of speculators in money and in law, would induce me to beseech you to trust no-body." [1]

This testimony to swarming speculators was supported by Augustus John Foster, secretary to the British minister, who wrote home that speculators had cut the ground in the Federal City into such small lots that space was lacking even for gardens. The capital contained other things that Foster did not like. He and the other diplomats yearned for a return of the stately ceremony and dress of Washington's and Adams's time. The simple modes that Jefferson had established revolted the Englishman. He accused Jefferson of "excessive vanity and speculative doctrines on imaginary perfection"; he wrote that Jefferson "flattered the low passions of a mere newspaper-taught rabble," and that as president Jefferson "seemed pleased to mortify men of rank and station." [2] He had seen the President ride through the streets and fasten his horse's bridle to the shop doors, and had been told that Jefferson had received the British minister "in yarn stockings and slippers."

Foster had to admit, however, that Jefferson could look well on state occasions, and at his second inauguration was elegantly dressed in black, with black silk stockings; [3] but "a very mixed company" came into the President's House, "some lolling about on couches and in dirty shoes, and even Negro servants were seen helping themselves to wine at the side table." The same sort of mixed company was to be seen at the Sunday services in the Hall of Representatives, which Jefferson and a secretary attended so regularly that two special seats were reserved for them. Mrs. Margaret Bayard Smith in her

[1] *Correspondence Between Thomas Jefferson and P. S. Du Pont de Nemours*, ed. Malone.

[2] Quoted by Margaret Bailey Turkcom, *William and Mary Quarterly*, VIII, 68–107.

[3] Compare William Plumer's note on the President's appearance, Dec. 3, 1803: "He was well dressed— A new suit of black-silk hose—shoes—clean linnen (*sic*), and his hair highly powdered." William Plumer's *Memorandum of Proceedings in the United States Senate*, ed. Brown, New York, 1923.

recollections thought these assemblages were highly interesting, being made up partly of "ladies in their gayest costumes," who, after listening a while to the Marine Band in scarlet uniforms, would push through the crowds and warm themselves at one of the huge fireplaces. Foster was disgusted, however, when an attending congressman, who found himself short of money when the collection plate came up, wrote out a check payable "to Jesus C."

But even the Britisher had to admit that some things at the capital were not bad. There was good snipe and partridge shooting on either side of Pennsylvania Avenue, and ducks and fish could be found nearby in Potomac waters. He found even among the Democrats "many highly respectable and worthy persons," and among the members of Congress were "several droll, original but unoffending characters." When delegations of Indians came to visit Jefferson, his fatherly attitude toward them amazed Foster. This is his picture of one of these occasions:

"Mr. Jefferson was as much attached to them from Philanthropy and because they were Savages as if they were his own children. . . . Just as we arrived the Indians were going out. The President was bowing to them; he made a bow also to me and to Mr. Merry, asking him how he did but said nothing more to us." [4] Foster liked the racing at Georgetown and the card-playing in the evening. "Brag" was favored by the men, while "Loo was the innocent Diversion of the Ladies who when they were looed pronounced the word in a very mincing manner."

The British secretary seems to have invaded the camp of the enemy in summer, for his memoirs remark that at Monticello the breakfast hour was eight o'clock. Guests were then left free till 4 P.M. when dinner was served. Jefferson played with his grandchildren till dusk when tea was brought in, afterward wine and fruit—"the peaches were excellent." Foster thought poorly of Jefferson's wines,[5] and heard his host admit that his wine barrels were sometimes tapped and water substituted. Life was carried on at Monticello very informally, and Foster was amazed when Jefferson

---

4 "Memoirs," Library of Congress.

5 Compare Plumer: "His [Jefferson's] dinner was elegant and rich—his wines very good—there were eight different kinds."

Randolph, Martha's sixteen-year-old son, came into the drawing room one evening barefooted.

Foster never forgave Jefferson for what he deemed an affront to his chief, the British minister, Anthony Merry. One evening the Merrys were invited to dine with the President. When dinner was announced, Jefferson, who had already made it known that formal etiquette would be abolished at the President's House, gave his arm to Mrs. Dolly Madison instead of Mrs. Merry. The latter, expecting precedent to be followed, was outraged and next day prevailed on her husband to take the case to the British foreign office. To offset any ill effects, Secretary of State Madison apprised James Monroe, then United States minister in London, of the facts. No official notice was taken, but the affair got into the gossip at the capital, where Mrs. Merry's horror of republican customs had been unconcealed. In fact, Mrs. Merry wrote to the poet Moore concerning the first meal served in her American home:

"Neither his Britannic Majesty's Minister or Mistress Merry could eat a morsel that was served. . . . Mr. M. frets and every moment exclaims: 'Why, it is a thousand times worse than the worst parts of Spain.' " [6] Mrs. Margaret Bayard Smith, Jefferson's admirer, disposed of the Merrys by saying Mrs. Merry was "so entirely the talker and actor in all companies that her good husband passes quite unnoticed; he is plain in his appearance and called rather inferior in his understanding." [7] In short, Mrs. Merry wore the trousers: as soon as the capital understood that, it laughed and passed on to a consideration of more serious matters like the composition of Jefferson's first cabinet.

For secretary of state Jefferson had named James Madison of Virginia; for secretary of war, General Henry Dearborn of Massachusetts; for attorney general, Levi Lincoln of Massachusetts; for secretary of the navy, Samuel Smith of Maryland; for postmaster general, Gideon Granger of Connecticut; and for secretary of the treasury, Albert Gallatin of Pennsylvania. These were the men of whom Jefferson wrote to John Dickinson:

"A just and solid republican government maintained here will

[6] *Records of the Columbia Historical Society.*
[7] *The First Forty Years of Washington Society.*

be a standing monument and example for the aim and imitation of the people of other countries."

The nation deemed it a worthy cabinet, particularly strong at the State and Treasury posts. Madison's abilities were well known; Gallatin's less so, but Jefferson in choosing him to design financial policy showed genius, for Gallatin was strongest where Jefferson was weakest —in business and finance.

Gallatin was Swiss-born. As a youth he came to America, taught French at Harvard College, went to the Middle West and made money speculating in land, settled in Pennsylvania, went into politics and served in the Pennsylvania legislature and in Congress. As head of the Treasury he quickly adopted a decisive financial policy. Alexander Hamilton's notion had been to create a great national debt and maintain that debt as the central pillar of government; Gallatin's policy was anti-war, anti-taxation and, above all, anti-debt. Jefferson welcomed this aim.

"The discharge of the debt is vital to our destinies," he wrote Gallatin, adding that all other objects might be "subordinate to this." [8]

From Gallatin's detailed letters to his wife we catch glimpses of what he called "Washington City" as it was in Jefferson's day.

"It requires more fortitude to live here in a humble way than it did in Philadelphia," he wrote her, and warned her not to come to the capital unless she was willing to put up with hardships. Gallatin was in all respects a practical man, and he proved to be just the man to relieve Jefferson of vexations within that sphere of finance for which, despite his love for figures and statistics, Jefferson was unfitted, and thus free his hands for the tasks immediately ahead of him.

The first of these tasks, as Jefferson saw it, was to free the infant nation, of which he had just been elected the head, from the clutch and influence of Europe. America, in Jefferson's view, must learn to stand on her own feet, grow in her own way, and achieve her own destiny. To do this America must develop her own institutions and cut loose from those of England and the rest of the Old World. In

---

[8] Adams, *Life of Gallatin*, p. 270.

the letters and papers of this period again and again he emphasized his primary aim:

"I consider Europe at present as a world apart from us."

. . . . .

"What is the whole system of Europe towards America but an atrocious and insulting tyranny?"

. . . . .

"We consider the interests of Cuba, Mexico, and ours as the same, and that the object of both must be to exclude all European influence from this hemisphere."

. . . . .

"The comparison of our governments with those of Europe is like a comparison of heaven and hell. England, like the earth, may be allowed to take the intermediate station."

. . . . .

Thus was foreshadowed that Monroe Doctrine which was now but partly outlined by Jefferson, but which attained full form under one of his chief pupils, James Monroe, when president of the United States. Jefferson saw the national government as fitted to deal with foreign nations; domestic affairs, he argued, should be in charge of the states.

Above all, Jefferson held, there must be no war. Give the United States a minimum of eight years of peace, and then it would be strong enough to cope with any likely enemy. Yet almost at that very moment the war tocsins sounded over Europe, and Napoleon gave the order for the building up of France's colonies in the New World. And Europe's monarchs were inclined to applaud Napoleon because they deemed the time ripe for a curbing of the burgeoning republicanism on the other side of the Atlantic. If republicanism succeeded in the New World, how long would the Old World be safe from its contaminations and infiltrations?

Determined as Jefferson was to see the country grow strong before engaging in any war, he was not able to maintain a peace policy with the Barbary States on the north coast of Africa; Algiers,

Morocco, Tunis and Tripoli for years had demanded and got tribute money from the chief naval powers before their ships could ply the Mediterranean. Under both the Washington and Adams administration large sums had been paid to these piratical little nations. This is a bill for captured Americans sent by the Barbary pirates to Jefferson when he was minister at Paris in the Washington administration:

3 captains, $6,000 each	$18,000
2 mates, $4,000 each	8,000
2 passengers, " "	8,000
14 seamen, $1,400 each	27,600
	$53,600
For custom, 11 p.c.	5,896
Total	$59,496

It is not on record that Jefferson ever paid this ransom money, for Congress had authorized him to offer only two hundred dollars a man. Finding that negotiations and conciliatory letters were useless, Jefferson as president decided to challenge the corsairs. Early in 1801 he sent Commodore Dale with four vessels to the Barbary coast with definite orders to protect American commerce. Dale captured a Tripolitan cruiser and instituted armed convoys in such a way as to frighten the pirates, who for the time being withdrew to their lairs. Eventually they gave up their predatory ways, but not until after Jefferson had left the presidency.

CHAPTER 52

HELP FOR THE FORLORN

IN THE COURSE of his first term as president, Jefferson several times
was called upon to show sympathy for, or otherwise help, some of
those raffish and eccentric or forlorn characters for whom he often
had a secret admiration. When Thomas Paine, who was becoming
old and poor in a vain effort to have his ideas and inventions accepted
in France, wanted to come home, Jefferson offered to give him passage
on a returning naval vessel. When Dr. Joseph Priestley, scientist and
religious writer, was mobbed in England and his home destroyed
owing to his political and religious views, Jefferson welcomed him
to America and to the capital.

"I should claim the right to lodge you," he wrote Priestley on his
Pennsylvania farm. It was to Dr. Priestley that Jefferson addressed
his *Syllabus of an Estimate of the Merit of the Doctrines of Jesus
compared with others,* a document often quoted, in which he said:

"To the corruptions of Christianity I am, indeed, opposed; but
not to the genuine precepts of Jesus himself. I am a Christian, in the
only sense in which he wished any one to be; sincerely attached to
his doctrines in preference to all others; ascribing to him every human excellence; and believing he never claimed any other."

To Colonel Benjamin Hawkins, United States agent among the
Indians, Jefferson wrote often, showing his anxiety about the red
men's future. He foresaw that the game of the fields and woods
would soon be gone, and he hoped the Indians would learn agriculture and home crafts, also that eventually "our settlements and theirs
[might] meet and blend together."

Near the end of Jefferson's first term two events occurred which caused him major shocks. His daughter, the lovely Maria, Mrs. John Wayles Eppes, after a lingering illness during which her father wrote to her anxiously every few days, drooped and died. To a sympathetic letter from his boyhood friend, John Page, Jefferson answered:

"Others may lose of their abundance, but I, of my want, have lost even the half of all I had."

Maria died in April, 1804. In July of that year Aaron Burr, maddened and frustrated by Alexander Hamilton's supposed interference with Burr's ambitions, shot and mortally wounded him in a pistol duel on Weehawken Heights in New Jersey across the river from New York.

To Jefferson, Hamilton's theories and financial programs had been things of detestation, but toward the man he could be, and was, charitable. Socially they had often met in friendly intercourse, and Hamilton's bust was among the few that Jefferson installed in the hall at Monticello. As for Burr, his disintegration began with the duel at Weehawken. He had a feeling that he was a small man among such giants as Jefferson, Hamilton and Washington, and that only by grasping power could he be regarded as on a level with such figures. His weakness was that he could not think in terms of any man's welfare but his own; and so Burr repeatedly got in the way of Burr, and at last Burr ruined Burr.

At the end of his first term Jefferson was able joyfully to announce that "fourteen of the seventeen States are completely with us" and that he would be a candidate again because "tory calumnies" had obliged him to appeal to the country once more "for a justification." In the election Jefferson won by 162 electoral votes against 14 for Charles C. Pickney of South Carolina, who got the support of only three states—Connecticut, home of some of Jefferson's most virulent critics, political and clerical; Delaware and Maryland.

Jefferson began his second term with his enemies temporarily silenced and with a prosperous nation looking up to him with gratitude and admiration.

CHAPTER 53

ADAMS ACID

JEFFERSON'S ADDRESS at the opening of his second term on March 4, 1805, pointed with pride to the success of the principles which he had proclaimed at his first inauguration.

"With nations, as with individuals," he said, "our interests, soundly calculated, will ever be found inseparable from our moral duties."

"Moral duties"—that was a phrase which should have been pleasing to such rigid onlookers as John Quincy Adams, who had never liked Jefferson even when his parents had. Adams had been elected to the Senate from Massachusetts. When a youth he had been befriended by Jefferson in Europe, but J. Q. Adams was not a man to be swayed by sentiment and he could never bring himself to approve of Jefferson either as man or president. But because of his very prejudices, we owe to Adams, who himself lived to become president of the United States, vivid pictures of Jefferson in the President's House during his second term. On November 23, 1804, Adams dined with Jefferson, who said he would "give the creation" for a young lawyer with ability and a knowledge of French to go to New Orleans as a Superior Court judge, at a salary of two thousand dollars. Jefferson went on to discuss the French Revolution and wished the French would return to constitutional government and to "the old family"; he thought all young Americans should learn French and Spanish, and remarked that he himself had learned Spanish in nineteen days by taking advantage of a sea voyage and a copy of *Don Quixote*.

At this point Adams wrote in his diary: "Mr. Jefferson tells large stories. . . . You can never be an hour in this man's company without something of the marvelous like these stories." [1] The evening

[1] *Diary*, ed. Nevins, 1928, pp. 25–26.

291

ended with a display by Jefferson of a natural history of parrots, with beautiful colored plates.

Soon after the new year, 1805, Adams again dined with Jefferson, who at first seemed to have something on his mind and then gave way to his "itch for telling prodigies." He told, wrote Adams, of seeing the cold in Paris at 20° F. below zero, where it stood, or nearly so, for six weeks.

"He knows better than all this," remarked Adams, "but he loves to excite wonder." At another time Adams enjoyed "one of the most agreeable dinners" he ever had in Jefferson's company. There was some talk, "not very edifying," on wines, and then Jefferson praised the philosophy of Epicurus, "misunderstood and misrepresented" though it had been.

The President agreed with Senator Mitchill, who was present, that Fulton's new inventions, the steamboat and torpedo, were of great importance.

CHAPTER 54

BURR REACHES FOR POWER

THUS FAR THE Union of states had met all of Jefferson's expectations, but one thing was still uncertain. Would the Union stand up under the divisive tendencies that had so plainly exhibited themselves almost from the natal day of the republic? Would the Union endure attack from within as well as without?

One doubt, small and hidden, remained in Jefferson's mind from his reading of Montesquieu. The French philosopher had taught that a republican form of government was suited only to small areas, and this argument had made an impression on Jefferson while his absorptive mind was still young and plastic.

Were the United States too large and expansive to be held together by a republic?

Would their splitting tendencies become worse as new and distant states were added?

An answer was given in Jefferson's second administration. It came through a man whom Jefferson was slow to suspect—Aaron Burr, his own vice-president. Some of Jefferson's friends doubted Burr's character, but no one doubted his ability. He was a son of a president of Princeton College. He had been an active officer in the chief battles of the Revolutionary War. He had proved his political astuteness in the political wars of New York State. Yet somehow Burr, though burning with ambition and thirsty for power, had never been able to reach the top places. He was full of frustrations and resentments. He had removed one of his chief obstacles by killing Alexander Hamilton, only to find himself charged with murder in New York and New Jersey. As presiding officer of the United States Senate he was often absent or inattentive. It was plain that something was on his mind.

Soon after Jefferson's second inauguration Burr went on a Western visit. He stopped at Pittsburg, again at Blennerhasset's Island in the Ohio river, at Lexington, at Nashville and finally at New Orleans. Here the commander of the American forces was General Wilkinson, a military swaggerer and high liver who loved wines, feasts, money and prominence. Years later it came out that Wilkinson was for sale, and was in fact already on the payroll of the Spanish government. It was one of Jefferson's criticisms of Burr that he was "always at market." Did Burr recognize in Wilkinson a fellow-traveler who would be ready to listen to schemes?

In 1806 Burr made a second Western trip and contracted to purchase a large tract of land near Nachitoches known as the Bastrop tract. Thereafter matters developed rapidly and men began to drift toward the Burr banner, some believing that they were only to settle the Bastrop tract, others that they were to help rescue the oppressed residents of Louisiana, and still others that they were to be founders of a Western empire that might extend into Mexico and have its capital at New Orleans.

Jefferson was slow to believe in Burr's guilt, but at last he issued a proclamation. By the time it reached the Mississippi valley, the states of Ohio, Kentucky, Tennessee and Mississippi were all aroused against Burr, and eventually he was arrested at a place on the Mississippi side of the river, now near Wakefield, Alabama. At that point Burr had left his command of one hundred men and nine boats. Since there was a question of jurisdiction, Burr was sent under escort to Richmond, Virginia. Jefferson was elated by this display of loyalty. He wrote to Governor Tiffin of Ohio on February 20, 1807:

"The hand of the people has given a mortal blow to a conspiracy which, in other countries, would have called for an appeal to armies, and have proved that government to be the strongest of which every man feels himself a part." He even wrote to General Wilkinson of "the public confidence in you." It is not on record if Jefferson ever learned that Wilkinson had been for years in the secret pay of Spain.

When Burr was arraigned before Chief Justice Marshall at Richmond, the latter would not allow him to be charged with high treason, but only with a misdemeanor. He permitted Burr to give bail and attended a dinner given by the Richmond lawyer, John Wickham, where he and Burr sat at the same table, a circumstance that Jefferson's friends—and enemies too—did not fail to notice. Jefferson himself foresaw that Burr would be acquitted, but wrote: "If his punishment can be commuted now for a useful amendment of the Constitution, I shall rejoice in it." He explained that he meant "the error . . . which makes any branch [meaning the judiciary] independent of the nation."

The investigation of Burr was conducted in an atmosphere of fashionable gaiety. He himself wrote his daughter, Theodosia Burr, whom alone among human beings he loved and trusted, of being treated in jail to gifts of "oranges, lemons, pineapples, raspberries, apricots, cream, butter, ice, and some ordinary articles."

One of the spectators at the grand jury investigation was the author Washington Irving, "on an informal retainer from one of the friends of Col. Burr." At one stage Irving wrote his friend, Mrs. Matilda Hoffman, that the grand jury had been "dismissed the day before yesterday for five or six days, that they might go home, see their wives, get their clothes washed, and flog their negroes." He added this about Burr: "I am very much mistaken if the most underhand and ungenerous measures have not been observed toward him." The Richmond ladies, he said, showed open sympathy for Burr; and some of these ladies "think you absolutely at their command; they conclude that you must, of course, be fond of moonlight walks, and rides at daybreak, and red-hot strolls in the middle of the day . . . they expect you to talk sentiment and act Romeo." [1]

The jury's verdict was that the accused had not been "proved to be guilty . . . by any evidence submitted to us," and Burr fled to Europe. He returned to live a shadowy life till 1834, eight years after Jefferson's death. Burr's beloved daughter Theodosia perished in 1812 in a gale off the North Carolina coast on a voyage between Charleston and New York.

Jefferson's supporters lost the Burr case, but they won a new belief in the firm union of American states. And foreign nations took note. To Jefferson, the conduct of Justice Marshall in the Burr case was only further proof that the enemies of rule by the people, defeated

---

1 *Life and Letters*, 1864, I, 193–203.

at the polls, had taken refuge in the judiciary. Marshall's name had already caused Jefferson to see red because Marshall had held in Marbury *vs.* Madison that the Supreme Court could interpret the Constitution in relation to the laws passed by Congress, even to the extent of declaring such laws null and void.

To Jefferson's mind this was abolishing the offset of one branch of the government by the others, and was consolidating supreme power in the nation's judges. There was no way under the Constitution to remove a judge except through impeachment. In 1804 the first attempt was made when old and battered John Pickering, a district judge in New Hampshire, was brought before the United States Senate on charges of drunkenness, profanity and personal abuse on the bench. He was duly impeached.

The Republicans then moved on to higher game. Samuel Chase of Maryland had been a signer of the Declaration of Independence and had been appointed to the Supreme Court by President Washington. In cases involving the Alien and Sedition Acts, Chase, who was a political reactionary, had lost his head and not only had helped to punish dissenters but had openly showed his scorn for Jefferson's tenets by attacking "democracy," "mobocracy," "universal suffrage" and other doctrines "fatal to all security for property and personal liberty."

Spurred by Jefferson, the House voted impeachment of Chase, and John Randolph of Roanoke headed the prosecution. But the necessary two-thirds vote of the Senate was not won, and just before Jefferson began his second term, Chase had been pronounced by Aaron Burr, presiding over the Senate, "not guilty."

Jefferson knew he had lost the battle; the rich and well-born, he feared, would keep intact their influence on the judiciary; but he kept up for life his warfare against the power of judges to "usurp legislation."

"It is a misnomer," he wrote James Pleasants twenty years later, "to call a government republican in which a branch of the supreme power is independent of the nation."

As for Marshall, he had written of Jefferson to Alexander Hamilton only a few weeks before Jefferson's inauguration: "By weakening the office of president he will increase his personal power; the morals

of the author of the letter to Mazzei cannot be pure," while Jefferson
continued to speak of Marshall's "gloomy malignity." It was ironical
that this, one of Jefferson's chief enemies, was the son-in-law of the
woman whom Jefferson had once admired, and almost proposed to,
as "Belinda"—Rebecca Burwell, who had married the mature Jacquelin Ambler while the boy Jefferson had vacillated.

CHAPTER 55

A SUBSTITUTE FOR WAR

WHEN JEFFERSON began his second term, the national revenues were growing so fast—upward of fifteen million dollars in 1806—that it was evident the Revolutionary War debt would soon be paid off and a surplus created. Jefferson wanted to use this surplus to provide for the general welfare by setting up improved means of education, also communication, so as to cement the Union by ties of roads, canals and rivers.

Congress responded with an appropriation for the Cumberland Road across the Alleghenies, the first of the national highways pointing westward. But Congress was not ready for a national university and Jefferson temporarily laid aside his plan without relinquishing it.

Peace and prosperity might have continued indefinitely except for two events. One was the British naval victory at Trafalgar, which ensured that Britannia could not only rule, but police, the waves without further fear of France or any other country. Thereafter British manners on salt water became short and short-sighted, and Jefferson had to struggle manfully to preserve his peace policy while British ships were stopping American vessels to take off and impress needed seamen, regardless of birth.

The other event was the Berlin Decree by which Napoleon Bonaparte ordered a blockade of the British Isles and prohibited all commerce with them. The British government retaliated by proclaiming that all ports which should shut out British ships would be subject to similar restrictions.

Jefferson well knew, and so did most of his countrymen, that the little United States with its six million people and its little navy,

consisting chiefly of economical gunboats, could not do battle with
those two monsters, England and France, which had thus begun a
final and mortal struggle for mercantile supremacy throughout the
world.

"Those moral principles and conventional usages which have here-
tofore been the bond of civilized nations," he wrote the Ketocton
Baptists, "have given way to force, the law of barbarians, and the
nineteenth century dawns with the vandalism of the fifth."

But the excitement caused by Napoleon's Berlin Decree and the
British Orders in Council was minor beside that aroused on June 19,
1807, when off the Virginia capes the British ship *Leopard*, seeking
British deserters, fired on the United States ship *Chesapeake*, killing
three men and wounding eighteen others. The consequence was a
national outburst of resentment, particularly strong in Virginia and
particularly weak in Connecticut where the Federalists, always
strongly pro-British, refused to sign pledges of support to the government.

Jefferson, clinging to peace but fearing the war party would sweep
the country, played for time.

"If we go to war now," he wrote, "I fear we may renounce forever the hope of seeing an end of our national debt. If we can keep
at peace eight years longer, our income will be adequate to any war."

The British, seeing his reluctance, were slow in making repara-
tions, and in fact did not settle accounts with the United States government until 1811; and even then did not stop miscellaneous im-
pressments. This fact remained a burning issue right up to the War
of 1812. And finally the pacific Jefferson gave way to his feelings and
wrote concerning the repeated impressment of American citizens:
"We must sacrifice the last dollar and drop of blood to rid us of that
badge of slavery; and it must rest with England alone whether it is
worth eternal war, for eternal war it must be if she holds to the
wrong."

In this atmosphere of tension, matters drifted along until Jefferson called a cabinet meeting to consider an embargo. Various
students of history have pronounced this to be the cardinal mistake
of Jefferson's presidential career; owing not only to the fact that the
embargo when adopted was more ruinous to American than to Brit-

ish trade, but also to Jefferson's failure to realize that an economic problem could not be solved by a political instrument. Madison, who at this stage had great influence with Jefferson, favored the embargo because one had been successfully employed in 1794, when for thirty days no American vessel had been permitted to clear for a foreign port. Only Gallatin warned that "government prohibitions do always mischief," and wanted to impose a time limit on any embargo adopted.

Jefferson favored an embargo because there were only two other alternatives, neither of which was to be thought of at the moment: one was submission, the other was war. Some form of coercion, he thought, must be employed; but in young America's weak condition it was best to make it "peaceable coercion."

"Our commerce is so valuable to them [European nations]," he wrote, "that they will be glad to purchase it when the only price we ask is to do us justice. I believe that we have in our hands the means of peaceable coercion; and that the moment they see our government so united as that they can make use of it, they will for their own interest be disposed to do us justice." The British reply came in the form of an editorial in the London *Times:*

"Right is power sanctioned by usage."

The Embargo Act as drawn by Madison in December, 1807, passed the Senate by a 22 to 6 vote and the House by 82 to 44. It prohibited all American vessels from leaving their ports for Europe. Jefferson was amazed to see that peacetime trade had its corruptions as well as wartime trade, and was astonished to behold the blighting effect of the embargo at home in Virginia as well as in New England. The shipping interests were the most immediate sufferers, but they could and did evade the act by extensive and ingenious smuggling. But on the cotton, rice and tobacco farmers of the South, dependent on export trade to England and the Continent, the effect was ruinous. Exports fell in value from $48,700,000 in 1807 to $9,433,000 in 1808.

Said John Randolph of Roanoke: "We have hanged ourselves for spite, in hopes that they [the British] would cut us down . . . they preferred to let us dangle in our garters." William Cullen Bryant, the poet, exhibited the indignation of his native heath by writing satirical verses plainly aimed at Jefferson. This was one:

"Go, wretch! Resign the Presidential chair,
Disclose thy secret measures, foul or fair;
Go search with curious eyes for horned frogs
'Mid the wild waste of Louisiana bogs;
Or where Ohio rolls his turbid stream
Dig for huge bones, thy glory and thy theme."

The Embargo Act, however, did have one emphatic effect: it promoted and established home manufactures. Cut off from European supplies, little farm-surrounded towns became industrialized, and small specialty and mechanical shops were set up all along the seaboard, especially in New England.

Jefferson had wit enough to see that this development was inevitable, and at this stage he was not slow to recognize industry and trade as having no less importance than agriculture.

"An equilibrium," he wrote, "of agriculture, manufactures, and commerce is certainly become essential to our independence."

The embargo experiment in centralized power hung on until Timothy Pickering, Federalist leader, joined with the Essex Junto of Connecticut to threaten the secession of at least three of the New England states. The New England papers howled for resistance to the embargo. The cabinet split on the question of maintaining it, but there was no question in the minds of the shipping and trading interests. They resisted and evaded the act for fifteen months until Jefferson finally gave up and permitted the embargo to be replaced by a non-intercourse act. His enemies called this another failure; his friends argued the embargo had been merely experimental, and at least had kept the country out of war. John Adams later wrote to Jefferson: "Your administration will be quoted by philosophers as a model of profound wisdom; by politicians as weak, superficial, and shortsighted." Adams's son, John Quincy Adams, called the embargo "the only shelter from the tempest."

As Jefferson's second term ended, he refused to consider a third one and happily turned his seat over to James Madison. He recognized that his ideal of a government "just and wise for the many" had not been attained, but he was convinced the American form was closer to it than any other. He was satisfied to receive from the Virginia legislature "a respectful and affectionate farewell" in an address which recited his unparalleled achievements as president.

Now at the age of sixty-six he could go back to Monticello with its five thousand acres and to Poplar Forest with its four thousand acres; back to family, books, birds, gardens and leisure. From Monticello he wrote back to Madison, who was facing the future wanly, what might have been a review of the national and international situation, but what he said was: "No oats sown, not much tobacco-seed. . . . Flour is said to be at eight dollars at Richmond."

CHAPTER 56

PLOUGHS AND HARROWS

AMONG THE HEROES of the Revolution who enjoyed a continued friendship with Jefferson was General Thaddeus Kosciusko, and to the great Pole the owner of Monticello now wrote an outline of his daily schedule:

"My mornings are devoted to correspondence . . . breakfast to dinner I am in my shops, in my garden, or on horseback [about this time Jefferson recommended to a friend as a cure for intestinal complaints two or three hours daily on horseback] . . . from dinner to dark with my neighbors and friends . . . from candlelight to early bedtime I read . . . I talk of ploughs and harrows . . . and feel at length the blessing of being free to do and say what I please." He mentioned being able to advise the young men of the neighborhood about their reading, giving them the use of his library, and keeping "their attention fixed on the main objects of all science, the freedom and happiness of man."

But his contentment was cut down by his discovery that his financial condition, after eight years in the presidency, had sunk far lower than he had suspected. On top of a series of poor crops, his income from his several plantations, because of the embargo on tobacco exports, had been steeply reduced and he was obliged to apply for a loan from a Richmond bank.

"Since I have become sensible of this deficit," he wrote his agent there, "I have been under an agony of mortification. . . . My intervening nights will be almost sleepless, as nothing could be more distressing to me than to leave debts unpaid." Further on the same theme he said:

"We can make indeed enough to eat, drink and clothe ourselves;

303

but nothing for our salt, iron, groceries and taxes which must be paid in money. For what can we raise for the market? wheat? we can only give it to our horses, as we have been doing since harvest. Tobacco? it is not worth the pipe it is smoked in. Some say whiskey; but all mankind must become drunkards to consume it."

At the end of his first year as president, Jefferson, who was a meticulous bookkeeper, had made out a report to himself on his debits and credits, showing that his salary of twenty-five thousand dollars, plus small profits from tobacco and his nail factory, had failed to meet his expenses by a considerable margin. The biggest expense was for provisions, $4,504.84. "Lands, horses and carriages" cost $4,712.74. Wines were charged at $2,797.28, groceries $2,003.71, and servants $2,675.84. "Charities (in cash)" were put down at $978.20.

The total expense for the year was $33,634.84—no great sum, even by the then existing standards, but one which troubled him not a little when he thought of the gradual accumulation of other debts.

Edmund Bacon, for twenty years Jefferson's plantation superintendent, observed in his recollections that his master kept at the President's House eleven servants brought from Monticello, besides a French cook, a French steward and an Irish coachman.

"He was perfectly tired out with company. He had a very long dining-room, and his table was chockfull every one of the sixteen days I was there. . . . Mr. Jefferson's steward was a very smart man, well educated, and as much of a gentleman in his appearance as any man. . . . Lamar told me that it often took $50 to pay for what marketing they would use in a day."

From the moment he returned to Monticello, Jefferson began a struggle to keep his income up to the level of his outgo. He knew no way to reduce expenses, for they must be kept up as long as hospitality was to be maintained. And to reduce hospitality was not to be thought of by a Southern gentleman of the old school.

CHAPTER 57

RECOVERY AT MONTICELLO

ON HIS RETURN from Washington, Jefferson was deeply discouraged by evidence of neglect at Monticello, Poplar Forest and other farms, and he began the work of restoration by keeping detailed records. From these figures we know that at Monticello in 1809 he had two work horses, ten mules, six cows, thirty-five sheep, sixty pigs and twenty-two beef cattle. At other farms he kept animals in proportion to the acreage and the demands of laborers. From Poplar Forest in the summer of 1810, he received sixty-eight hams, eighty-one shoulders, seventy-five middlings and twenty-four pieces of beef.

He noted that "we require annually 600 yards of woolen and cotton" and "800 yards of linen." He estimated that three hundred pounds of wool might be spun by a spinner in a year, and that from January 1 to November 1 two hundred barrels of corn at four and one half barrels a week would be needed to feed ninety persons. His *Farm Book* [1] is filled with the most voluminous and minute figures on farming operations. One wonders how Jefferson found the time to record such matters while carrying on the tremendous correspondence and other duties that he took upon himself after his retirement. Yet this laborious record-keeping did not make his farms profitable.

It was Jefferson's delight to have as his housekeeper at Monticello his surviving daughter, Martha, wife of Thomas Mann Randolph. She was of a cheerful temper and, like her father, went about humming a tune or singing to herself. Like him, too, she was always busy, and she taught her daughters housekeeping duties as fast as they

---

[1] Presented by the Massachusetts Historical Society, and reproduced in 1953 as edited by Edwin Morris Betts for the American Philosophical Society.

grew up. Her father was fond of having her sit in his room while she sewed or read aloud. She had a clear, bright complexion and blue eyes. She became the mother of eleven children—six daughters and five sons. A few were blond but most of them had the Randolph complexion and features—dark from a supposed descent from Pocahontas.

Jefferson found that while he was president, many things at Monticello had deteriorated; and Martha helped him restore the flower beds and shrubbery, and plant new species brought from Georgetown; for eleven grandchildren and playmates could and did devour quantities of vegetables, berries and fruits of all kinds. The variety of plants was widened by a present of seven hundred species of seed from Jefferson's old friend in Paris, Superintendent Thouin of the Royal National Garden. The detail of Jefferson's knowledge of plants and their uses was astonishing, and his instructions for handling them were often minute. For example, thorn bushes to fill holes in the hedges must be planted just six inches apart; four purple beech trees must be planted at the spots marked by sticks lettered No. IV; robinias were to be set at sticks marked V; prickly ash was to be set at the northwest and southwest angles of the house; six Spitzenberg apple trees and five peaches were to be planted in the southeast orchard; and ground must be provided for five hundred October peach stones and a box of "peccan nuts."

"Mr. Perry must immediately extend the paling," he wrote, "so as to include these, and make the whole secure against horses." [2] And so on with other directions regarding the mill, the weaving shop, the nailery (one of the few things that Jefferson established which paid a substantial profit), the orchards, the animals, the pastures, the fields, and food and housing for the servants. He even thought of providing whisky, some for the house and some "for the people"—about thirty gallons would last a year. His imported animals were not used to make money, but to improve the breeds owned by his neighbors; for Jefferson could think not only individually but collectively.

Hardly second to his family was Jefferson's delight in horses. When he was president, he sometimes drew critical fire by going to the races at Georgetown, but at Monticello he had no sour spectators.

[2] Pierson, *Jefferson at Monticello.*

Bay horses were his choice. He owned five that became famous in the family chronicles: Diomede, Brimmer, Tecumseh, Wellington and Eagle.

Diomede and Brimmer were from imported sires. The former had been bought at eighty pounds for Jefferson by his son-in-law, John W. Eppes. Brimmer was good for both saddle and harness.

Tecumseh had belonged to old Davy Isaacs, who kept a store in Charlottesville. Jefferson saw the horse in a field one day and sent his chief overseer, Edmund Bacon, to buy him.

Wellington was pulling a wagon for a Dutchman named Imboden when Bacon rescued him.

Eagle was the last horse that Jefferson was able to ride in his old age—a tall horse with white hind feet.

He used these horses on his visits to Washington, to James Madison at Montpelier and to Poplar Forest, his summer farm ninety miles below Monticello, near Lynchburg. After finishing his two terms at Washington, he had a carriage built at home according to his own plans. The woodwork, metal work and painting were done by his Negro workmen. When taking a carriage ride, he always brought along a fifth or spare horse ridden behind by his servant, Burwell, and he never allowed a driver to take the reins but placed servants on the harnessed horses, each servant guiding a pair.

Though he was fortunate with his livestock, he made a failure of his flour mill. He hoped it would meet the community's needs, but it was far too costly in every part, including the four-story building, the dam on the Fluvanna river and the canal that brought the water three-quarters of a mile. Much of the digging and blasting had to be done through solid rock. The flour sold readily at Richmond when floated down by bateaux 250 to 300 barrels at a time, sometimes for fourteen dollars a barrel, but at last a freshet came down the river and ruined everything. Jefferson had visitors at the time, but never allowed them to think the loss was anything but a passing incident. Whenever the flour was sold at Richmond, Overseer Bacon took the money in bills fresh from the United States Bank. When handing it to Jefferson, Bacon once remarked that it was pretty money.

"Yes," said Jefferson, "and very convenient if people would only use it properly. But they will not. It will lead to speculation, inflation, and trouble." [3]

As a farmer Jefferson was sometimes successful and sometimes not, but even so he far surpassed his son-in-law, Thomas Mann Randolph. Randolph became a member of Congress and then governor of Virginia, but on the farm somehow he could not make ends meet. He was a good producer but an indifferent salesman and finally ended in bankruptcy, obliging Jefferson to support Martha and her eleven children as well as little Francis Eppes, son of the lovely Maria so lately dead.

Jefferson found consolation for Randolph's failures in the abilities of his eldest grandson, Thomas Jefferson Randolph. As he was Martha's most promising child, his grandfather took marked pride in his growing abilities and when the lad was fifteen, sent him to Philadelphia to be educated by the painter, C. W. Peale, who had an art and curio museum there. The boy on departing was advised by his grandfather to cultivate four essentials: (1) good humor, (2) integrity, (3) industry, (4) science.

Explaining the first, Jefferson remarked that "we had all rather associate with a good-humored, light-principled man than with an ill-tempered rigorist in morality." He defined politeness as "the giving a pleasing and flattering turn to our expressions which will conciliate others and make them pleased with us as well as themselves. . . . When this is in return for a rude thing said by another, it brings him to his sense, it mortifies and corrects him in the most salutary way, and places him at the feet of your good nature. . . . I never saw an instance of one or two diplomats convincing the other by argument."

The peace that Jefferson had looked forward to at Monticello failed at last. A burden of correspondence from all parts of the Union and foreign countries fell upon him, but with it came a much greater burden of visitors. Edmund Bacon, his overseer, once testified to the extent of his master's hospitality.

"I have killed a fine beef," said Bacon, "and it would all be eaten in a day or two. There was no tavern in all that country that had so much company."

Statesmen like Madison and Monroe, foreign visitors like Chastel-

[3] Pierson, *Jefferson at Monticello.*

lux, and scientists like Correa de Serra, were Jefferson's delight; but intruders and curiosity appeasers irked him and made him glad to welcome summer when he could take his gig or carriage and escape to Poplar Forest.

In the house at Monticello, Ceracchi's bust of Jefferson stood facing a bust of Hamilton. There were other busts of Napoleon and Emperor Alexander of Russia opposite those of Voltaire and Turgot. Around the walls were portraits of Columbus, Newton, Locke, Bacon, Washington, Adams, Franklin and Madison. On the left of the hall was a sitting room and behind that Jefferson's room with its reclining study-couch and a bed built in an alcove between bedroom and library. To the left of the library was a piazza containing Jefferson's work-bench for use when he was mechanically inclined.

To the right of the hall lay four rooms—Martha Randolph's and one called Madison's room, a dining room and tea room. Each wing gave onto terraces ending in pavilions. Beneath the terraces and out of sight were stables, offices, serving and storage rooms, and servants' rooms. On the lawn of the north terrace, in good weather, Jefferson loved to sit and talk with his friends. In his bedroom he always made his own fire and when he took his daily ride it was without attendants.

The house at Poplar Forest was in plan somewhat similar except there was no dome, but the slope of the ground caused it to be one story in front and two stories behind. The front portico looked out on a circular driveway and a grove of poplars, some of which, giants in size, are still standing just as Jefferson planted them. The rear looked out upon a great lawn and wide fields. In the center of the building was a square living and dining room. From this opened four bedrooms, a pantry and a dumb-waiter. Stairways led to the kitchen and servants' quarters in the basement. The over-all design was classic and octagonal, and Tuscan in feeling. It was believed to have influenced Robert Mills, designer of the Octagon Unitarian Church in Philadelphia and of the Washington Monument. Jefferson made the plans originally for his daughter Maria in 1804, but hardly were they completed when she died. He did much writing there and assembled his *Notes on Virginia* while recovering from a fall from his horse Caractacus. The situation was charming and secluded among the mountains, and doubtless it helped to prolong his life. He praised it in a letter to his favorite medical friend, Dr. Benjamin Rush of Philadelphia, saying:

"I have fixed myself comfortably, keep some books here, bring others occasionally, am in the solitude of a hermit, and quite at leisure to attend to my absent friends. . . . Having to conduct my grandson through his course of mathematics, I have resumed that study with great avidity. It was ever my favorite one."

At this very time Dr. Rush, with his original and pungent character, was secretly devising methods for bringing together those two old but estranged friends, Jefferson and John Adams. One of the doctor's devices was the relation of a dream of reconciliation to Adams, who replied: "I have no other objection to your Dream, but that it is not History. It may be Prophecy." At length Rush boldly wrote to Jefferson: "I am sure an advance on your side will be a cordial to the heart of Mr. Adams. Tottering over the grave, he now leans wholly upon the shoulders of his old Revolutionary friends." [4] To this Jefferson replied: "I knew him always to be an honest man, often a great one, but sometimes incorrect and precipitate in his judgments."

On New Year's Day, 1812, Adams wrote Jefferson a friendly letter saying he was sending to him as "a friend to American Manufactures . . . two Pieces of Homespun lately produced in this quarter." These proved to be two volumes of lectures by John Quincy Adams. Jefferson in reply emphasized his unchanged affection and respect, saying Adams's letter had carried him "back to the times when, beset with difficulties and dangers, we were fellow-laborers in the same cause, struggling for what is most valuable to man, his right of self-government."

That began a long and detailed correspondence of which one of the most debated topics was that of aristocracy, its composition and uses. Jefferson introduced the topic thus in a letter dated June 27, 1813:

"Whether the power of the people or that of the aristocracy should prevail, were questions which kept the states of Greece and Rome

---

[4] *Letters of Benjamin Rush,* ed. Butterfield.

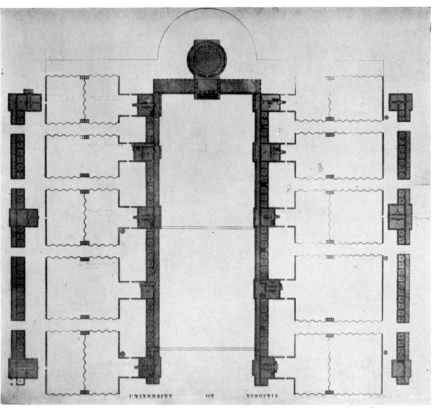

Reproduction of Jefferson's drawings for the lay-out of the University of
Virginia

Birds-eye view of original buildings designed by Jefferson for the University of Virginia

Jefferson, aged eighty-two. Bronze from life mask by John H. I. Browere

in eternal convulsions, as they now schismatize every people whose minds and mouths are not shut up by the gag of a despot. And in fact, the terms of whig and tory belong to natural as well as civil history. They denote the temper and constitution of mind of different individuals."

To this Adams replied: "But who are these aristocracy? Who shall judge? Who shall select these choice spirits from the rest of the congregation? Themselves? We must find out and determine who themselves are. In a collection of moral sentences from all the most ancient Greek poets . . . I read . . . a couplet, the sense of which was 'Nobility in men is worth as much as it is in horses, asses, or rams; but the meanest-blooded puppy in the world, if he gets a little money, is as good a man as the best of them.' Yet birth and wealth together have prevailed over virtue and talents in all ages. The many will acknowledge no other aristocracy."

In August, 1813, Adams enlarged his views on birth and wealth thus:

"My friend Curnis, when we went to purchase horses, asses, or rams, we inquire for the well-born, and every one wishes to procure from the good breeds. A good man does not wish to marry a shrew, the daughter of a shrew, unless they give a great deal of money with her. . . . Has science, or morals, or philosophy, or criticism, or Christianity, advanced, or improved, or enlightened mankind upon this subject, and shown them that the idea of the 'well born' is a prejudice, a phantom, a point-no-point, a Cape Flyaway, a dream?

"I say it is the ordinance of God Almighty, in the constitution of human nature, and wrought into the fabric of the universe. Philosophers and politicians may nibble and quibble, but they never will get rid of it. Their only recourse is to control it. Wealth is another monster to be subdued. Hercules could not subdue both or either. . . . We call this sentiment [of aristocracy] a prejudice, because we can give what names we please to such things as we please; but, in my opinion, it is a part of the natural history of man."

In a later letter Adams clinched his argument with this observation: "The five pillars of aristocracy are beauty, wealth, birth, genius, and virtue. Any one of these three first can, at any time, overbear any one of the two last."

In reply Jefferson referred to a passage quoted by Adams and wrote:

"This passage particularly seems to be a reproof to man, who, while with his domestic animals, he is curious to improve the race, by employing always the finest male, pays no attention to the improvement of his own race, but intermarries with the vicious, the ugly, or the old, for considerations of wealth or ambition. . . . The natural aristocracy [of virtue and talents] I consider as the most precious gift of nature, for the instruction, the trusts, and government of society."

At this point Jefferson returned to a favorite contention of his: that the United States had given to the world a new kind of man, fit to govern himself, as against the European who was limited and corrupted by monarchy and feudalism.

"Before the establishment of the American States," he wrote, "nothing was known to history but the man of the old world, crowded within limits either small or overcharged, and stupid in the vices which that situation generates. . . . [Here] every one, by his property, or by his satisfactory situation, is interested in the support of law and order. And such men may safely and advantageously reserve to themselves a wholesome control over their public affairs, and a degree of freedom, which, in the hands of the *canaille* of the cities of Europe, would be instantly perverted to the demolition and destruction of everything public and private. . . . The American example has kindled feelings of right in the people. An insurrection has consequently begun, of science, talents, and courage, against rank and birth, which have fallen into contempt."

Herein is exhibited that distrust of the urban proletariat which was characteristic of Jefferson's thinking and which no doubt had been heightened by the printed accounts of episodes in the French Revolution. Also therein is a reference to the ownership of property as a support of social stability which is very rare in Jefferson's writings. Adams in reply insisted on giving his own definition of an aristocracy.

"Pick up the first hundred men you meet," he wrote, "and make a republic. Every man will have an equal vote; but when deliberations and discussions are opened, it will be found that twenty-five, by their talents, virtues being equal, will be able to carry fifty votes. Every one of these twenty-five is an aristocrat in my sense of the word; whether he obtains one vote in addition to his own, by his birth, fortune, figure, eloquence, science, learning, craft, cunning, or even his character for good fellowship, and a *bon vivant*. . . . Your distinction between natural and artificial aristocracy, does not appear to me founded. Birth and wealth are conferred upon some men as imperiously by nature as genius, strength, or beauty . . . and both artificial aristocracy and monarchy, and civil, military, political, and hierarchical despotism, have all grown out of the natural aristocracy of virtues and talents." Adams admitted he had thought an hereditary aristocracy was the best bulwark against political corruption.

Adams soon steered the correspondence toward religion, in which he was far more interested than aristocracy; and he began his own views thus:

"Philosophy looks with an impartial eye on all religions. I have examined all, as well as my narrow sphere, my straightened means, and my busy life would allow me; and the result is, that the Bible is the best book in the world. It contains more of my little philosophy than all the libraries I have seen; and such parts of it as I cannot reconcile to my little philosophy, I postpone for future investigation."

On this Jefferson made no immediate comment. He preferred to bring up his favorite aversion, Plato, and castigate him. Plato's *Republic* he deemed a compound of "whimsies, puerilities and unintelligible jargon." Adams replied that "your reflections upon him [Plato] so perfectly harmonize with mine"; and remarked that after laboring through various translations of Plato "my disappointment was very great, my astonishment was greater, and my disgust was shocking." He did not say why. And then Adams resumed his reflections on religion.

"The question before the human race is, whether the God of nature shall govern the world by His own laws, or whether priests and kings shall rule it by fictitious miracles. Or, in other words, whether authority is originally in the people? or whether it has descended for 1800 years in a succession of popes and bishops, or brought down from heaven by the Holy Ghost in the form of a dove, in a phial of holy oil?"

The question of Plato and his influence on Christian tenets kept intruding itself, and finally Adams wrote:

"Plato borrowed his doctrines from Oriental and Egyptian philosophers, for he had travelled back into India and Egypt.

"The Oriental philosophy, initiated and adopted, in part, if not the whole, by Plato and Philo, was:

"1. One God the good.

"2. The ideas, the thoughts, the reason, the intellect, the logos, the ratio of God.

"3. Matter, the universe, the production of the logos, or contemplations of God. This matter was the source of evil. . . .

"4. This logos of Plato seems to resemble, if it was not the prototype of, the *Ratio and its Progress* of Manilious, the astrologer; of the *Progress of the Mind* of Condorcet, and the *Age of Reason* of Tom Payne. . . ."

Adams at times outwrote Jefferson at the rate of four letters to one, and he continued the discussion by blasts against religious intolerance, thus:

"It is very true that the denunciations of the priesthood are fulminated against every advocate for a complete freedom of religion. Communications, I believe, would be plenteously pronounced by even the most liberal of them, against Atheism, Deism, against even man who disbelieved or doubted the resurrection of Jesus, or the miracles of the New Testament. . . . Poor weak man, when will thy perfection arrive?"

In his next letter Adams guided the debate to a comparison of his own and Jefferson's administrations:

"Your character in history may easily be foreseen. Your administration will be quoted by philosophers as a model of profound wisdom; by politicians as weak, superficial, and shortsighted. Mine, like Pope's woman, will have no character at all."

Jefferson was often impatient with those persons, including John Adams, who failed to see in Jesus Christ a simple and homely teacher.

"In extracting the pure principles which he taught," he wrote Adams, "we should have to strip off the artificial vestments in which they have been muffled by priests, who have travestied them into various forms, as instruments of riches and power to themselves."

Jefferson was insistent that Jesus was to be respected primarily for his moral precepts and for his doctrines of man not only as an individual but a social being.

Then Adams was reminded of George Washington's administration, which had preceded his own, and wrote in a vein which could not have been displeasing to Jefferson:

"The impious idolatry to Washington destroyed all character. His legacy of ministers was not the worst part of the tragedy; though by his own express confession to me, and by Pickering's [5] confession to the world, in his letters to Sullivan, two of them, at least, were fastened upon him by necessity, because he could get no other. The truth is, Hamilton's influence over him was so well known, that no man fit for the office of State or War would accept either. He was driven to the necessity of appointing such as would accept. . . .

"The fundamental article of my political creed is that despotism, or unlimited sovereignty, or absolute power, is the same in a majority of a popular assembly, an aristocratical council, an oligarchical junto, and a single emperor."

Jefferson in reply wrote that national morality through the sixteenth, seventeenth and eighteenth centuries had been rising by means of the arts and sciences whose "natural effect is, by illuminating public opinion, to erect it into a censor, before which the most exalted tremble for their future, as well as present fame. With some exceptions only, through the seventeenth and eighteenth centuries, morality occupied an honorable chapter in the political code of nations."

Adams in his next letter suddenly changed the subject and asked, "Would you go back to your cradle, and live over again your seventy years?" To this Jefferson replied:

"You ask if I would agree to live my seventy or rather my seventy-three years over again. To which I say, yea. I think with you, that it is a good world on the whole; that it has been framed on a principle of benevolence, and more pleasure than pain dealt out to us . . . how much pain have cost us the evils which have never happened! My temperament is sanguine. I steer my bark with Hope in the

---

[5] Timothy Pickering was a leader of the New England Federalists.

head, leaving Fear astern. My hopes, indeed, sometimes fail; but not oftener than the forebodings of the gloomy. There are, I acknowledge, even in the happiest life, some terrible convulsions, heavy set-offs against the opposite page of the account. I have often wondered for what good end the sensations of grief could be intended. All our other passions, within proper bounds, have an useful object. And the perfection of the moral character is, not in a stoical apathy, so hypocritically vaunted, and so untruly too, because impossible, but in a just equilibrium of all the passions. I wish the pathologists then would tell us what is the use of grief in the economy, and of what good it is the cause, proximate or remote."

Adams was not the man to evade a philosophical question, however difficult, and he replied at length under date of May 6, 1816:

"When I approach such questions as this, I consider myself like one of those little eels in vinegar, or one of those animalcules in black or red pepper or in the horseradish root, that bite our tongues so cruelly, reasoning upon the το παν. Of what use is this sting upon the tongue? Why might we not have the benefit of these stimulants without the sting? Why might we not have the fragrance, beauty of the rose, without the thorn?

"In the first place, however, we know not the connections between pleasure and pain. They seem to be mechanical and inseparable. How can we conceive a strong passion, a sanguine hope, suddenly disappointed, without producing pain or grief? Swift, at seventy, recollected the fish he had angled out of water when a boy, which broke loose from his hook, and said, 'I feel the disappointment at this moment!' . . . It should seem that grief, as a mere passion, must be in proportion to sensibility.

"Grief drives men into habits of serious reflection, sharpens the understanding, and softens the heart; it compels them to rouse their reason, to assist its empire over their passions, propensities and prejudices, to elevate them to a superiority over all human events, to give them the *felicis animi immotam tranquillitatam;* [6] in short, to make them stoics and Christians.

"After all, as grief is a pain, it stands in the predicament of all other evil, and the great question occurs, what is the origin, and what

---

6 Immovable tranquillity of a happy mind.

the final cause of evil. This, perhaps, is known only to Omniscience. We poor mortals have nothing to do with it, but to fabricate all the good we can out of all inevitable evils, and to avoid all that are avoidable; and many such there are, among which are our own unnecessary apprehensions and imaginary fears. Though stoical apathy is impossible, yet patience, and resignation, and tranquillity may be acquired, by consideration, in a great degree, very much for the happiness of life."

These not very definite conclusions were dismissed by Jefferson with the simple statement that "to the question indeed on the utility of grief, no answer remains to be given."

Adams evidently hoped that Jefferson would ask for his own views on the pains and pleasures of life, but when he did not, Adams addressed to Jefferson his own imaginary interview:

"J. Would you agree to live your eighty years over again?

"A. Aye! and *sans phrase*.

"J. Would you agree to live your eighty years over again for ever?

"A. . . . I own my soul would start and shrink back on itself at the prospect of an endless succession of boules de savon,[7] almost as much as at the certainty of annihilation. What is human life . . . I have had more comfort than distress, more pleasure than pain, ten to one; nay, if you please, a hundred to one. . . . But, after all, what is human life? A vapor, a fog, a dew, a cloud, a blossom, a flower, a rose, a blade of grass, a glass bubble, a tale told by an idiot, a *boule de savon*, vanity of vanities, an eternal succession of which would terrify me almost as much as annihilation."

"J. Would you live over again once or forever rather than run the risk of annihilation, or of a better or a worse state at or after death?

"A. Most certainly I would not."

"Ninety-nine hundredths of the pleasures and pains of life are nothing but hopes and fears. . . . The Maker of the universe, the cause of all things, whether we call it *fate,* or *chance,* or God, has inspired this hope. . . . Let us, then, wish for immortality at all hazards, and trust the ruler with his skies."

Jefferson answered briefly and dryly. Referring to grief, he said,

---

[7] Cakes of soap.

"We may consider its value in the economy of the human being, as equivocal at least." And then on the subject of afflictions he added this clinching comment:

"Those afflictions cloud too great a portion of life to find a counter-poise in any benefits derived from its use."

Adams, probably recognizing that the debate on the uses of grief had brought them to no definite conclusion, shifted the question to the *abuses* of grief and offered a few examples. One dealt with the death of Washington. Said he:

"The old Tories, the hyperfederalists, the speculators, set up a general howl. Ovations, prayers, sermons, mock funerals, were all employed, not that they loved Washington, but to keep in continuance the funding and banking system."

And that reminded him of Alexander Hamilton's death, which had produced similar expressions of grief.

"And why?" asked Adams. "Merely to disgrace the Old Whigs, and keep the funds and banks in countenance."

He also cited the death of Fisher Ames, one of the most vocal of Federalists, which caused "a general mourning."

"And why?" asked Adams. "To glorify the Tories, to abash the Whigs, and maintain the reputation of funds, banks, and specula-tions."

In reply Jefferson wrote a letter longer than that he ordinarily composed in the course of this correspondence, but he switched the subject to the French student of philosophy, Destutt Tracy, whom he adjudged "the ablest living writer on intellectual subjects, or the operations of the understanding." Tracy had written three volumes on ideology which he had to confess he had not read entirely "be-cause," he wrote, "I am not fond of reading what is merely abstract and unapplied immediately to some useful science." And then Jef-ferson added a statement of one of his cardinal tenets: "I gather from his other works that he adopts the principle of Hobbes, that justice is founded in contract solely, and does not result from the construc-tion of man. I believe, on the contrary, that it is instinct and innate, that the moral sense is as much a part of our constitution as that of feeling, seeing, or hearing; as a wise creator must have seen to be necessary in an animal destined to live in society; that every human mind feels pleasure in doing good to another; . . . virtue does not consist in the act we do, but in the end it is to effect . . . The essence of virtue is in doing good to others."

Adams was given to tangents, and he was off on one when he wrote apropos of nothing: "When People talk of the freedom of Writing, Speaking or Thinking, I cannot choose but laugh. No such thing ever existed. No such thing now exists; but I hope it will exist."

In the autumn of 1818 came an abrupt change in the tone of this correspondence. In October Adams wrote to Jefferson concerning the mortal illness of his wife, Abigail—she who at first admired Jefferson almost extravagantly, then turned chilly toward him, and finally was friends with him again. On November 13 Jefferson wrote Adams this letter:

"I know well, and feel what you have lost, what you have suffered, are suffering, and have yet to endure. The same trials have taught me that for ills so immeasurable, time and silence are the only medicine . . . God bless you and support you under your heavy affliction."

The two old ex-presidents exchanged many more letters, Adams writing oftener than Jefferson because of the latter's stiffening wrists, until they came to the year 1826. In March of that year Jefferson wrote a note of introduction to Adams for his grandson, Thomas Jefferson Randolph, eldest son of Martha. Adams replied cordially in April. This was their last exchange. Within a few weeks, on July 4, 1826, they died on the same day and within an hour of each other. Adams was in his ninety-first year. Jefferson was eighty-three.

CHAPTER 58

WRONG ON THE WAR

JEFFERSON, BEING A MAN and not a god, was occasionally mistaken in his opinions and judgments, but seldom was he so completely wrong as events proved him to be concerning the War of 1812. Although it was not his but Madison's government which declared war, Jefferson favored hostilities.

"Surely," he wrote James Maury in England, "the world will acquit our Government from having sought it. Never before has there been an instance of a nation's bearing so much as we have borne. Two items alone in our catalogue of wrongs will forever acquit us of being the aggressors; the impressment of our seamen and the excluding us from the ocean." He held that it was part of the American "social compact" to give the protection of government to persons and property.

As regards England, he was wrong again when he predicted in writing to Kosciusko that "our present enemy would have the sea to herself, while we should be equally predominant at land, and should strip her of all her possessions on this continent." Jefferson could not help exulting a little as he pictured the United States extending its rule over Canada, for he had long believed there could be no peace until the English were driven from North America.

"The acquisition of Canada this year as far as the neighborhood of Quebec," he wrote the editor, William Duane, "would be a mere matter of marching, and would give us experience for the attack of Halifax the next, and the final expulsion of England from the American Continent."

He was confident that the American army, made up chiefly of militia, would be able to break through the Canada frontier with ease, and was equally confident it would be a mistake to confront Britain's navy of a thousand vessels with America's scant handful of ships. The clash of arms proved to be wrong on both counts. Treachery and poor judgment brought the army's early attempts to invade Canada to fiasco and disaster; while the United States's unseasoned navy did well against England's veteran ships.

"Upon the whole," wrote Jefferson in a blind outburst of patriotism, "I have known no war entered into under more favorable auspices." But it was only a little while before he was obliged to write:

"The delivery of the fort and army of Detroit by the traitor Hull; the disgrace at Queenstown, under Van Rensselaer; the massacre at Frenchtown under Winchester; and surrender of Boerstler in an open field to one third of his own numbers, were the inauspicious beginnings of the first year of our warfare. . . . I see that our men are good and only want generals."

Then when better news came, he began to brag like any dyed nationalist, even exulting in the growth of industry, saying:

"We have taken their Upper Canada and shall add the Lower to it when the season will admit; and hope to remove them [the English] fully and finally from our continent. And what they will feel more, for they value their colonies only for the bales of cloth they take from them, we have established manufactures not only sufficient to supersede our demand from them but to rivalize them in foreign markets."

But British armies, and particularly the British blockade of Hampton Roads and the Delaware river, continued to succeed until Jefferson was gloomily convinced that the war had become one of "conquest, to be waged until she [England] conquers from us our fisheries, the province of Maine, the Lakes, states and territories north of the Ohio, and the navigation of the Mississippi."

And then came an event which shocked the nation but seems to have had no such effect on Jefferson, who was used to New England enmity and could not be astonished by anything the Federalists there might do. In 1814 the state of Massachusetts called for delegates from the other New England states to meet at Hartford, Connecticut, to discuss the war and future plans regarding it. Everybody knew what would be the underlying thought of the convention: secession.

It was an idea not new in this part of the United States; New England had been muttering threats of secession ever since Washington and Jefferson had been chosen out of Virginia to become presidents; and no further back than the Louisiana Purchase, New England orators had threatened to leave the Union if their interests suffered because of the accession of Louisiana. The Federalists in New England were averse to the War of 1812 for two reasons: (1) they loved England and English life; and (2) they were suspicious of democracy and disliked rule by persons living below the Potomac. Josiah Quincy of Massasachusetts had already described the invasion of Canada as a "cruel, wanton and wicked attack . . . upon an unoffending people, bound to the Americans by ties of blood and good neighborhood." In return for such favorable views, England had exempted Massachusetts from her blockade of the American coast.

Five New England states sent delegates to Hartford—Massachusetts twelve, Connecticut seven, Rhode Island four, New Hampshire two, Vermont one. The convention voted for several drastic constitutional amendments as follows: that no new state be admitted to the Union without concurrence of two-thirds of Congress's membership (this was obviously aimed at the Louisiana Purchase); that Congress should not have the power to impose an embargo for more than sixty days; that the same person should not be elected president a second time, nor should the president be elected from the same state two times in succession.

The legislatures of Massachusetts and Connecticut sent commissioners to Washington to urge Congress to adopt these amendments. They arrived February 13, 1815, only to learn that Andrew Jackson had beaten the British at New Orleans, and that a peace treaty had been signed at Ghent the day before Christmas. The ridicule that ensued, and the fear of treason charges, finally killed the Federalist party. But in a sense it was no longer needed, for in a few years the rise of industrial capitalism had made up to New England all its losses in shipping and trading. America went on to enlarge the political democracy preached by Jefferson, but by adopting machine industry she also evolved a class of landless proletarians.

At the threatened secession by the New England states Jefferson was not alarmed. Of the defection of Massachusetts he wrote:

"It is a disagreeable circumstance but not a dangerous one. . . . Their own people will put down these factionists."

Much more distressing was the news of the burning of the Capitol, the White House and library at Washington by the British army under Admiral Cockburn. Jefferson offered to restore the library by selling to Congress his collection of nearly ten thousand books. "They may be valued," he wrote, "by persons named by themselves [Congress], and the payment made convenient to the public . . . so as to spare the present case of our country, and await its days of peace and prosperity."

Eventually a bill was passed by Congress ordering the sum of $23,950 to be paid Jefferson for his library, to replace that burned by the British. And it rests in the Library of Congress now with its numerous annotations by Jefferson still intact and legible. When the bill came before the House, Cyrus King of Massachusetts moved an amendment authorizing the library committee to remove from Jefferson's collection "all books of an atheistical, irreligious and immoral tendency, if any such there were, and send the same back to Mr. Jefferson." He afterward withdrew this motion. Ordinarily the sum thus earned would have relieved Jefferson's straitened means, but he was obliged immediately to pay back $10,500 to William Short, formerly his secretary at Paris, for money borrowed, and $4,870 to John Barnes, another friend, for the same reason.

In a letter to Lafayette about this time, Jefferson made a charge against Great Britain that has not received the due attention of historians. It was a charge he later repeated in different forms. In substance it was that the British government had brought on some of the worst excesses of the French Revolution by sending into France agents well provided with money for the express purpose of aborting the revolution or twisting its course; and that similar agents carrying British money had been at work politically in Massachusetts. Jefferson told Lafayette:

"The Marats, the Dantons, and Robespierres of Massachusetts are in the same pay, under the same orders, and making the same efforts to anarchize us, that their prototypes in France did there. I do not say that all who met at Hartford were under the same motives of money, nor were those of France. Some of them are Outs, and wish to be Ins; some the mere dupes of the agitators, or of their own party passions, while the Maratists alone are in the real secret; but they have very different materials to work on."

Whether Jefferson was thus giving way to partisan heat, or whether he really knew more of the secrets of the French Revolution than he had previously indicated, cannot now be said. At any rate, this accusation is a measure of his deep dislike of certain British governments and their apparent wish to see the American republic fail. At the same time he wrote to John Adams concerning the British:

"Were they once under a government which should treat us with justice and equity, I should feel myself with great strength the ties which bind us together, of origin, languages, laws and manners. . . . A purer government . . . will see in us what we really are, their natural friends and brethren, and more interested in a fraternal connection with them than with any nation on earth."

The peace which Jefferson hoped for was indeed begun at the end of the Ghent meeting and lasted a hundred years. Under this peace Americans forgot Europe and absorbed themselves converting the riches of a continent into cash until the shock of war in 1914 brought America and Britain not only into an understanding but also an alliance.

CHAPTER 59

FIREBELL IN THE NIGHT

THE HUNDRED YEARS of peace that followed the Treaty of Ghent was not the creation of statesmen or an accident of circumstances. It was due in some part to the preoccupation of Americans with the westward movement that began with Jefferson's purchase of the Louisiana territory; to the opening of free or cheap land across the Mississippi; and to the mounting difficulty of maintaining profitable farms in the Eastern states. New England, which was the center of opposition to Jefferson's doctrines, watched the transfer of power westward with jealous eyes and obstructionist tactics.

"If this bill passes," shouted Josiah Quincy in Congress concerning the proposal to admit Louisiana as a state, "it is my deliberate opinion that it is virtually a dissolution of this Union; that it will free the States from their moral obligation; and, as it will be the right of all, so it will be the duty of some definitely to prepare for a separation, amicably if they can, forcibly if they must."

Such threats were repeated more or less constantly for years. But the westward movement did not stop. It rolled on, shaggy and aggressive and irreverent, until it established Andrew Jackson in the White House.

The migration of settlers from the Eastern states across the Mississippi brought up new and unexpected questions, and one of the fiercest of these questions ended in the celebrated Missouri Compromise. It involved a problem that frightened Jefferson and caused his enemies to sneer at him for an alleged refusal to face it completely.

The drama arose when in 1819 Missouri applied for statehood. An attempt was made to insert in the granting act a clause forbidding the extension of slavery in the new territory. Concealed emotions—economic, political, social and geographical emotions—all exploded in furious debate not only on the floor of Congress but wherever men gathered. A bill eventually passed both houses providing that north of the line marked by 36 degrees 30 minutes latitude, slavery should be forever prohibited but permitting slave fugitives to be reclaimed.

"We never had so ominous a question," wrote Jefferson to John Adams, and added in a letter to John Holmes, a former Federalist who had turned Republican: "This momentous question, like a firebell in the night, awakened and filled me with terror." And then he explained:

"A geographical line, coinciding with a marked principle, moral and political, once conceived and held up to the angry passions of men, will never be obliterated; and every new irritation will mark it deeper and deeper."

But five months later he had changed his mind and viewed the question as not a rending one but merely political. "The Missouri question," he wrote William Pinckney, "is a mere party trick," and went on to accuse the Federalists of using a geographical line to split parties and create confusion in which they could gain their own ends.

But at this point Jefferson's usually keen insight either failed him, or on his mountain top three miles from Charlottesville, Virginia, his informants and advisers let him down. For what may indeed have been begun as a political maneuver soon disclosed itself as having massed behind it an avalanche of political fear, sectional jealousy and economic uncertainties. The Northeastern states saw the rise of strength in the West as menacing to their carefully built up economic domination through banks and trade with Europe. The South, seeing slavery only as a symbol of a prized way of life, solidified itself behind a front line of younger orators like Clay and Calhoun. The nascent West looked on and whooped.

Jefferson continued to deny that the question of slavery in Missouri was a moral question. It was "one merely of power"; he wrote Lafayette: "All know that permitting the slaves of the south to spread into the west will not add one being to that unfortunate condition, that it will increase the happiness of those existing, and by spreading them over a larger surface, will dilute the evil everywhere, and facilitate the means of finally getting rid of it, an event more anxiously wished by those on whom it presses than by the noisy pretenders to exclusive humanity."

At length a compromise resolution was passed by a fairly close vote in both houses of Congress providing for the admission of Missouri "on an equal footing with the original States, in all respects whatever," on condition that the clause in the Missouri constitution concerning the emigration of free Negroes into the state should never be construed to authorize the passage of any law by which "any citizen of either of the States of this Union should be excluded from the enjoyment of any of the privileges and immunities to which such citizen is entitled under the Constitution of the United States."

But considerations of politics took up only a fraction of Jefferson's time at Monticello. Far greater was his satisfaction with farm and family, and above all with gadgets. Never did a man take more pleasure in the invention of gadgets than Jefferson. Some of them were time-saving, others were designed to impress visitors, and although his correspondence took an ever greater share of his energy he found time to create *Jefferson's Bible,* which was a book made up from cuttings of the four gospels whereby all the sayings of Jesus were preserved but his so-called miracles omitted. He wrote about it to his friend Charles Thomson, old secretary of Congress in Revolutionary times, who had been using some of his leisure in making a new translation of the Pentateuch. Of his own book he said:

"It is a document in proof that I am a *real Christian,* that is to say, a disciple of the doctrines of Jesus, very different from the Platonists, who call me infidel and themselves Christians and preachers of the Gospel, while they draw all their characteristic dogmas from what its author never said nor saw. They have compounded from the heathen mysteries a system beyond the comprehension of man, of which the great reformer of the vicious ethics and deism of the Jews, were he to return on earth, would not recognize one feature."

At this period of Jefferson's retirement an English visitor, Lieutenant Francis Hall, visited Monticello where he found Jefferson "tall in person, but stooping and lean with old age . . . with an unabated flow of conversation on the most interesting topics discussed in the most gentlemanly and philosophic manner." His own capacities Jefferson described in a letter to Charles Thomson:

"Rather feeble to walk much, but ride with ease, passing two or three hours a day on horseback.

"Eyes need the aid of glasses by night, and with small print in the day.

"Hearing not quite so sensible as it used to be.

"No tooth shaking yet.

"Greatest oppression in a correspondence afflictingly laborious."

On reaching the age of seventy-six Jefferson was able to write to various correspondents about himself and his habits that:

He could not walk far, but could ride six or eight miles a day, and sometimes thirty or forty.

He could read ordinary print without spectacles in the daytime, but used them at night.

He slept from five to eight hours nightly, always rising with the sun.

He ate chiefly vegetables, using animal food as a condiment.

He doubled his doctor's prescription of a glass and a half of wine daily, but drank weak wines only. "No nation is drunken where wine is cheap."

He never used ardent spirits in any form.

He rarely had catarrhs or fevers, but occasionally had persisting headaches.

He never went to sleep without reading "something moral" for a half-hour to an hour.

He preferred ancient history to contemporary newspapers.

As he wrote John Adams, "It is of some comfort to us both that the term is not very far distant, at which we are to deposit in the same cerement, our sorrows and suffering bodies, and to ascend in essence to an ecstatic meeting with the friends we have loved and lost, and whom we shall still love and never lose again."

CHAPTER 60

MARIA COSWAY AGAIN

IN 1819 CAME two other events that had a particular interest for Jefferson. One was a national financial depression of the kind which at fairly regular intervals has afflicted the United States economy.

The other event was the receipt of a letter from Maria Cosway. For thirty years that Anglo-Italian lady had refused to allow her correspondence with Jefferson to lapse except during wars. In 1801, the year of his inauguration as president, she had written him in her quaint English from London:

"Would you not receive the congratulations of an old friend, *qui vous sincèrement dévouée?* [1] . . . This is enough: words cannot express all I should say on the subject and you have to much of that sympathizing sentiment to inable you to Conceive more than I can write what the occasion would require."

This letter was brought to Jefferson by her brother, George Hadfield, who had had some architectural training and who with Jefferson's recommendation was able to obtain employment in Washington. The most conspicuous of his architectural designs that remains is that which resulted in the Robert E. Lee home at Arlington. The next year Maria wrote again from Paris:

"Surely you have not forgotten such an old friend! I am now in the place which brings me to mind every day, our first interview, the pleasing days we passed together."

Jefferson gave his answer to Monroe, who was going over to Paris on the mission that eventuated in the Louisiana Purchase. The letter referred to that first interview mentioned by Maria which, said Jefferson, "has produced an attachment which has never been diminished.

---

[1] Who is sincerely devoted to you.

. . . Be assured of my deepest and sincere affection and respect."
Maria was silent for a time, during which she established a religious
school for girls at Lyons, France. And then she wrote:

"It is very difficult to give up some friends, tho' time goes apace
with distance. We cannot forget those we have once highly esteemed.
. . . What is become of my Brother he never writtes to any of his
family."

Wars, embargoes and enmities interfered with this exchange of
letters. Meantime Maria gave birth to and lost a child. She retreated
to Italy where at Lodi she founded a college for girls which is still
in existence.[2] And then at news of a breakdown in her husband's
health she returned to London from where she wrote Jefferson in
1819:

"Often I have read your name in the papers, therefore have been
acquainted of your proceedings in that honorable way which was
expected of you. . . . Oh! how often have I thought of America!
wished to have exerted myself there. Who would have imagined, I
should have taken up this line? it has afforded me satisfaction unfelt
before; after having been deprived of my own child. . . . Forgotten
by the Arts, suspended the direction of education (tho' it is going on
vastly well in my absence) I am now exercising the occupations of
a Nurse. Happy in self gratification of doing my duty, with no other
consolation. In your Dialogue your head would tell me, *that is
enough,* your heart perhaps will understand, I might wish *for more.*
God's will be done. . . . May I flatter myself to hear from you?
Give me some account of yourself as you used to do, instead of Chal-
liott [3] & Paris taulk to me of *Monticello* &c. Accept of the best wishes
from one, who, ever retains with the deepest sense of gratitude your
kindness to her & wishes most ardently to find a place in your remembrance as one who will be yours most sincerely & affy., Maria
Cosway."

This letter of Maria's, written in April, 1819, was not answered
by Jefferson till December 27, 1820, when he explained by how much
he differed from the ardent young man who once had written to her

---

[2] In 1954 the Collegio Maria S.S. Bambina had as its directress the Sister Prosperina
Renzini, who furnished the picture which is our frontispiece.

[3] This was Mrs. Cosway's spelling for the Grille de Chaillot, Jefferson's Paris home.

from Paris the disguised love letter called *Dialogue Between my Head and my Heart* in October, 1786. In these thirty-four years he had become a white-haired ex-president of the United States, ailing and no longer able even to mount his horse unassisted. He told her of his poor health for two years, his imperfectly healed wrist which had made writing a "slow and painful operation," and of his living "like a patriarch of old" among eleven grandchildren and half a dozen great-grandchildren. News of the people of the old coterie in Paris showed them to be dead, diseased or dispersed.

"But," he wrote, " '*tout a qui est differé n'est pas perdu,*' [4] says the French proverb, and the religion you so sincerely profess tells us we shall meet again. . . .

"You have many good years remaining to be happy yourself and to make those around you happy. May these, my dear friend, be as many as yourself may wish, and all of them filled with health and happiness, will be among the last and warmest wishes of an unchangeable friend, Th. Jefferson."

His last known letter to Maria was dated October 21, 1822, and was written in a more cheerful tone owing to the glad announcement he was able to make:

"I am laying the foundation of an University in my native state, which I hope will repay the liberalities of its legislature by improving the virtue and science of their country, already blest with a soil and climate emulating those of your favorite Lodi.

"I have been myself the architect of the plan of its buildings and of the system of instruction. Four years have been employed in the former, and I assure you it would be thought a handsome and classical thing in Italy. I have preferred the plan of an academical village rather than that of a single massive structure. The diversified forms which thus admitted in the different Pavilions and varieties of the finest samples of architecture, has made it a model of beauty, original and unique. It is within view, too, of Monticello so it's a most splendid object, and a constant gratification to my sight. We have still one building to erect which will be on the principle of your Pantheon, a Rotunda like that but of half of its diameter and height

4 "All that which is postponed is not lost." This is from a letter preserved in the Alderman Library at the University of Virginia.

only. I wish indeed you could recall some of your by-past years and seal it with your approbation." Her reply came from Milan, June 18, 1823:

"I wish I could come and learn from you, was it the furthest part of Europe nothing would prevent me but that immense sea makes it a great distance. . . . What a change since you was here! I saw Mad. de Corny when at Paris, she is the *Same* only a *little* older, but well, we talked of you."

Mrs. Cosway's last letter to Jefferson was written from Florence on September 24, 1824, and was received on February 21, 1825. She said she wished to hear more of his "Seminary" and added:

"I am just setting out for my home, pray write to me at Lodi, and if this reaches you *Safe,* I will write longer by the same way. Believe me ever, your most oblgd and afftce. friend, Maria Cosway."

Ever is a long word, but in Maria's letter it was well justified, for she never gave up her friendship for Jefferson even through thirty-four years and a wide ocean had separated them. She survived Jefferson by twelve years and was buried in the church of Santa Maria della Grazie at Lodi where a tablet marks her grave and where in the *collegio* still hangs the little portrait of Jefferson painted especially for her by John Trumbull when they were all young and gay in the Paris of the old regime.

The financial depression of 1819 was foreseen by Jefferson long before it actually arrived. Ever since an economic upheaval, eventuating in Shays's Rebellion, had taken place near the end of Washington's presidency, he had sounded warnings like that he had once sent to John Taylor of Caroline:

"Banking establishments are more dangerous than standing armies."

After Hamilton's United States Bank had expired in 1811, Jefferson had issued many warnings in letters to his friends, and particularly to his former son-in-law, John W. Eppes. To the latter Jefferson wrote in 1813:

"He who lent his money to the public or to an individual, before the institution of the United States Bank, twenty years ago, when wheat was well sold at a dollar the bushel, and receives now his nominal sum when it sells at two dollars, is cheated of half his fortune; and by whom? By the banks, which since that, have thrown into circulation ten dollars of their nominal money where there was one at that time."

Jefferson's grievance against the banks, state and private, was that through loans and note issues they could and did produce through their increase of the money supply inflations difficult or impossible to control. An instance could be found in the sale value of Pennsylvania lands which in 1809 sold for $39 an acre; $150 an acre in 1815 when speculation, supposed to be encouraged by loosely managed banks, was rising; and $35 an acre in 1819 after the crash came.[5] In 1817 Jefferson wrote to Dr. G. B. Stuart:

"The bank mania . . . is raising up a moneyed aristocracy in our country which has already set the government at defiance, and although forced at length to yield a little on this first essay of their strength, their principles are unyielded and unyielding. These have taken deep root in the hearts of that class from which our legislators are drawn."

The second United States Bank was established in 1816, but it did little to correct the unsettled conditions that followed the War of 1812, and finally when all the banks except those in New England had refused any longer to pay specie, a depression descended that wrecked countless enterprises. Jefferson thus analyzed it in a letter to John Adams:

"The paper bubble is burst. This is what you and I, and every reasoning man, seduced by no obliquity of mind or interest, have long foreseen. We were laboring under dropsical fullness of circulating medium. Nearly all of it is now called in by the banks, who have the regulation of the safety valves of our fortunes, and who explode them at their will."

Not even sequestered Monticello, where an advanced state of self-containment had been achieved, was able to remain unaffected by this financial collapse, for we find him writing with a note of pathos to a friend: "I offer for sale a merchant mill which would pay every

5 Wildman, *Money Inflation in the United States.*

dollar I owe in the world, but I know not when I may meet with a purchaser." [6]

For the ruptured banking system Jefferson had no regrets. As he wrote to Dr. Thomas Cooper: "The crisis of the abuses of banking is arrived. The banks have pronounced their own sentence of death."

But though badly shattered, the banking system then in vogue did not die. Reformed in some parts but not essentially rectified, it lingered on until 1933 when it collapsed utterly and had to be rescued by the government of F. D. Roosevelt.

[6] *Farm Book,* p. 408.

CHAPTER 61

INFORMING THE PEOPLE

THERE WAS ONE other great event in Jefferson's life in 1819, and that was one of the most rewarding of his career. "Whenever the people are well informed," he had written in 1789, "they can be trusted with their own government." The condition, indeed, which he always attached to his advocacy of government by the people was this —they must be informed. It was to enable the people to be informed of every advancement in science—by which he usually signified knowledge or learning—that he had begun in 1779 to advocate a more general diffusion of knowledge, the main object of which was "the freedom and happiness of man." Knowledge, he wrote George Ticknor in 1817, is not only power, but "knowledge is safety, knowledge is happiness"; and instruction should lead not only to self-government but "to the practice of the social duties."

But even had he been less convinced of the benefits of proper instruction, he would almost certainly have made one more great effort to confer some signal blessing on his fellow-men before age and failing powers should come upon him. Losing confidence in his alma mater, William and Mary College, because of its class and religious bias, he had begun while still a young man to dream of setting up in his native state an institution of learning not inferior to those of Europe. To this end in 1794 he supported a proposal to move the College of Geneva in Switzerland to Virginia; but that notion came to nothing.

By 1814 he was convinced a university, "which should comprehend all the sciences useful to us," could be established in his own neighborhood, and he summoned all the energies of his still powerful mind to carry out this idea. In 1814 five trustees decided to use a lottery scheme to launch a school to be called the Albemarle Academy, and Jefferson was invited to join them. Eagerly he drew a sketch showing buildings grouped along three sides of a square, each section to have a pavilion containing a classroom and an apartment for a professor.

Probably at Jefferson's prodding, the academy was converted into Central College, at the same time he let it be known that he considered it appropriate that an institution with such a name should be centrally situated—that is, in his own vicinity; and that it should have on its board of visitors sympathetic members such as James Madison and James Monroe. When elected, their presence gave the board three former presidents of the United States—a circumstance unique in educational history.

There was one other member of this board whose abilities quickly drew the attention of Jefferson. This was Joseph C. Cabell, a young lawyer and legislator who in pursuit of health had spent three years in European countries studying the arts and natural sciences and sitting under famous European teachers. He had met Volney and Kosciusko, and had rambled with Robert Fulton and Washington Irving over Europe. His wife was an heiress, stepdaughter of St. George Tucker, the jurist.

"No one could be much with Mr. Cabell," wrote T. H. Ellis in the Richmond *Whig*, September, 1856,[1] "without seeing that he had taken George Washington for his model. In his principles and his conduct, in the dignity of his character, and even in the gentlemanly and becoming particularity of his dress, you could not fail to observe the resemblance."

Cabell's energy and idealism were just what Jefferson was looking for, and the older man was not slow in making him his chief lieutenant and agent in building and procuring the money for the university that was to be the last great work of his life. In fact, Cabell was scarcely less a father of the University of Virginia than the sage of Monticello.

Jefferson was also fortunate in enlisting the intelligent service of another young man in the same enterprise. This was Francis Walker Gilmer, who gave the last measure of his strength to further Jefferson's unrelaxing plans for a central university. Gilmer was born

---

[1] Quoted by Bruce, *History of the University of Virginia.*

across the river from Monticello, was the son of a doctor who had
been Jefferson's close friend, and had spent much time at the home
of the Thomas Mann Randolphs where he had studied French under
Jefferson's daughter Martha. He had prepared himself for the law,
but was much more fascinated by botany and philosophy. If it was
Cabell who helped Jefferson obtain the public interest and the funds
that built the university, it was Gilmer who went abroad to procure
the faculty. Indeed, these two young men became to Jefferson in the
realm of education what Madison and Monroe had been to him in
political life.

As early as 1800 Jefferson had written to Dr. Priestley: "We should
propose to draw from Europe the first characters in science." Because
he preferred teachers brought from Europe, Jefferson was at the time
much criticized, but as a matter of fact one of his first choices for the
University of Virginia faculty was Dr. Thomas Cooper, who had
been a resident in America for years.

Cooper was one of those raffish and eccentric characters who,
though society might look at him askance, was always sure of a share
of Jefferson's attention and hospitality. He once declared that Cooper
had "more science in his single head than all the colleges of New
England, New Jersey and, I may add, Virginia put together," but
John Adams called him a "madcap."

Cooper, who was a born reformer, had come to the United States
from Manchester, England, as a result of the fright and repression
that had followed the French Revolution. Though a chemist and
mineralogist, he had a weakness for politics and on establishing himself in Pennsylvania, he was convicted of seditious libel against the
government during the presidency of John Adams. After serving
several months in jail, he was elected a district judge and then was
chosen for the chair of chemistry at Dickinson College. He held other
academic posts and at length, sponsored by Jefferson, was confirmed
as professor of chemistry, mineralogy and natural philosophy at the
unborn University of Virginia. Cooper was known as a critic of
Calvinism, having ridiculed "its horrid criterion, the doctrine of
election and reprobation," and he had numerous enemies.

No sooner had Cooper accepted the post than he was attacked by
the Virginia clergy, especially the Presbyterians, for alleged "ma-

terialism" and sympathy with Unitarianism. To attend a meeting of the university board at Montpelier where Cooper's case was to be discussed, Jefferson rode on horseback at the age of seventy-six over snow-clogged roads; but his most eloquent pleas failed to save his friend from the talons of the offended Presbyterians. They won, and Cooper's appointment was canceled. In his chagrin Jefferson wrote to Cooper:

"I must explain to you the state of religious parties with us. about ⅓ of our state is Baptist, ⅓ Methodist and of the remaining third two parts may be Presbyterian and one part Anglican. the Baptists are sound republicans and zealous supporters of their government. the Methodists are republican mostly, satisfied with their government, medling with nothing but the concerns of their own calling and opposing nothing. these two sects are entirely friendly to our university. The anglicans are the same. the Presbyterian *clergy* alone (not their followers) remain bitterly federal and malcontent with their government. they are violent, ambitious of power, and intolerant in politics as in religion." [2]

And in the course of his correspondence with John Adams, Jefferson let loose a blast at the father of Presbyterianism, John Calvin. "The Being described in his five points," wrote Jefferson, "is not the God whom you and I acknowledge and adore, the Creator and benevolent Governor of the world; but a daemon of malignant spirit."

Cooper's rejection at Charlottesville did not end Jefferson's interest in the eccentric professor. When Cooper moved on to South Carolina College at Columbia, Jefferson sent his grandson, Francis Eppes, to study under him and applauded when the "Old Coot," as the students called him, was made president of the college. Cooper lived to become an arrant conservative, opposing nearly everything that Jefferson had once advocated. He repudiated the Declaration of Independence, urged absolute state rights, ridiculed the emancipation of Negroes, and opposed universal suffrage. "Rights," he proclaimed, "are what society acknowledges and sanctions, and they are nothing else." His latter end, in fact, proved that John Adams was more nearly right about him than Jefferson.

Despite these disappointments, Jefferson, assisted by Cabell, went

---

[2] Jefferson habitually began sentences with small letters.

ahead with the project which was to be the crown of his old age. In 1818 the Virginia assembly passed the bill approving a state university. Then came the momentous question of its location. Several cities and towns made offers, but Jefferson's mind was already made up. A board of twenty-four commissioners was named to choose the site. They were called to meet at Rockfish Gap in the Blue Ridge Mountains near Charlottesville, an elevation symbolic of Jefferson's lofty ideas, and also the dividing line between east and west. The meeting was held around a rough table in a country tavern. Jefferson was chosen to preside, which he did in the spirit of "taking things by their smooth handle." Those present considered a report which was supposed to have been drawn up by six members, but no one doubted that its chief provisions had been written down by Jefferson himself. Chief among them were these proposals:

1. That the setting and design should be that which had already been laid down for the Central College, based on a continuous and linked group of buildings around three sides of a square containing dormitories and pavilions.

2. That the curriculum should embrace ancient and modern languages, mathematics and the physical sciences, government, municipal law, and the fine and literary arts.

The most unexpected recommendation was that which opposed any form of coercion upon the students. The report said—and here we see the distinct hand of Jefferson:

"The human character is susceptible of other incitements to correct conduct more worthy of employ and of better effect. Pride of character, laudable ambition, and moral dispositions are innate correctives of the indiscretions of that lively age. A system founded on reason and comity will be more likely to nourish in the minds of our youth the combined spirit of order and self-respect."

Meantime Cabell acted as public relations counsel, and procured publication of favorable views in Jefferson's favorite newspaper, the Richmond *Enquirer*. The Rockfish Gap report was embodied in an act that won over all opposition in the assembly, which placed the university at Charlottesville and fixed its annuity at fifteen thousand dollars. When the news was brought to Jefferson of this, one of the salient triumphs of his life, he simply said, "I sincerely join in the general joy." [3] He was appointed chairman of the board of visitors and then rector.

One thing on which Jefferson prided himself in the university was its "distinguished scale in structure" and its architectural reliance on "chaste models taken from the finest remains of antiquity." In fact, it might be said he poured into his designs all the confined architectural yearnings that had beset him ever since he was old enough to study the illustrations in European books on architecture. In being guided by the Roman classical tradition, he based one pavilion (a professor's residence) on the Doric of the Diocletian baths, another on the Corinthian of Palladio, a third on the Ionic of the same, a fourth on the Doric of Palladio, and a fifth on the Ionic of the Temple of Fortuna Virilis.

On the other side of the lawn was one on the Ionic of the same, another on the Doric of Albano, a third on the Ionic of the Theater of Marcellus, a fourth on the Corinthian of the Baths of Diocletian, a fifth on the Doric of the Theater of Marcellus. Finally came the crown of all, the Rotunda modeled after the Pantheon at Rome. These buildings and their setting resulted in a total unrivaled in America.

Jefferson not only designed these structures, including the serpentine walls, but wrote out the specifications and superintended the building operations. In accordance with his respect for European artisans, especially Italians, he procured from Italy two stonecutters named Micheli and Giacomo Raggi to work on Tuscan bases and capitals. But the native stone which was employed as far as possible proved to be refractory or brittle, and eventually Ionic and Corinthian capitals of marble were imported from Italy.

These were vexatious setbacks and delays, and enemies and critics of the whole university scheme were not wanting. In 1822 after years of toil on the project, Jefferson wrote to Dr. Cooper, who was his chief confidant at this time:

"The time of opening our University is still as uncertain as ever. All the pavilions, boarding houses, and dormitories are done. Nothing is wanting but the central building [the Rotunda] for a library and other general purposes. For this we have no funds, and the last

[3] Bruce, *History of the University of Virginia*, p. 235.

legislature refused all aid." Supporters upon whom he had relied
proved to be fickle and lest Cabell, his chief lieutenant, might withdraw, Jefferson urged him on with fatherly letters:

"The gloomiest of all prospects," he wrote, "is in the desertion of
the best friends of the institution, for desertion I must call it . . .
but I will die in the last ditch."

His fierce determination was applied even to minor details, such
as preparing tests, deeds and contracts; designing the gardens in the
rear of the ten pavilions; building the waving walls around them to
a height of six or seven feet though originally only half a brick in
thickness; and the ordering of a college clock which must be heard
"at a distance of two miles, because this will ensure its being heard
at Charlottesville."

There was a stage when Jefferson was accused of extravagance in
building the university, even, as Cabell confessed, by the "intelligent
circle of society," although he was proposing to construct the 104
dormitories for only $350 each and had estimated that the entire
group of buildings, excluding the Rotunda, which was not completed
until after his death, would cost only $162,304. In procuring ap-
propriations, Jefferson had to deal with various forms of opposition
arising not only from his political and clerical enemies but from the
rivalry of other existing Virginia institutions and from much provincial indifference.

Of this last factor he made capital by pointing out "the heavy
tribute we are annually paying to other states and countries for the
article of education." The economic factor that made an impression,
the burden of obtaining money from the legislature, fell chiefly upon
Cabell in the senate, who worked under such a physical and mental
strain that he became ill and went to bed with a heart condition;
Jefferson could not help him even with a few well-aimed letters, for
he had to confess "the joints of my right wrist and fingers, in consequence of an ancient dislocation, are become so stiffened that I can
write but at the pace of a snail. . . . The letter I am writing has
taken me two days." But he managed to keep before Cabell, urging
him to keep it before all legislators, that "the great object of our aim
from the beginning has been to make the establishment the most
eminent in the United States."

The next step was the procuring of a faculty. Jefferson's mind was already made up as regards two requirements: each professor "should be educated as to the sciences generally" and he must be "of the first order." He well knew that teachers of the first order must come from the Old World, that they would not be attracted by dismal barracks or a log college such as was then popular in certain parts of the United States; hence his insistence that the university not be opened until visitors could gain an impression of the dignity of the whole arrangement.

However, he considered two American professors properly qualified and encouraged offers to George Ticknor, traveler and writer, and Nathaniel Bowditch, mathematician and navigator, both of Massachusetts. Both declined, and Jefferson then knew that on account of the common language, he must look to the Old Country for teachers. As his agent to go abroad and find the right man, he selected Gilmer, who in tastes and ideals was nearly the counterpart of the elegant Cabell. Gilmer, who was a brother-in-law of William Wirt, federal attorney general and conspicuous figure in the Burr trial, was well read in law, science and literature; and when Jefferson wished him to take the chair of law at the new university, Gilmer hesitated but, despite frail health, did consent to go to Great Britain and search for distinguished professors. In 1824 Gilmer sailed for England carrying letters of introduction to Dr. Samuel Parr, classical scholar; to Major John Cartwright, liberal lawyer and to Dugald Stewart, the philosopher.

The first professor engaged by Gilmer was Dr. George Blaetterman, of German descent, who took the chair of modern languages at Virginia at a salary of one thousand five hundred dollars a year. But later choices were much more difficult. At both Oxford and Cambridge universities Gilmer learned that education was a class enterprise; that, in fact, it was, as he wrote Jefferson, "almost exclusively confined to the nobility and opulent gentry," whose members were not inclined to leave England or teach in an uncompleted university in a raw country. Even in Edinburgh where he found "needy young men, living miserably up 10 or 12 stories, in the wretched climate," the prospects were poor.

However, he procured at Cambridge the services of Thomas

Hewett Key, son of a London physician, as professor of pure mathematics; and George Long, who described himself as not "a man of rank and property," as professor of classical languages; and had further luck in obtaining Dr. Robley Dunglison, a writer on medical subjects, as professor of anatomy; and Charles Bonnycastle, son of a professor of mathematics at Woolwich, as professor of natural philosophy.

But though hospitably received everywhere, his exertions wore Gilmer out and he came down with a pulmonary complaint from which he never recovered. When he reached New York late in 1824, he described himself to Jefferson as "emaciated to a shadow" and in the grip of a violent fever. For a year and a half he struggled with exhaustion and feeble strength, meantime writing Jefferson hopeful notes of filial respect, but early in 1826 he died. He was only thirty-six years old.

As if this were not discouraging enough to Jefferson, John Adams wrote him his disapproval of tutors fetched from Europe. Said Adams:

"They are all infected with Episcopal and Presbyterian creeds and confessions of faith. They all believe that great principle which has produced this boundless universe, Newton's universe, and Herschell's universe, came down to this little ball to be spit upon by the Jews. And until this awful blasphemy is gotten rid of there never will be any liberal science in the world." From Maria Cosway in Italy, now three years a widow, came a more cheerful letter:

"I wish much to hear from you, and how you go on with your fine Seminary. I have had my grand saloon painted with the representation of the four parts of the world. . . . I have left a hill bare where I would place Monticello and the Seminary. . . . Pray write to me at Lodi, and if this reaches you *Safe,* I will write longer by the same way. Believe me ever, your most obliged and affectionate friend, Maria Cosway."

Jefferson by now had discarded breeches for pantaloons and wore overalls when he went for his daily ride on his horse, Eagle. He had also cut off his eighteenth-century queue. But he declined to shorten his waistcoats and, rejecting nineteenth-century cravats, clung to his stocks, or neckcloths, of white cambric. He also continued to sign his letters in the old-fashioned way: "Your most obedient and humble servant."

The university first opened its doors to classes early in 1825, and Jefferson had the satisfaction of daily looking through his Monticello telescope down upon its first students crossing the lawn in their prescribed dress of Oxford gray, swallow-tailed coats, cotton or linen pantaloons, white or black neckcloths and round black hats. Such a vision was the crowning triumph of a life not self-centered but generous to fellow-men. And it was a new thing in academic life: an institution created not for a thin upper stratum but for a numerous democracy, and established not to further a religion but the whole field of learning.

Students were allowed a dignified form of self-government; and debasing punishments, like the public whippings prescribed at Harvard, were forbidden. But the serpent of disorder was not long creeping into this Eden and the university was not a year old when a band of students, by Jefferson called an "unworthy few," rioted one night on the lawn. When the leaders were brought before the board of visitors, Jefferson arose to speak but was overcome with weakness and emotion; his voice failed him and he was obliged to let another member utter his rebuke. Four guilty youths were then expelled; but for some years illicitly peddled alcohol, added to youthful exuberance, continued to interfere with academic decorum.

Jefferson never prevailed with his earlier plan for dividing the counties into hundreds, or a later plan for dividing the state into college districts of eighty miles square; but this victory over political prejudice, denominational ill-will, mossy habits and petty localism satisfied him. "I do most anxiously wish," he wrote, "to see the highest degrees of education given to the highest degrees of genius, and to all degrees of it, so much as may enable them to read and understand what is going on in the world, and to keep their part of it going on right; for nothing can keep it right but their own vigilant and distrustful superintendence," thus "advancing the happiness of man."

The Dr. Dunglison who was made professor of anatomy at Charlottesville, on his arrival at Monticello, wrote notes of his first impressions and incidentally pointed out one of Jefferson's weaknesses as an architect:

"The venerable ex-President presented himself and welcomed us with that dignity and kindness for which he was celebrated. He was then 82 years old, with his intellectual powers unshaken by age, and the physical man so active that he rode to and from Monticello, and took exercise on foot with all the activity of one twenty or thirty years younger. . . . The houses [the university pavilions] were much better furnished than we had expected to find them, and would have been far more commodious had Mr. Jefferson consulted his excellent and competent daughter, Mrs. Randolph, in regard to the interior arrangements, instead of planning the architectural exterior first and leaving the interior to shift for itself. . . . At all times dignified, and by no means easy of approach to all, he was generally communicative to those on whom he could rely; in his own house he was occasionally free in his speech, even to impudence, to those of whom he did not know enough to be satisfied that an improper use might be made of his candor."

CHAPTER 62

· VISITORS TO MONTICELLO

WHILE THESE THINGS were going on, visitors flocked to Monticello in mounting numbers, some of them to consult the owner, others simply to stare. Hospitable traditions obliged Jefferson to see them all when possible, and even to offer them food and shelter, but two visitors gave particular pleasure. One was the Abbé Joseph Correa de Serra, Portuguese scientist and diplomat; the other was Lafayette.

Correa's liberal views when he was living in Portugal brought on him the sinister attentions of the Inquisition, inducing him to flee to England. In 1813 he came to the United States and like so many intellectual foreigners, he sought out Jefferson, who was delighted with his learning and urbanity. At Monticello Correa met young Francis W. Gilmer, and when each found the other to be an amateur botanist, they dropped everything and went on a botanic tour of the South, including Georgia and South Carolina.

"He is the most extraordinary man now living, or who perhaps, ever lived," wrote Gilmer of his companion. Correa often visited Jefferson both at Monticello and Poplar Forest and eventually when he was appointed minister to Brazil by the Portuguese government, Jefferson proposed to him the germ of what later matured into the Monroe Doctrine of 1823. In 1820 Jefferson mentioned his haunting dream of a partition walling off the Americas from Europe in a letter to William Short, his old secretary at Paris:

"From many conversations with him [Correa], I hope he sees, and will promote in his new situation, the advantages of a cordial fraternization among all the American nations, and the importance of their coalescing in an American system of policy, totally independent of and unconnected with that of Europe. The day is not distant, when it may formally require a meridian of partition through the ocean which separates the two hemispheres, on the hither side of which no European gun shall ever be heard, nor an American on the other; and when, during the rage of the eternal wars of Europe, the lion and the lamb, within our regions, shall lie down together in peace."

After an absence of forty years, Lafayette returned in 1824 to the United States. He was sixty-seven years old. Jefferson wrote to him at New York:

"What a history have we to run over, from the evening that yourself, Mousnier [Mounier], Barnave, and other patriots settled, in my home in Paris, the outlines of the constitution you wished. And to trace it through all the disastrous chapters of Robespierre, Barras, Bonaparte, and the Bourbons! These things, however, are for our meeting."

On arriving at Charlottesville Lafayette was escorted in an open barouche to Monticello by 120 mounted men. Jefferson wanted to go down the mountain to meet him, but weakness kept him on the steps of his house. When Lafayette stepped down from his carriage, the spectators saw that he was stout and ruddy, and walked with a limp, and that Jefferson's long frame was bent at the shoulders. The two old men stumbled forward and clasped each other, their eyes wet. As they entered the house, the crowd at the entrance broke up in silence. None ever knew what the two men talked about.

The royal welcome given to Lafayette everywhere caused Congress to vote him a gift of two hundred thousand dollars and a township (twenty-four thousand acres) of land.

Among the other visitors who came to Monticello as Jefferson was watching through his mounted telescope the last few touches being given to the University of Virginia, was George Ticknor, traveler, New Englander and author of a history of Spanish literature. He was accompanied by the young Daniel Webster. Webster afterward put down a few notes on Jefferson's appearance as the latter neared his eighty-second birthday:

"His mouth is well formed, and still filled with teeth; it is strongly compressed, bearing an expression of contentment and benevolence.

"His walk is not precise and military, but easy and swinging.

"His general appearance indicates an extraordinary degree of health, vivacity, and spirit. His sight is still good, for he needs glasses only in the evening. His hearing is still good, but a number of voices in animated conversation confuse it.[1]

"His diet is simple, but he seems restrained only by his taste. His breakfast is tea and coffee, bread always fresh from the oven, of which he does not seem afraid.

"In conversation, Mr. Jefferson is easy and natural, and apparently not ambitious; it is not loud, as challenging general attention, but usually addressed to the person next to him."

That part of Webster's report which attracted most attention was his version of what Jefferson said about Andrew Jackson, candidate for president of the United States in competition with John Quincy Adams, Henry Clay, John C. Calhoun and William H. Crawford of Georgia, a former Federalist. Jefferson would take no sides in this campaign, but his friends said he favored Crawford. Webster thus reported Jefferson's opinion of Jackson:

"I feel much alarmed at the prospect of seeing General Jackson president. He is one of the most unfit men I know of for such a place. He has had very little respect for laws or constitutions, and is, in fact, an able military chief. His passions are terrible." Thomas Jefferson Randolph, who was always in the confidence of his grandfather, was inclined to be skeptical about this report, and believed if Jefferson had doubts as to Jackson they were due only to an habitual distrust of military men in high civil posts.

Young Randolph, incidentally, had taken over the management of his grandfather's farms and had proved himself more capable of staying out of debt than his erratic father, Thomas Mann Randolph, who meantime had served as governor of Virginia. The older Randolph for a time, owing to some unknown cause, had ceased to speak to Jefferson even when they sat at the same table, and for a long period stayed away from his home and his wife, the long-suffering Martha.

Jefferson's letters at this period show occasional spells of worry about debts and hard times. To a lessee of his flour mill he wrote:

---

[1] For this reason Jefferson preferred to sit at a separate table even in the family dining room.

"The distress in which I am to meet debts of the most pressing urgency obliges me to remind you of the arrearages due to me on the mill account." For some years his nailery (in which a trained slave could make twelve pounds of nails a day) was profitable, bringing in two thousand dollars a year, but the War of 1812 shut off his supply of nail-rod, and then nails exported from England made such severe competition that by 1823 homemade nails were no longer in demand.

At this period Jefferson found it harder and harder to deal with his burdening correspondence. Occasionally he employed one of his granddaughters to help him, but he answered most letters in person, although a fall from his horse, Eagle, left both wrists swollen and aching, and although sometimes he was obliged to spend the entire morning from daylight to 2 P.M. at his writing desk. He told Nathaniel Macon he felt "a much greater interest in knowing what has passed two or three thousand years ago, than in what is now passing." He confined his newspaper reading to one journal, the Richmond *Enquirer*, edited by Thomas Ritchie, which he called the best paper in America.[2]

---

2 Ritchie successfully conducted a liberal Republican paper in a Federalist stronghold. He followed Jefferson in an announced determination to rid Virginia of the last relics of feudalism. When the Negroes in San Domingo revolted, however, to spare the feelings of slaveholders he suppressed all news and comment on the progress of the rebellion.

CHAPTER 63

THE LAST ENEMY

By THE TIME the year 1826 had opened it was known among Jefferson's friends that he had summoned his energies to give battle one more time to his old enemy—debt. His hair now was long and white; unaided he could no longer mount a horse; and though his intelligence was still high, his strength had passed its peak.

At this stage one wonders that Congress, well aware of his undemanding services to his country, did not come to his relief with a generous grant that would have met all his obligations. It was estimated that eighty thousand dollars would have freed him of all financial burdens; and indeed this sum at one time was considered by the Virginia legislature as a donation, free of interest, from the public treasury; but opposition arose and at length a bill was drawn up merely allowing Jefferson to dispose of his property by a lottery. He had written about the proposed lottery to Cabell at the first of the year as "almost a question of life and death" and explained why he had been obliged to send his grandson, Thomas Jefferson Randolph, to the legislature to ask for permission.

"My own debts were considerable," he wrote, "and a loss was added to them of $20,000 by indorsement for a friend." This unnamed friend was Wilson Cary Nicholas, father-in-law of Thomas Jefferson Randolph and former United States senator and governor of Virginia. Nicholas was one of the speculating Virginia gentlemen of the period—he had been caught by the 1819 depression and died in debt.[1] He had been one of Jefferson's political supporters and

---

[1] "While he was Governor," said Edmund Bacon, Jefferson's old overseer, "he once sent out an agent to meet the droves of hogs that were coming in to Richmond, and buy them up; and the butchers were compelled to buy them all of him. They were so

when he asked the sage to endorse a note for twenty thousand dollars, Jefferson consented, thereby adding just enough weight to a great burden of debt to break him. Jefferson's debts had been growing ever since his days as minister at Paris; they increased while he was president for eight years; and they were augmented after he left the presidency by the effects of the embargo, by the general fall in farm prices, following the 1819 depression, and by the deterioration of his lands under slave labor.

Although lotteries were not unknown in the various states and were indeed commonly used for educational and charitable purposes, Jefferson was so desperate that he felt moved to justify his own proposal for a lottery by saying that although lotteries were games of chance which were frowned upon by good society, they had been found "useful on certain occasions, and injurious only when carried beyond their useful bounds." He cited the case of Colonel Byrd, master of the estate at Westover, who through a lottery in 1756 had been "made competent to pay his debts." He added: "If it [permission for a lottery] can be yielded in my case, I can save the house of Monticello and a farm adjoining, to end my days in, and bury my bones. If not, I must sell house and all here, and carry my family to Bedford, where I have not even a log hut to put my head into." [2]

In a letter to Thomas Jefferson Randolph, his grandfather confessed his fears, saying: "You kindly encourage me to keep up my spirits; but oppressed with disease, debility, age, and embarrassed affairs, this is difficult. . . . My dear and beloved daughter, the cherished companion of my early life and nurse of my age, and her children, rendered as dear to me as of my own from having lived with me from their cradle, left in a comfortless situation, hold up to me nothing but future gloom."

In February, 1826, Jefferson wrote to Madison confessing that the interest of one thousand two hundred dollars a year which he had been obliged to pay on Nicholas's debt had been a kind of *coup de grâce*,[3] and he added as if saying farewell: "To myself you have been

mad . . . that one night they covered the fence with hogs' entrails."—Pierson, *Jefferson at Monticello*.

[2] This statement was made after he had sold part of his Bedford county property.

[3] Randall in his *Life of Thomas Jefferson* says Nicholas in his last hours testified that Jefferson had never alluded to his loss by him.

a pillar of support through life. Take care of me when dead, and be assured that I shall leave you with my last affections."

At this point came the news from Cabell that the lottery bill had passed, and almost at the same time came voluntary contributions from other states—eight thousand five hundred dollars from Philip Hone, mayor of New York; five thousand dollars from Philadelphia and three thousand dollars from Baltimore. These sums were not enough, but Jefferson's spirits rose again and he was happy to exclaim:

"No cent of this is wrung from the taxpayer—it is the pure and unsolicited offering of love." And it was in this belief that his debts would be met that Jefferson watched with serenity his strength decline.

As the spring came on, Jefferson's doctors noticed that his food no longer nourished him, and whenever he bade his grandchildren good-night, his embrace and kiss were tender and lingering. On March 16 he wrote out his will and the next day added a codicil. He called in his grandson and chief reliance, T. J. Randolph, and talked with him at length. When an artist, Browne, came to take a cast of his features, Jefferson was so weak that he was all but suffocated by the plaster over his face without being able to signal his distress.

As July, 1826, approached, he received from General Wrightman, mayor of Washington, an invitation to attend a celebration of the fiftieth anniversary of the Declaration of Independence. His reply was written with great care. It was the last long letter that he ever wrote. It had the old ring. He hoped that men everywhere eventually would "assume the blessings and security of self-government."

"All eyes are opened, or opening," he wrote, "to the rights of man. The general spread of the light of science has already laid open to every view the palpable truth, that the mass of mankind has not been born with saddles on their backs, nor a favored few booted and spurred, ready to ride them legitimately, by the grace of God."

On the same day he wrote to Dr. Dunglison asking him to call and admitting he was not well. The doctor, who had been treating him for diarrhea and a glandular affection, saw that his physical powers were waning and gave orders that he was to remain in bed. His daughter Martha was with him almost constantly by day; at night his servants and the doctor visited him at nine, twelve and four o'clock. He perfectly realized his condition and talked freely, with a clear mind, of events during the Revolution.

"I am like an old watch," he said, "with a pinion worn out here, and a wheel there, until it can go no longer."

He wondered who would succeed him as rector of the University of Virginia, and hoped it would be James Madison, who at the age of fifteen had become the closest friend of Jefferson, who was then twenty-three.

On July 2 he fell into a stupor, with moments of wakefulness, but on the third the watchers in his room saw that he was sinking. His eyesight became indistinct and although the doctor was at his bedside, he called out, "Ah! doctor, are you still there?" He recalled the Revolutionary Committee of Safety. "Let it be warned," he cried.

In clearer moments he was aware that it was the eve of July 4 and evidently hoping he would live to see the anniversary, he kept asking, "Is it the Fourth?"

At 4 A.M. on the morning of the Fourth he spoke distinctly for the last time. At ten o'clock he mutely signaled that his head should be raised, and at eleven he showed gratitude for a wet sponge laid to his lips. From then on, his breath became labored, his extremities turned clammy, and at fifty minutes past noon July 4, 1826, he ceased to breathe.

Within two years his personal property and lands had been sold in a vain endeavor to meet his debts, which were eventually cleared by T. J. Randolph; and his only child, Martha Randolph, would have been dependent upon charity had not two states, South Carolina and Louisiana, voted her ten thousand dollars each. Monticello fell into the hands of people who did not respect it, and at one time it was used as a storage place for hay. Its trees and shrubs were cut down and the grounds neglected. These owners were succeeded by Jefferson M. Levy of New York, who did his best to preserve the estate. He refused offers of seven hundred and fifty thousand dollars and then of one million by the Thomas Jefferson Memorial Foundation, which was formed in 1923 and which eventually raised a fund and obtained title to Monticello and much of its ground.

One might write many pages concerning Jefferson's aims, ideas and achievements, and enlarge upon the history of his period while bringing it up to the present, and yet do no better than Abraham Lincoln when on April 6, 1859, he wrote from Springfield, Illinois, to H. L. Pierce and others at Boston declining an invitation to attend a celebration of Jefferson's birthday. After reminding them that Jefferson advocated the personal rights of men, "holding the rights of property to be secondary only, and greatly inferior," Lincoln declared:

"But, soberly, it is now no child's play to save the principles of Jefferson from total overthrow in this nation. One would state with great confidence that he could convince any sane child that the simpler propositions of Euclid are true; but nevertheless he would fail, utterly, with one who should deny the definitions and axioms. The principles of Jefferson are the definitions and axioms of free society. And yet they are denied and evaded, with no small show of success. One dashingly calls them 'glittering generalities.' Another bluntly calls them 'self-evident lies.' And others invidiously argue that they apply to 'superior races.' These expressions, differing in form, are identical in object and effect the supplanting the principles of free government, and restoring those of classification, caste, and legitimacy. They would delight a convocation of crowned heads plotting against the people. They are the vanguard, the miners and sappers, of returning despotism. We must repulse them, or they will subjugate us. This is a world of compensation; and he who would be no slave must consent to have no slave. Those who deny freedom to others deserve it not for themselves, and, under a just God, cannot long retain it. All honor to Jefferson—to the man who, in the concrete pressure of a struggle for national independence by a single people, had the coolness, forecast, and capacity to introduce into a merely revolutionary document an abstract truth, applicable to all men and all times, and so to embalm it there that today and in all coming days it shall be a rebuke and a stumbling block to the very harbingers of reappearing tyranny and oppression." [4]

---

[4] *Letters and Addresses of Abraham Lincoln,* ed. Bell, New York, 1903.

CHAPTER 64

JEFFERSON'S ULTIMATE OPINIONS

IN THE MORE than twenty-seven thousand pieces of manuscript by Jefferson which have been preserved, the word "democrat" is used only three times as follows:

1. To Du Pont de Nemours in 1816:

"We of the United States are constitutionally and conscientiously Democrats."

2. To Henry Lee in 1824:

"The appellation of aristocrats and democrats is the true one expressing the essence of all [political parties]."

3. To William Short in 1825:

"Democrats consider the people as the safest depository of power in the last resort; they cherish them, therefore, and wish to leave in them all powers to the exercise of which they are competent."

Jefferson has often been described by hostile critics as a radical and leveler. He was neither. He was a republic-man. As a participant in the revolt against England he favored self-government as against government by kings, nobles, priests or aristocrats because, in his view, although monarchy might occasionally furnish good government, such government was accidental and tended to deterioration, whereas self-government permitted and encouraged growth and progress. He had confidence in the average man and favored "what will secure and enlarge his freedom."

"The event of our experiment," wrote Jefferson in 1802, "is to show whether man can be trusted with self-government." He saw the United States as acting not "for ourselves alone, but for the whole human race."

Government by caste had failed and became oppressive; self-government alone remained to be tried. Theorists like James Wilson, Burlamaqui, Locke, Hooker, Harrington and Blackstone had often discussed liberty as an inborn and natural right, but no nation covering a large area had enjoyed liberty through self-government. America must prove it could be done or fail the onlooking human race. Jefferson believed in natural law and identified it with moral law.

"Every man, and every body of men on earth, possesses the right of self-government," he wrote in 1790. "They receive it with their being from the hand of nature." Two years previously he had written to George Washington from Paris: "There is not a crowned head in Europe whose talents or merit would entitle him to be elected a vestryman by the people of any parish in America." By 1820 when he was an old man he had not altered this opinion; he still believed in democracy, and in the people, except that he thought the people should be informed and educated.

"I know of no safe depository of the ultimate powers of the society," he wrote, "but the people themselves; and if we think them not enlightened enough to exercise their control with a wholesome discretion, the remedy is not to take it from them, but to inform their discretion by education. This is the true corrective of abuses of constitutional power."

Jefferson did not deem every people ready for self-government. He advocated a process of gradualism to prepare them for it. He wrote Dr. Walter Jones in 1801: "When we reflect how difficult it is to move or inflect the great machine of society, how impossible to advance the notions of a whole people suddenly to ideal right, we see the wisdom of Solon's remark, that no more good must be attempted than the nation can bear." Government, as he saw it, must be adapted to society, not society to the government. In 1815 he reminded Lafayette that he had urged on the French patriots such reforms as freedom of the press, trial by jury, the writ of habeas corpus and a national legislature, saying: "This was as much as I then thought them able to bear, soberly and usefully for themselves," but he had to admit that subsequent events had "proved they were equal to the constitution of 1791."

Finally, Jefferson can be understood only as an advocate of the continuation of ancient British liberties. He believed that the thread that began with King Alfred somehow must be picked up, restored and carried on. The English common law, introduced by the Saxons when they settled England, was the unwritten law which grew out of the customs and natural rights of the people. It was alive, flexible and adaptable to the changing needs of the people. But when the land was no longer owned by the "folk right," feudalism came in, bringing in its train kings, nobles and priests, and ultimately sycophants, who perverted the common, unwritten law into a written law framed to suit the purposes of rulers. When this statute law became fixed and no longer responsive to the needs of the people, oppression resulted followed by revolt.

Jefferson was determined that this feudal, unadaptable structure of society should not be brought from the Old World into America. He fought it in Virginia and he fought it in the nation. He wanted to keep America free for a great experiment which should convince mankind that the basic principles which governed the Saxon tribes in their Germanic forests could be applied to a virgin continent. Through this he foresaw illumination for the whole of mankind.

The cast and temper of Jefferson's mind was almost wholly political. In mastery of political thought and philosophy he was far ahead of any contemporary American. But he could not foresee that economic power would eventually dominate political power. And when he was brought up against the workings of economics he was bewildered and depressed.

But such axioms of a free society as he laid down became the permanent possession of the American people. They have been often ignored and brushed aside, but never buried.

In another age Jefferson would have been called a man of the Renaissance, relying less on heaven than on the intelligent use of human powers. He came to maturity at an era when men were forsaking revelation for science and for technical achievement. He was a man nourished on Europe's accumulated learning, and yet he perceived that America, in order to make its own original contribution to the total scheme of things, must break with the Old World politically and if possible economically, but not culturally. He wanted to retain whatever was rich and fertile in Europe's past, but use it as a base from which to erect a freer and more creative civilization than history had yet seen.

CHAPTER 65

LIVING PORTRAITS OF JEFFERSON

As seen by Joseph Story, Associate Justice of the United States Supreme Court in Life and Letters of Joseph Story, *by W. W. Story:*

"Jefferson is tall and thin, of a sallow complexion, with a fine intelligent eye. . . . His language is peculiarly appropriate and his manner very unaffected. . . . The President is a little awkward in his first address, but you are immediately at ease in his presence. His manners are inviting and not uncourtly; and his voice flexible and distinct. He bears the marks of intense thought and perseverance in his countenance. . . . His smile is very engaging and impresses you with a cheerful frankness. His familiarity, however, is tempered with great calmness of manner and with becoming propriety. Open to all, he seems willing to stand the test of inquiry, and to be weighed in the balance only by his merits and attainments. . . . If he chooses, he cannot fail to please. If he cannot awe, he will not sink into neglect."

As seen by William Maclay, United States Senator from Pennsylvania, 1789–91, in Journal of William Maclay:

"Jefferson is a slender man; has rather the air of stiffness in his manner; his clothes seem too small for him; he sits in a lounging manner on one hip commonly and with one of his shoulders much above the other: his face has a sunny aspect; his whole figure has a loose, shackling air. . . . Yet he scattered information wherever he went, and some of even brilliant sentiments sparkled from him. . . . Hamilton has a very boyish, giddy manner, and Scotch-Irish people could well call him a 'skite.' Jefferson transgresses on the extreme of stiff gentility or lofty gravity."

As seen in 1782 by the Marquis de Chastellux in Travels in North America:

"I found his first appearance serious, nay, even cold; but before I had been two hours with him, we were as intimate as if we had passed our whole lives together. . . . A conversation always varied and interesting, always supported by that sweet satisfaction experienced by two persons who in communicating their sentiments and opinions, are invariably in unison, and who understand each other at the first hint, made four days pass away like so many minutes."

As seen in 1796 by the Duke de la Rochefoucauld-Liancourt, former President of the National Assembly of France:

"I found him in the midst of the harvest, from which the scorching heat of the sun does not prevent his attendance. His negroes are nourished, clothed, and treated as well as white servants could be. . . . He animates them by rewards and distinctions; in fine, his superior mind directs the management of his domestic concerns with the same abilities, activity, and regularity which he evinced in the conduct of public affairs, and which he is calculated to display in every situation in life."

As seen by Senator William Plumer of New Hampshire in "Memorandum of Proceedings in the United States Senate, 1803–1807":

"I found the President dressed better than I ever saw him at any time when I called on a morning visit. Though his coat was old and threadbare, his scarlet vest, his corduroy small clothes, and his white cotton hose were new and clean—but his lennen [sic] was much soiled, and his slippers old— His hair was cropped and powdered.

"His conversation was vapid—mere commonplace observations on the weather—crops and sickness of particular districts. From these he went into an elaborate defence of Horse-racing—he said it was an effectual means to improve the breed of horses—that all people will have their amusements—that horse racing is less injurious to the people than playing at cards or dice as the Bostonians do" . . . *December 3, 1804:* "He was well dressed—a new suit of black silk hose—shoes—clean linnen [sic], and his hair highly powdered. His dinner was elegant and rich—his wines very good. . . . There were also exposed on the table two bottles of water brought from the river Mississippi, and a quantity of the Mammoth cheese. This cheese, was one made by some Democrats in Massachusetts two three years since, and presented to Mr. Jefferson. It weighed 1200 lb. & is very far from being good. . . . His table furnished a great variety of pies, fruit and nuts. He performed the honors of the table with great facility."

As seen in 1809 by Mrs. Margaret Bayard Smith in "The First Forty Years of Washington Society":

"His tall and slender figure is not impaired by age, though bent by care and labor. His white locks announce an age his activity, strength, health, enthusiasm, ardor, and gaiety contradict. His face owes all its charm to its expression and intelligence; his features are not good and his complexion bad, but his countenance is so full of soul and beams with so much benignity, that when the eye rests on the face, it is too busy in perusing its expression to think of its features or complexion. . . . But his manners—how gentle, how humble, how kind."

THE END

INDEX